MGF AND TF
DAVID KNOWLES

THE CROWOOD PRESS

First published in 2010 by
The Crowood Press Ltd
Ramsbury, Marlborough
Wiltshire SN8 2HR

www.crowood.com

© David Knowles 2010

All rights reserved. No part of this publication may be reproduced or transmitted in any form or by any means, electronic or mechanical, including photocopy, recording, or any information storage and retrieval system, without permission in writing from the publishers.

British Library Cataloguing-in-Publication Data
A catalogue record for this book is available from the British Library.

ISBN 978 1 84797 202 6

Dedication
To the memory of Brian Griffin (spiritual father of the MGF and MG TF)

Unless otherwise stated, illustrations are from the author's collection.

Typeset by Bookcraft Ltd,
Stroud, Gloucestershire

Printed and bound in Singapore by
Craft Print International

Acknowledgements
Producing any book is an intense process but one that is dependent upon the goodwill, support and enthusiasm of others. This book has been no exception, and there are many people I need to thank, quite apart from my ever patient and supportive family. These people (together with their relevant roles at the time of their involvement) include: Keith Adams, Austin Rover website; Greg Allport, Rover Group MG Brand Manager, later Head of MG Rover Group PR; David Arbuckle, Senior Designer, MG Rover Group; Roy Axe, Rover Group Design; Erik Baekelant, Belgian MGF and TF enthusiast; Chris Bangle, BMW Group Design Director; Rob Bell, MGCC and MGF/TF enthusiast and expert; Peter Brooking, MG Motor UK; Denis Chick, Rover Group PR; Stephen Cox, MG Motor UK; Eleanor De la Haye, MG Motor UK; Marek Djordjević, Designworks; Ian Elliott, Rover Group External Affairs; Graham Fairhead, MG Rover Group, 'Project Director, Sports Cars Product Development' (2001); Adrian Guyll, MG Rover Group safety engineer; Richard Hamblin, Rover Group Design; Steve Harper, Rover Group and MGA designer; Ben Hooper, TWR Designer; Tony Hunter, Rover Group MG Designer; Colin Jones, Dove Company; Guy Jones, MG Motor UK; Kevin Jones, MG Rover Group Public Relations Manager; Tony Williams-Kenny, SAIC UK; Dieter Koenekke, MGF Register; David Lindley, SAIC UK and former MG Rover senior engineer; Gerry McGovern, Rover Group Design and MGF designer; Graham Morris, Rover Group Director; Tim Morris, Chairman, MGF Register; Jon Moulton, Chairman of Alchemy Partners; Rob Oldaker, MG Rover Group Design & Development Director; David Paveley, DPRS; Ian Pogson, SAIC UK and former MG Rover senior engineer; Julian Quincey, Rover Group MG Designer; Andrew Roberts, MG expert, writer and good friend; David Saddington, Rover Group Senior designer; Neil Simpson, TWR Design; Gordon Sked, Rover Group Design Director; Kevin Spindler, MG Rover Design; Nick Stephenson, Phoenix Venture Holdings (MG Rover Group) Director; Peter Stevens, MG Rover Group Design Director; Phil Turner, Chassis engineer on MGF through to current MG TF; Geoff Upex, Rover Group Design Director; Wolfgang Vollath, BMW Group (Mini & MG Brand Management in 1999); Barrie Wills, Chapman-Arup and Project Kimber; David Woodhouse, Rover Group designer on the MGF Super Sports and record cars; and Wolfgang Ziebart, BMW Engineering Director to 2000.

Contents

Introduction 4

1 The Modern MG Legacy 5
2 Return of the MG Sports Car 27
3 Route of Destiny 53
4 Dreams Realized: The New MG*F* 87
5 Another New Start 118
6 Eastern Promise 176
7 MG Clubs and Specialists 193

Appendix   Specifications 197
Index 204

Introduction

For several years, following the demise of the famous dedicated sports car factory at Abingdon, the MG sports car appeared to have become nothing but a fading memory, a product of a blighted company whose focus had, of necessity, moved away from the seemingly frivolous world of open-top two-seaters to the serious business of high-volume family and executive motoring. In the wake of the demise of the MG Midget, MGB and then the Triumph TR7 (and, with the latter, the end of any prospect, good or bad, of an MG-badged derivative) there seemed – from the perspective of the early 1980s, at least – little prospect for the MG badge beyond the possibility of being used as a kind of 'GTi' badge for various Austins and Rovers. However, thanks to the determination of a few people – and an enduring affection in public hearts – the tale would have a happier ending. This is the story of that journey – from desolation to rebirth, just like the phoenix from which the project that created the MG*F* took its name.

In 2009, MG celebrated eighty-five years of sports car history with the MG TF 85 LE, practically the ultimate evolution of the MG*F* and MG *TF* story told in this book. (MG Motor)

chapter one

The Modern MG Legacy

MG HERITAGE

The MG sports car had its roots in a limited run of specials based on the products of William Morris's eponymous factory at Cowley, a suburb of Oxford. Morris (later Lord Nuffield) had retained private ownership of his original Morris Garages business while he developed the Morris Works. A new manager who joined that garage business in 1922, Cecil Kimber, hit upon the idea of 'customizing' Morris cars for a discerning clientele initially drawn largely from Oxford's prosperous leafy suburbs.

Business took off and before long evolved into the creation of bespoke sports cars bearing a distinctive octagonal 'MG' badge, which was first seen in Morris Garages advertisements in 1923 and gradually applied in a modest way to cars in the following years. Before the end of the decade, MG Midget sports cars

The archetypal MG sports car in many minds is the MGB – and with over half a million built perhaps that is hardly a surprise. (MG Rover Group)

THE MODERN MG LEGACY

would be emerging in series production from a dedicated factory at Abingdon-on-Thames and by the mid-1930s MG was a household name in sports car terms.

Despite a setback in 1935, when Kimber perhaps overreached himself and Morris clipped his wings by selling MG to the principal Nuffield Motors business, the MG sports car continued to rise in both popularity and sales: by the onset of the Second World War, MG was arguably the leader of the whole market sector. MG sports cars formed part of Nuffield's export drive immediately after the war, and in a climate hungry for new product and driven by a national need to earn currency from exports, MG thrived with first the TC, TD and TF Midgets and later the revolutionary (in MG terms) MGA and MGB sports cars of 1955 and 1962, respectively.

Both the latter models would go on to set sales records and even today, when the owners of other sports car model names claim higher total sales, it is still the MGB that retains the record of the highest production run for what was basically the same sports car bodyshell, with well over half a million built over an eighteen-year period. Of course with the MGA lasting only seven years, it was obvious that the MGB should really have been replaced by around 1969. In the event, for reasons that will become apparent, this never happened, and so the Abingdon-built car soldiered on for a further twelve years – but not without a number of ideas arising along the way.

MGD: THE MID-ENGINED MG THAT GOT AWAY

The MGF may have been the first mid-engined volume-built sports car with an MG badge, but as we shall see in the early part of this book, it was hardly the first time that such a concept had been explored. Had circumstances been different at the end of the 1960s, there could have been a really modern, innovative mid-engined sports car in MG dealerships across the world instead of yet another MGB facelift. In the dying days of BMC independence, MG had been given authority to work on a prototype intended to replace both the MG Midget and the MGB in one model – a recurrent theme in the company's history.

Given official MG prototype status by being badged as EX234, this project, which originally dated from 1964, built on MG Midget-based studies by MG's Syd Enever aimed at marrying the Hydrolastic suspension of the ADO16 MG1100 with a traditional MG rear-wheel drive layout. The crowning glory of the EX234 project was a rather pretty one-off Pininfarina prototype, which, despite being finished in MG's traditional prototype colour of metallic green, could well have passed muster on Mulholland Drive as a replacement for the Alfa Romeo Duetto Spider.

The prototype featured an MG Midget 'A' series engine, but the theory was that production versions would also have been offered with the new five-bearing 1798cc 'B' series from the MGB; the chief differentiation in the showroom would have been in terms of trim and equipment, although the rather lame contemporary execution of this philosophy proved to be one of the bugbears of the MGC when measured against the MGB. As a rather gamine sports car, EX234 was clearly not intended to embrace the more butch MGC or big-Healey end of the BMC sports car family: that role would have been filled by other projects, especially after Jaguar joined the fold in 1966.

Unfortunately for MG, the EX234 project – driven from Abingdon with support from Longbridge, rather than vice versa – was too far down the growing list of concerns that BMC Chairman Sir George Harriman already had on his mind, and so EX234 gathered dust alongside other MG might-have-been exercises. By the time that the British Leyland merger came along in the spring of 1968, EX234 had become little more than a pretty but outdated relic of the old order: Lord Stokes and Harriman had much bigger issues to tackle,

THE MODERN MG LEGACY

The ADO21 prototype of 1969–70 could have become the first production mid-engined MG sports car had there been different circumstances: instead, the MGB got a facelift. (Paul Hughes)

with the whole sports car family inheritance part of the debate.

For about a year, discussions about the future direction for British Leyland Motor Corporation's sports car family focused mainly on rationalization and general policy issues: the fate of the MGC was decided in this time, the Karmann-styled Triumph TR6 facelift project moved nearer completion, and there were discussions about how to reduce the proliferation of sports car lines while meeting marque loyalties, franchise obligations and the burgeoning automotive legislation in the critically important North American sports car market.

There was also a strong view, held especially by Lord Stokes, that as a forward-looking company British Leyland's next sports cars should be vanguards (no pun intended) for the whole company, and in that context the traditional sports car, exemplified by the MGB and TR5, was seen as backward-looking and consequently, like the Austin Healey 3000, targeted for extinction due to fashion, legislation or simple corporate edict.

As a former minor outpost of the vast BMC conglomerate, the role of the MG Abingdon team in these forward-looking policy debates was nominal at best, whereas in complete contrast, many of the Triumph people were at the heart, since they had already been right at the forefront of Leyland's car-making experience prior to the merger.

As Triumph had already carried out a lot of work on a new sports car range intended to replace the GT6 and TR families (and one that was also closely aligned to a proposed new Triumph saloon range), it is perhaps hardly surprising that the engineers from Canley were authorized to develop the basis of a new corporate sports car intended to replace not only the Triumph TR6 but also the MGB, the latter rightly seen as most important as the highest-selling sports car in the Corporation's portfolio.

However, if Triumph was about to be rewarded with the project to develop, and eventually to engineer, the replacement for the MGB and TR6, the question about the future of the smaller sports cars – the Sprite, Midget, Spitfire sector of the market – remained open. There were relatively few rivals to these small and rather primitive sports cars outside the corporation (although Honda offered a very

From the rear, Paul Hughes' proposal for ADO21 looked like a Ferrari and would have been as far a leap forward for MG as had been the MGA in its day, fifteen years earlier. Note the 'DGT' badge on the tail panel. (Paul Hughes)

good product in this sector) yet they were seen by the US importers as a very important part of the product portfolio, providing a first rung on the ladder for many of their younger customers.

In the United States, many Midgets and Spitfires were purchased by indulgent and wealthy parents for their offspring, often as a reward for graduation from school, and a small English sports car was seen as a relatively inexpensive low-powered way to achieve mobility and street credibility. Clever sales and marketing built on the youthful premise, and the hope was that infatuation with a Midget or a Spitfire might later translate to purchase of a larger and more profitable vehicle from the corporate British Leyland fleet.

While the Spitfire had been a clever spin-off of the Triumph Herald, it had many flaws and the Triumph engineers had made no recent serious headway towards a direct replacement (although none of this prevented it carrying on until 1980). The MG Midget was even more antediluvian, with origins in the 1958 Austin Healey Sprite, but both MG and BMC had worked on potential 'new Midgets', which included not only EX234 but a variety of ADO15 Mini-based concepts for front-wheel drive sports cars. If anyone in the newly enlarged British Leyland was going to look into a new small corporate sports car, it seemed logical that it should be the Abingdon and Longbridge teams.

In theory, a front-wheel drive sports car made production engineering and manufacturing sense, but there were serious concerns about the way that such a vehicle would be seen in a market sector still dominated by rear-wheel drive: this would be another recurring theme. Studies already undertaken included ADO34 and British Leyland would also commission ADO70, both Mini-based projects. However there was also some impetus for the rather more exotic and exciting prospect of a mid-engined sports car, using the Issigonis transverse drivetrain to good effect by cleverly packaging engine and transmission behind the driver.

British Leyland created quite a stir at the Earls Court Motor Show with the Austin Zanda concept of 1969, which promulgated the idea of a mid-engined sports car using the new Maxi 'E'-Series powertrain, while the low-volume specialist Unipower GT, based on the Mini Cooper powertrain, had also generated interest out of all proportion to likely sales when it made

THE MODERN MG LEGACY

its debut three years earlier at the 1966 Racing Car Show.

Over in the United States at the British Leyland offices, Sales and Marketing man Bruce McWilliams, who had joined the organization from Rover via the Leyland Motor Corporation, had also championed the striking Rover P6BS/P9 prototype for a mid-engined Rover sports car using the ex-Buick alloy 3.5-litre V8. This exciting project had been abandoned, partly at the behest of Jaguar's Sir William Lyons, but also in all probability because of budget constraints and doubts about the need for a Rover sports car, but not before McWilliams tried to rebrand the project as the new Leyland Eight.

The Rover P9/Leyland Eight was obviously on an entirely different sports car plateau from that occupied by the MG Midget, but its existence did at least demonstrate that there were some people within the North American sales organization who were keen on the idea of a mid-engined British sports car. This layout also promised the kind of exotic image that Lord Stokes and his management team could see had the right sort of ring to it for a British Leyland sports car for the 1970s, even if some of the engineering and marketing people could see the risk involved in straying from tried and tested formulae.

Accordingly Austin Morris and MG were given the task of developing a proposal for a mid-engined sports car intended primarily to replace the MG Midget and Triumph Spitfire, with a choice of engines and exterior bodywork as part of the game plan. The project code was ADO21 and serious work started in the autumn of 1969, with a potential launch optimistically pencilled in for the spring of 1973, by when it was anticipated that both the Midget and Spitfire would be pensioned off.

From the outset the engine choice was restricted to 'BMC' units. This was surely not just Longbridge protectionism but tacit realization that only the Mini and Maxi units offered a logical route to a transverse mid-engined layout. By the time that engineering and styling work began, the project book defined the engine choice as 'A' series or 'E' series in a range of engine capacities that in theory could have easily stretched from 1098cc to 1748cc. Don Hayter from MG's Abingdon design office was temporarily seconded to Austin Morris headquarters at Longbridge and was tasked by ex-Triumph man Harry Webster to flesh out ADO21.

For suspension, Hayter and his MG chassis colleague Terry Mitchell eschewed the received logic of Hydrolastic, and went for a De Dion rear suspension and conventional MacPherson struts at the front. Before long a rather curious-looking MGB GT was running around with a false rear bulkhead behind the driver's seat, behind which was an Austin Maxi engine and gearbox complete with the latter's dreadful cable operation. So Heath Robinson was this prototype that the gear changes were all back to front, which made driving the beast something of an experience in itself, but as a workmanlike 'mule' it was not so far removed from the philosophy behind the converted Metro vans (see Chapter Three).

While the idea of fitting a front-wheel drive Austin engine behind the cockpit was fine in theory, one of the key challenges in aesthetic terms would be accommodating the remarkably tall Maxi engine and gearbox package. A high centre of gravity was only part of the problem: the real issue was in packaging the bulky unit in a car that had to look low and sleek. Many sketches were drawn up by Harris Mann, Rob Owen, Paul Hughes and others in the Austin Morris design studios, but eventually the one that found favour was a sharp-nosed shape by Paul Hughes, which in some of his sketches wore 'MGD' badges – surely the model name that MG versions would have worn in production.

Hughes cleverly concealed the height of the 'E'-Series engine by the *trompe l'œil* of flying buttresses, which managed to hide the engine bay cover within external panelwork with lower wing 'creases'; the effect was certainly exotic, although the combination of a fixed roof, a

THE MODERN MG LEGACY

Lord Stokes was more sold on the idea of advanced styling than on the concept of exotic engineering; as a consequence, the stylists behind ADO21 were asked to work their magic on the Triumph Bullet to create the Triumph TR7. (Alisdair Cusick)

narrow slot-like rear window and the substantial rear haunches would have made rear three-quarter visibility marginal at best. The styling was unquestionably striking, however, and if produced ADO21 would have been one of the most revolutionary sports cars in its sector.

Some encouragement came when the Italian designer Bertone showed a mid-engined sports car concept, the Autobianchi A112 Runabout at the 1969 Turin motor show; this would later form the basis of a mid-engined Fiat sports car. From October of the same year, of course, there was also interest in the BL Zanda styling concept (referred to on page 8).

By early 1970, however, the odds were beginning to stack up against ADO21. An obvious handicap was the 'E'-Series engine, for even though it was being produced in some numbers in a brand new but as yet underutilized state-of-the-art factory at Cofton Hackett, and offered the bonus of a compact 6-cylinder version – artfully schemed into the ADO21 plan – there were no immediate plans to make the engine compliant with US emissions legislation.

This had not always been the case: at one stage there had been a plan to use the engine in the new ADO28 Marina, but that idea was dropped in the case of both European Morris and North American specification Austin Marinas, launched in 1971 and 1973 respectively, the latter being exclusively fitted with the trusty 'B' series shared with the MGB. In the end the only Marinas to see the 'E'-Series engine would be the Leyland Australia and South Africa versions, and the engines in those cases would be locally built.

The 'A'-Series engine shared with the Mini and ADO16 ranges would still have been a logical choice, but by now ADO21 had grown to be rather larger than a basic Midget, and so a bigger capacity engine would be needed – and the 'A'-Series was at its practical capacity limit already at 1275cc. The size of ADO21 was arguably in itself a problem, for in scheming a potential replacement for the MGB as well as the Midget, the Austin Morris and MG people had strayed dangerously close to Triumph's MGB replacement brief. Coupled with size, of course, was cost, and the relative complexity

THE MODERN MG LEGACY

of the exotic ADO21 did it no favours if it was supposed to take over sales from the Midget and Spitfire.

By the end of 1969 it was obvious from internal documents that the struggle to contain costs against a backdrop of competing British Leyland programmes was going to militate against ADO21; the contemporary MG Midget and Triumph Spitfires sold for around $2,000 and $2,400 respectively, and it looked very unlikely that the mid-engined car could be built profitably to retail at that price.

By the following spring, all prospects of ADO21 becoming the basis of a new Midget had been blown right out of the water by cost estimates. Engineering assessments placed the costs of building ADO21 as even higher than those of the MGB GT, which meant that the mid-engined car could only be viewed as a potential replacement for the MGB. While the folk at Longbridge and Abingdon may have been sanguine about this idea, in the context of the sports car master plan, the idea of Lord Stokes sanctioning both a new Austin Morris-engineered mid-engined MGB replacement as well as a rival Triumph-engineered front-engine, rear-wheel drive MGB replacement was surely in the province of cloud cuckoo land.

Various corporate assessments and viewings followed through the summer and autumn of 1970, by when Triumph designers were at a reasonably advanced stage with their comparatively primitive but entirely logical Bullet/Lynx programme (not be confused with the later more familiar TR7 versions with those code names). Notes of meetings record polite interest and latent enthusiasm for the exotic ADO21, but waning prospect of the project being given the essential green light. Perhaps the final blow came after a fact-finding visit to California by Spen King and Mike Carver, which revealed that many of those they spoke to were much more in favour of a conventional front-engined sports car than one with a mid-engine.

In October 1970 the minutes of a product policy meeting recorded:

a mid-engined model (ADO21) has been investigated but it hardly justifies development independent of Triumph's plans. As yet there is little, if any, joint model planning but the establishment of Product Planning Co-ordination Department at Berkeley Square should at least ensure that overlapping programmes don't get approved.

At the start of the next month, ADO21 was viewed along with a more conventional prototype for a front-wheel drive Mini-based sports car, known as 'Calypso' (ADO70). Referring to ADO21, it was recorded that 'the front end was unanimously admired, but there were some reservations about the rear end. However, in view of the corporate sports car policy, it was decided that no more work is to be done on this programme'.

Just under a fortnight later, the wooden ADO21 model was trundled into the studio again for a viewing alongside Triumph's 'Bullet' (not to be confused with the later TR7), the Calypso and Triumph's 'Lynx' coupé (again, not to be confused with a later TR7-based project). The management saw merit in Calypso as a small sports car and Lynx as a large one, but there was only room for one in between, and as Bullet and ADO21 were 'too expensive as shown', it was decreed that both models would be revised and shown again a month later (14 December 1970), the date of studio photos of ADO21. But the costs could not be reduced, and so the project was considered unviable.

Thus was the MGD strangled at birth, and so the idea of a mid-engined MG sports car would have to wait for different circumstances and a parent company changed almost out of all recognition. Meanwhile Fiat and its styling partner Bertone continued to forge ahead with their own miniature Ferrari, launched as the Fiat X1/9 in 1972, just three years after that initial Autobianchi concept, and following the same pattern of using conventional saloon components (in this case from the Fiat 128) in a mid-engined format. The X1/9 – marketed

THE MODERN MG LEGACY

ADO21 versus MGF

	ADO21	MGF
Length	Not finalized	3,910mm
Wheelbase	2,108mm	2,380mm
Width	1,549mm	1,630mm
Height	1,194mm	1,270mm
Front track	1,372mm	1,400m
Rear track	1,372mm	1,410mm
Fuel tank capacity	48ltr (10.5 Imp gal)	
Wheels	5Jx12 or 5Jx13 inch diameter	
Tyres	155/70R-12 or 165/70R-13	
Engine capacities	1275cc, 1485cc or 1748cc 4-cylinder (later also 2227cc 6-cylinder)	

Paul Hughes produced a variety of sketches for ADO21: this is one of his dating from November 1969. (Paul Hughes)

variously as a Fiat or a Bertone product – would go on to register a healthy 200,000 sales.

All eyes at British Leyland, meanwhile, turned to marrying the avant-garde styling themes of ADO21 with a conventional front engine rear-wheel drive platform in the form of a new Triumph-engineered but Longbridge-styled 'Bullet', approved by Lord Stokes in the summer of 1971 and launched in 1975 as the Triumph TR7. Promised MG offshoots, however, never materialized.

MG SPORTS CARS: IDEAS FOR THE 1980s

The Triumph TR7, launched in the United States in 1975 and the rest of the world a year later, was intended to be British Leyland's light sports car challenger for the next decade, stretching into the 1980s and building a platform for continued success as long as demand for sports cars continued. Therein lay the rub, however, since from the vantage point of 1971, proposed automotive legislation changes in the USA seemed to suggest that the sports car might have only a limited future.

For much of the decade a replacement for the MGB was variously on and off again, and the TR7 proved to be a poor market substitute, hampered as much by rejection of its controversial looks as by a poor reliability record. Coupled with the corporate woes that led British Leyland into 99 per cent public ownership in 1975, this meant that the company's sports car programme sputtered on for just a few years before the MGB's survival became an economic impracticality and the TR7 followed suit.

THE MODERN MG LEGACY

Throughout the life of the Triumph TR7, there were various attempts to create an MG derivative, but all were destined to end in failure: here is one of Michelotti's proposals dating from around 1979.

Thus the end of the MGB, swiftly followed by the TR7, seemed to signal the demise of the small high-volume British sports car. There had long been low-volume specialists such as Morgan, Lotus and TVR, but these were usually quirky cars built in smaller numbers, often with much hand-building and reliance on bought-in components from volume manufacturers. However, while the Abingdon MG story was nearing an end, so a new era was simultaneously unfolding for British Leyland, with the forging of an alliance with the Honda Motor Company in 1978.

Michael Edwardes (he would be knighted in June 1979) had swiftly come to appreciate, not long after he took over the hot seat at British Leyland at the end of 1977, that the company – then just two years into effective state ownership – was badly lacking a replacement for its larger-volume mainstream products.

The two key vehicles, the Austin Allegro and Morris Marina, had been in production for four years and six respectively, and yet no all-new successor for either had been developed sufficiently for production. Clay models and engineering prototypes may have been built, but very little had been done with regard to the crucial production investment necessary, despite the edict of the Ryder Plan of 1975 that seemed in essence to imply that British Leyland should 'spend, spend, spend'.

Decisions had already been made that effectively made the 'Mighty Mini', which would become the Metro (see below), the only de facto option for a first major volume-built vehicle launch of any significance. Despite those models and prototypes, however, the products needed in the mid-size sector to replace the Allegro and Marina were still further down the road (and in fact would not arrive until 1983/4).

THE MODERN MG LEGACY

As rivals came to market that would render the old British Leyland products ever more uncompetitive, it was obvious to Edwardes that the company needed a stopgap, at least until the new cars – part of the 'LC10' family – could be made ready: even then, the basic thinking behind LC10 already dated back almost to the nationalization of British Leyland.

Casting around for someone with whom to do business, Edwardes and his team explored alliances with a number of manufacturers. Some initially appeared to offer good opportunities, but in the end none of the fine words came to anything. In the end, the company that appeared to provide the best 'fit' with British Leyland (or BL, as the company was known from July 1978) was Honda: similarly sized, ambitious and with aspirations to expand its business into new sectors. From an informal approach a month after the name change to BL, followed by a first date in San Francisco in October 1978, the relationship soon blossomed and quickly produced a deal whereby BL would get swift access to a medium-sized Honda saloon derived from the well-respected Honda Civic part bin.

Honda was developing a sister car to the Civic that would eventually be sold mainly in the domestic Japanese market as the Honda Ballade. As a small, roughly Ford Escort-sized car with a typically sewing machine-like Honda 4-cylinder engine and silky-smooth transmission, the Honda Ballade seemed to be a perfect fit between the forthcoming LC8 Metro and the larger Austin, Morris, Rover and Triumph product ranges. As the deal was fleshed out over the spring of 1979, the discussion inevitably turned to what badge the 'British' Ballade would wear, while the project moved forward under the guise of the code name 'Project Bounty' (showing little doubt that BL thought that with this car, their boat had come in).

Rumours in the media that the MG factory doors were being closed for the last time suggested that the Honda 'Bounty' would wear an MG badge when it saw production. This engendered hot debate among MG fans still smarting from the destruction of the MGB. In truth, some of these rumours might have started because key members of the old MG design team took on responsibility for drawing up the production plans and schedules for the new car, and moved across to the Cowley works when Abingdon finally closed. In addition there was an understandable trade in rumours both inside and outside Britain's largest indigenous car maker about what the Honda relationship would mean in the future.

The concept of an MG derived from a Honda did not seem illogical on further analysis, even if the idea itself may have been unpalatable to some: the Honda marque had overtly sporting leanings and the Honda S800 roadster, with its high-revving engine, had always resembled someone's highly sophisticated interpretation of what a contemporary MG Midget could have been like. Some speculated that the new 'Bounty' was going to be a three-door MG hatchback coupé, perhaps along the lines of the contemporary Honda Accord coupé, but when this story broke it was swiftly denied by BL.

A memorandum of understanding was signed between BL and Honda on 15 May 1979, stipulating that the British version would wear a Triumph badge; when 'Bounty' did finally appear, it was as the Triumph Acclaim. Free-revving and smooth though the drivetrain undoubtedly was, there was nothing remotely sporting about the neat if innocuous four-door saloon when it arrived in October 1981. For the time being, therefore, ideas of new MG products outside the indigenous Austin Morris arena would remain flights of fancy.

However, this was not because of any lack of desire on BL's part: right from the early days of the Bounty programme, what was then still a semi-independent Rover Triumph group charged with getting the Bounty into production (at that stage, the old Triumph factory at Canley was the intended home for the new car) pencilled in the idea of a new MG sports car to be developed 'dependent on the future opportunity of developing a new sports car in collaboration with Honda'.

THE MODERN MG LEGACY

At this stage (1980) Rover Triumph was still clinging on with increasing desperation to a project called 'Broadside', intended to salvage as much of the TR7/TR8 programme as possible; the optimistic ambition in 1980 was that a new Honda-MG joint venture project could deliver a future but entirely hypothetical new sports car in 1987.

'Broadside', however, was a short-lived project that was barely outlived by Rover Triumph itself (for a full account, see the present author's *Triumph TR7 – The Untold Story*, The Crowood Press, 2008). By the time that the Triumph Acclaim was launched, the Honda transplant was a BL product, built at the old Morris home at Cowley. The Triumph Acclaim arrived in the same month as the last TR7 sports car was built: perhaps not the best omen for the future prospects for another sports car.

The Triumph name quietly slipped into oblivion just four years later. This was scant reward for the Acclaim, which in the meantime had earned itself the reputation of being BL's most reliable product.

METROMORPHOSIS

Just as British Leyland management were looking for a way to replace the Allegro and Marina, the same team was wrestling with the consequences of a previous management's decision to focus primarily on a functional replacement for the evergreen Mini. By late 1977, when Edwardes took charge, work on the Mini replacement – a stark and basic but extremely compact three-door known by the project code of ADO88 – was already at an advanced stage, with tooling and production facilities ordered and broadly on target for a 1979 launch.

However, customer clinics were returning a fairly poor showing for ADO88 prototypes against competitor products: Ford had only recently launched its Spanish-built Fiesta to rave reviews and roaring sales. In the space of a few months, therefore, ADO88 was reworked, improving the styling at the front, upgrading some trim and materials, lengthening the whole car and reformatting the whole project as 'LC8'. Those with a long memory might have recalled the time when Lord Stokes arrived at BMC in 1968 and instigated a crash redesign of ADO14, which had emerged a year later as the Austin Maxi.

In the event, LC8, which became the Austin Mini Metro when launched in October 1980, would prove to be a great success, built in an expensively refitted Longbridge factory. Despite state-of-the-art manufacturing, the guts of the new Metro (the Mini prefix would soon be dropped) still relied to some extent on old engineering. There was growing, if reluctant, realization that BL would either have to bite the bullet and invest in new powertrain or look to their new friends at Honda (creators of the stratified charge CVCC engine in the previous decade), who could unquestionably provide useful knowledge of light engine design – but at a commercial price.

With the MGB on the way out – some BL showroom catalogues briefly featured both the new Austin Mini Metro and the MGB – the future of the octagon seemed briefly uncertain. Especially after the abortive Aston Martin bid to buy the MGB had faded away, BL took great pains to stress its firm intention to keep the MG name for some unspecified future product; for a short time that might have been part of the 'Broadside' programme (see above), but with the collapse of Rover Triumph and the decision already made to build the Honda 'Bounty' as a Triumph, the sole remaining option in the short term was to apply the MG name to the new Metro.

The first stab at a road-going performance Metro came from outside BL, in the form of a private conversion by the Cooper garages, who saw potential in rekindling the magic of the old Mini Coopers with the new Mini Metro. Only a prototype Cooper Metro was ever seen; before production could get into swing, BL dealt it a death blow by launching

THE MODERN MG LEGACY

Arguably the first real sign of recovery for the nationalized British Leyland was the LC8 Metro – and the two MG variants (1300 and Turbo) were an important part of this. (Rover Group)

their own performance hatch, the MG Metro, in May 1982. The MG Metro – and the sharper Turbo version that followed – were, in concert with their time, decked out with stripes and red trim and the obligatory octagonal badges: under the bonnet, there was even a nod to classic MG sports car buffs by the fitment of a polished alloy valve cover and a slightly larger carburettor. Traditionalists grumbled, but the general public were enthusiastic and sales reached a healthy level.

The MG versions of the Metro, followed by the various octagon-badged versions of the Maestro and Montego in 1983 and 1984 respectively, offered life for the name, but for many enthusiasts, no matter how good the product may have been, this was hardly much better than the more cynical excesses of BMC's badge engineering policy of twenty years beforehand. The MG Metro Turbo and the often quite frightening MG Montego Turbo offered a sign that Austin Rover, the latest iteration in a long line of company names, was seriously intent on offering MG badged cars that were quite distinct in character and performance from their Austin relatives, but there was little optimism in MG enthusiast circles around 1984 that we would ever see another true MG sports car. Thankfully, we would prove to be quite wrong.

HONDA DREAMS

As we saw earlier, the idea of an MG derived from a Honda had some theoretical merit. So why was there no MG Honda sports car? The answer to that obvious question is that beyond the first joint venture, which was little more than a turnkey operation whereby BL got to

World Rally MG Contender: The MG Metro 6R4

Arguably the first green shoots of an MG resurgence came when Austin Rover's motor sports division, created from the ashes of the old Abingdon Competitions Department, which had folded with the closure of the TR7 rally programme, began casting around for something new to use as the basis of a motor sports campaign. It was pretty obvious around the time of the Metro launch that this fairly revolutionary small car – at least in British car making terms – would be something upon which to build both a motor sports vehicle and a sales and marketing campaign. Even the most fervent optimist, however, would have been hard pressed to imagine that a 1.3-litre hatchback could be teased far beyond the field of one-make racing championships and club racing.

The answer was to create something revolutionary but obviously based on the platform of the Metro. This would be achieved in a number of discrete stages. The first offering was a one-off version of the Metro (yet to receive MG badging on any versions) with a unique 16-valve engine and five-speed gearbox, which was shown during the Metro's public launch at the 1980 Motor Show and various other venues afterwards – mainly as a statement of intent that Austin Rover had serious sporting aspirations, and that these would be realized in exciting and unexpected ways. This was just the warm-up act, however: the real genie in the bottle would come later.

Towards the end of 1980, John Davenport, BL's Motorsports Director, was formulating plans for a special rally car that would help to raise the image of both the company and their new 'Mighty Metro'. The following February, Davenport commissioned Patrick Head of Williams Engineering to build a 'silhouette' car loosely based on the Metro but with a front engine – a V6 derived from the Rover V8 – driving the back wheels through a rear-mounted gearbox.

Rally legend Tony Pond became involved: when he found he was sitting so far back in the cockpit that he couldn't see the front of the car, the plan changed from June 1981 to a mid-engined layout, using the same engine but with four-wheel drive. It would never be a sports car in the traditional sense, but it most definitely could be sporting.

Continuing with Williams Engineering throughout 1982, a period that coincided with the May launch of the MG Metro 1300, the concept swiftly developed, but with the connection to the Metro being little more than the basic bodyshell, lights and some of the trim. This original prototype was first driven in anger in February 1983, with Tony Pond at the wheel.

By the time that the 6R4 was first revealed a year later, the MG badge was firmly back in the new car sales brochures and accordingly the mid-engined mongrel – ugly as sin but mad as a box of frogs – was christened the MG Metro 6R4. The full story of the Metro 6R4 (including the bespoke V6 engine created for it, hinted at during the press launch in February 1983 but not shown to the press until May 1985) is a fascinating tale that need not concern us in more detail here other than to call attention to its role in elevating enthusiasm both inside and outside Austin Rover for the idea of a truly exciting MG.

To the Austin Rover senior management the Metro 6R4 was very much a 'Metro' rather than an 'MG': better sales of Austin, MG and Rover badged hatchbacks and saloons was the 6R4 mission – but as far as the world was concerned, this was still an MG and was regarded as a potent indication of even more exotic products to come. Just how exotic would soon become apparent.

The weird and wonderful MG Metro 6R4, which promised a great deal and gave credence through its make-up to the idea of an exotic sports car – only to be stymied by changes in International Rallying rules. (Rover Group)

THE MODERN MG LEGACY

build a barely-altered Honda, both parties were keen to explore true joint ventures but only in areas where both could benefit equally.

The sector where Honda genuinely wanted to expand was in the larger car market, where they had no presence, while BL desperately wanted a modern replacement for the Rover SD1, which could also serve as the platform to stage a return to the North American market. Early in 1982 BL abandoned plans for a reskin for the Rover SD1 under the 'Bravo' code name, while Honda had begun to formulate plans for a bigger V6-powered flagship.

In 1982 design direction at the company had passed into the hands of former Chrysler man Royden Axe, but the concept for the new executive saloon started even before his arrival. The joint-venture programme was formally signed between Austin Rover Managing Director Mark Snowden and Tadeshi Kume (later to become President of Honda) in November that year. Known as 'Project XX', and mischievously dubbed the 'double cross', this programme would reach production in 1986 as the Rover 800 and Honda Legend. Honda had motor sport experience and aspirations of its own, and arguably while the idea of an MG Honda may have had some appeal, the need in such a relationship would have been rather more BL's than Honda's.

Of course these commercial realities did not stop the people at BL, especially in the company's advanced design studios, from toying with the idea of new MG products, especially in the wake of the MG Metro's successful launch in 1982. However, once more those same commercial realities, including the fact of state ownership (and, increasingly

The US magazine *Road & Track* sponsored a conversion of the Honda CRX Coupé into a spyder version by specialist Californian coach-builder Richard Straman (better known for Ferrari conversions) in 1984, and they cheekily commissioned one a few months later in British Racing Green and put MG badges on it. Straman went on to build 310 Honda CRX Spyders, but the 'MG CRX' remained a one-off. (*Road & Track*)

from 1979, a Conservative government hostile to the concept of long-term continuation of public funding), militated against these MG ideas getting much further than designers' sketchpads.

By 1984 the first new Austins had been launched in the wake of the Metro in the form of the five-door Maestro hatch and the closely related Montego four-door saloon, both with MG-badged versions in their ranges. These new models were seen as the first step in the revitalization of what, from September of that year, became known as Austin Rover. Jaguar had been privatized the previous month (the British government retained, for the time being, a so-called 'golden share' to prevent Jaguar being gobbled up by an overseas buyer) and the new management in charge of what would soon be exclusively Austin, MG and Rover affairs began looking at the company's future with a focus on making the business more attractive to potential private investors.

The relationship with Honda was going fairly well (Project XX was heading for a 1986 debut, somewhat behind the original programme), battles with the more militant elements of the workforce seemed to have been largely won, a midlife facelift of the Metro (including a five-door version) was on the cards, a new engine family was under development and, under the dynamic if sometimes overbearing leadership of Harold Musgrove, Austin Rover seemed at last to have begun to develop self-belief. Against this backdrop came the first seeds of what could have become an early rebirth for the open-top MG, without, it seems, any serious thoughts of a Honda input.

DAUGHTERS OF METRO: ECV3, AR6 AND THE MG MIDGET

Roy Axe had arrived too late to have any significant impact on the Maestro, or a great deal more on the Montego; he had overseen a major revamp of the 'XX' design at the start of that project, however, and had been able to completely overhaul and consolidate the disparate corporate design studios he had inherited. Alongside the main design studio function, Roy Axe facilitated an advanced design strand and, along with many other ideas that eventually foundered through lack of funding or corporate commitment, the studio created an advanced concept for what could have been the replacement for the Metro.

The Metro had been a marvellous achievement for a company on its knees, but the roots of LC8 lay in an even older project, ADO88, which had been created as a replacement for the almost antediluvian Mini, née 1959, and using much of the older car's running gear. The Longbridge engineers had worked marvels in updating the old BMC A-Series to create the 'A-Plus', but the old stager, with its gears-in-the-sump four-speed transmission, was losing ground to much newer opposition.

From 1984 Austin Rover was working with serious intent on an all-new engine, the K-Series, which would of course become crucial to the MG*F* story in due course, together with a five-speed gearbox based on a design bought in from Peugeot. A forward-looking BL subsidiary, BL Technology, based at BL's now research centre at Gaydon, had shown the press a concept for a future small car code-named 'ECV3' in December 1982, intended to be a showcase for the future and to show the world that BL Technology was looking ahead.

ECV3 (the letters stood for 'Energy Conservation Vehicle') was a 3,840mm long mobile test bed with an all-new 1113cc 3-cylinder engine, which, unbeknown to us at the time, gave some tentative clues to the future K-Series (even though the engines were not in any way related). Despite input from Ogle Design, ECV3 was not a styling tour de force, nor was that its intention: even so, it raised expectations for a future Metro less shackled to ADO15/ADO20 Mini technology.

As part of the future programme, the design studio at Canley was beginning to look at AR6,

THE MODERN MG LEGACY

Gerry McGovern led the creation of this concept for an MG Midget from the basis of another concept – for a possible future Metro. The 1979 MG Midget in the photo is from the last batch built at Abingdon. (Rover Group)

a projected replacement for the Metro. One of the design team involved in this new car was Gerry McGovern, a recent recruit to the company via Peugeot-Talbot from Chrysler, where Roy Axe had spotted and nurtured the ex-Royal College of Art student before enticing him to make the move to Canley.

Just as BL Technology had been used to raise the engineering research profile of BL, Roy Axe was keen to raise the company's design profile, particularly as the only production cars that his newly merged studio would have to show the general public until 1986 would be the Maestro and Montego, hardly candidates for the international car design trophy cabinet. Axe hit upon the idea of an open day for the press, but it was fairly obvious that it would be no good showing the assembled hacks a number of current cars posed unconvincingly on the studio floor.

As a consequence, what appeared on the face of it to be an obvious answer swiftly presented itself: the studio would work up a design proposal, highly hypothetical at this stage, for a possible future Metro replacement, aimed at around the year 1990. The theme of 'Project 90' (or 'Joe 90' as some wags in the studio dubbed it) would derive from ECV3 – thereby neatly linking the engineering and design themes – but could also point the way for the 'real' Metro replacement, AR6.

Various design proposals were sketched out for this future Metro, followed by scale and full-sized models. Along with Gerry McGovern's, there were various studies by other members of the design team, including Steve Harper and Dave Saddington. In the end, a full-sized model was made ready for display in a corner of the Canley design studio with the intention – successfully, as it happens – of piquing interest from the visiting journalists, keen to see the workings of the new Austin Rover facility under the direction of a newly imported director.

The visit took place early in 1984. From an article by journalist Daniel Ward headed 'Designs on the Future', published in the weekly magazine *Motor* on 25 February 1984, we learn that investment in the new Canley studio was already £5.2 million and that the staffing contingent was 110. Included with the article was a line drawing that was a pretty good rendition of the 'future Metro' that Ward had seen in the studio.

While assessing this future Metro, it was fairly logical to take the exercise a step further and look at the idea of a soft-top version; engineering and budget realities need not take a front seat when designers are exploring the boundaries of what might be possible, and Roy Axe was keen to see if some kind of 'modern Midget' could conceivably be spun off the Project 90/AR6 study.

It wasn't as if the idea was totally off the wall; a private company had made some modest sales by taking a production MG Metro and chopping the roof off – somewhat crudely and inelegantly, it has to be said (even if the idea of a soft-top version would come back much later in the Metro's life). Various pundits were asking why Austin Rover hadn't looked more seriously at a drop-top Metro, and so a studio study was a logical step to take.

Taking a copy of the original three-door hatch as its basis, the designers effectively lopped off everything above the waistline bar the windscreen, then dressed the grille aperture with an octagon, reshaped the bumpers, lower side aprons and sills, and cut a pair of broad louvres in the bonnet top. Finished in de rigueur bright red, but with a white finish to the lower body section (echoing the two-tone colour themes that would soon

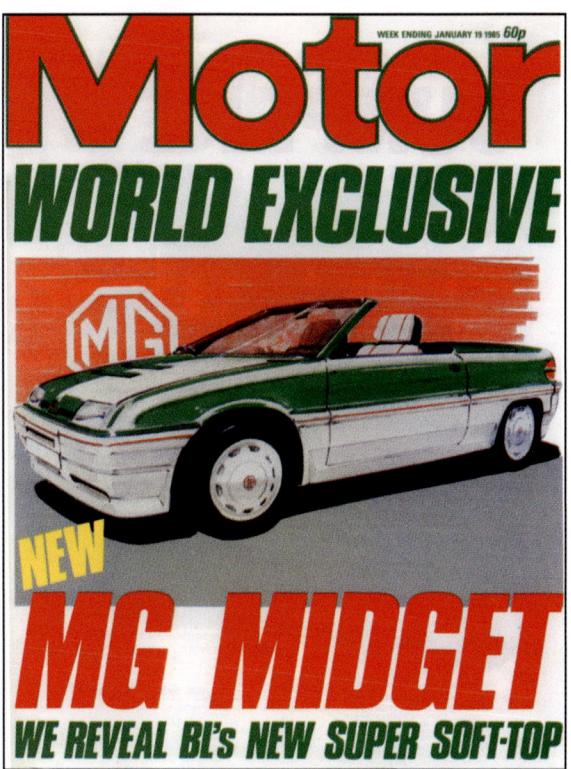

Motor magazine published a cover story scoop in January 1985, but wrongly claimed that the Midget was actually scheduled for production – and with Honda running gear.

be seen on some production Austins and Rovers), the little Midget certainly looked different.

Seen from the perspective of the twenty-first century, the style of the red and white Midget looks a little square-cut and awkward, but those sharp-edged lines were quite appropriate for the time, even if the prevailing mood in 1984 was returning to more aerodynamic curvaceous shapes (such as the Ford Sierra). The prototype was developed through the creation of a full-sized plastic bodyshell, manufactured by Specialised Mouldings of Huntingdon, and was eventually photographed for the archives, some shots also featuring one of the last rubber bumper MG Midgets.

According to Steve Harper, working in the studio at the time, this latter car took a little finding, but eventually one belonging to colour and trim designer Michelle Wadhams, the girlfriend of designer Rob Owen and later to become a key layout designer for the Heritage Museum at Gaydon, was used for the outdoor shots reproduced here.

This 'Metro Midget' was never shown to the press, but that did not stop a story appearing in *Motor* on 19 January 1985, again written by Daniel Ward and peppered with pretty accurate sketches clearly based on photos of the 'Metro Midget'. The suspicions of some of the former design team point towards a leak at Specialised Mouldings, based on the fact that the *Motor* sketches appeared to have been based on images of the car using the wheels only used for transport to the company. Since the prototype was just a shell, however, Ward had to be inventive with regard to the running gear.

During the previous year, a firm in California had started cutting the roofs off unsuspecting Honda Civic CRX coupés. *Road & Track* magazine featured this in their July 1984 issue and subsequent issues included various pleas from enthusiasts, the author among them, for Austin Rover to take a cue from this pretty little car and consider an MGD or a TR9.

It had therefore not taken much effort for the writers at *Motor* to put two and two together in January 1985 to make five, and to announce confidently that the 'Metro Midget' would be launched in the near future with Honda running gear. Sadly, it was all nonsense, however, although a cynic might be tempted to suggest that the continuing debate about a new MG Midget did relatively little harm to the arguments of those inside Austin Rover who wanted to see MG reborn in this way. *Road & Track* playfully commissioned one of the Honda CRX roadster conversions, had it finished in British Racing Green, stuck MG badges on it and showed the result in their May 1985 issue.

Mindful of the speculation that followed these various magazine articles, Harold Musgrove appeared unmoved and was certainly unequivocal when he was tackled about the subject in a later interview with Gavin Green for *CAR* magazine's June 1985 issue: 'we have no plans to build an MG roadster' he insisted, adding, 'it is not even in the concept stage. We would only build one again if we thought that it was profitable. At the moment, we don't think it is.'

According to Roy Axe, this corporate view stemmed largely from the Marketing section:

> They would always insist that MG was a 'brand of the past' and it was not a brand that a modern man or woman would relate to. They thought that it related to something like the MG TC Midget in terms of how the Americans saw it – which was quite right, as they did. But what they totally miscalculated with regard to America was that the Americans had their image of MG, but because of that, MG was on a pedestal, and you could have brought out a modern MG and it would have absolutely wiped the floor.

By the summer of 1985, when the *CAR* interview appeared, the MG Midget project was already old hat. AR6 was abandoned the following year, largely on cost grounds (although Graham Day would claim in an interview in July 1987 that the reason had been a lack of proper market research on the prototype), in favour of a thorough facelift of the original Metro platform. With the abandonment of AR6, this route to a possible open-top Midget was lost. In the meantime, however, something far more remarkable was being readied in the design studio, and this time there was a slight possibility that it might even see a public debut.

MG SUPERCAR: THE EX-E

As we have seen, when Roy Axe first arrived at BL, he found a fragmented, under-resourced and to some extent dispirited design function spread across several poorly equipped studios.

THE MODERN MG LEGACY

One could argue that they had achieved some pretty remarkable things with the resources available to them, but remarkable in this context is not necessarily a measure of greatness. Facelifted Marinas, Allegros and evolutionary products like the Austin Ambassador arrived at the start of the 1980s, but it was going to be a fairly lean time from Axe's arrival until the debut of the Honda Rover XX project.

For various reasons, XX became delayed and the launch slipped from 1985 to 1986. Roy Axe was worried that getting across the message that the new Austin Rover was a design-led company was going to prove almost impossible to achieve. Just as Axe used a 'future Metro' concept in February 1984 to excite press interest in the work of his designers, he began to think about an even more exciting concept that could help build up the excitement in Austin Rover design before the XX could be made public.

In the studio, designers were working on early sketches and models for a coupé version of XX, already being thought of as the 'Coupé Concept Vehicle' (CCV), but these designs were obviously tied to an executive car that had yet to enter production. Clearly it would not be practicable to show a prototype of XX or an offshoot without either giving the game away or providing a false sense of what was to come, and so Axe and his team hit upon the idea of a futuristic MG sports car: something at the same time forward-looking but with a production-feasible basis.

The process began towards the end of 1983, well before either the press open day or the 'Metro Midget', under yet another acronym: the 'Sports Concept Vehicle' (SCV). During 1984 there were further paper exercises, but before long the idea with the most obviously exciting potential was a mid-engined MG 'supercar' built on the platform and running gear of the

One of the early images for the 'Sports Concept Vehicle' project which became the basis of the EX-E of 1985.

THE MODERN MG LEGACY

MG Metro 6R4, then still under development and with a very real, if low-volume, production future ahead of it. Serious work on the SCV therefore started around Christmas 1984. For a while, designers continued to doodle a variety of low sleek shapes but none of them seemed to hit the spot; Roy Axe decided that a bit of direction was needed, and he brought along his own Ferrari 308GTB for inspiration and to show the kind of design that he wanted for the MG supercar.

By this stage, there were two separate studios at Canley: one for exteriors, led by Gordon Sked, and another for interiors, overseen by Richard Hamblin. While Sked and his team, which included Gerry McGovern, sought inspiration from contemporary fighter aircraft such as the Lockheed Martin Falcon F-16 and, a little more prosaically, Roy Axe's Ferrari, Hamblin oversaw the creation of a remarkable technology-led interior that would prove to be a riot of cream, grey and red leather, a state-of-the-art digital dashboard (sadly non-functional) and such novelties for 1985 as a CD player and a credit-card style keyless entry system.

As Gordon Sked remembers it, the MG supercar project was basically under himself and Richard Hamblin but both accountable directly to Roy Axe:

> Richard had overall responsibility for the interior and I had the same for the exterior. Gerry McGovern had been working with Richard but at that point he switched over to work under me on the exterior – Gerry and I worked in total concert on the exterior of that car.

In tandem with the design work, Stan Manton and his engineering team schemed out the intended mechanical package and the proposed advanced body construction, using modular units and a riveted and glued alloy structure, which would have been encased in an unstressed skin of polypropylene.

Richard Hamblin recalls that in order to motivate his team to more creative efforts for such a show car:

> I sent the designers off to see the film *Alien* to get some inspiration, which they had thought was a pretty cool idea, and after which they were churning out futuristic sketches by the dozen. The interior of the EX-E started from one of these sketches that a designer had discarded: I felt that this particular sketch, with modifications, would make for an exciting and sporty theme. In essence my input was to create a form (with the facia, seats and door trims) that gave a hexagonal – or even octagonal – space for the driver and another for the passenger. By the use of carpets with large woven logos the interior did not therefore just 'have' MG badges, but in effect 'was' MG badges ...

By the summer of 1985, the project had moved from a full-size clay model to a fully-glazed plastic 'skin' – made, like the 'Metro Midget', by Specialised Mouldings – fitted out with Richard Hamblin and his team's fully trimmed interior. To the average onlooker, the new super MG looked just about ready to launch off down the road in pursuit of the nearest Italian supercar. In fact the car was a long way from being roadworthy; other than ensuring some package protection for the Metro 6R4 running gear, only virtual engineering work had been done. There were tentative plans to build one or more running prototypes and, depending on a positive corporate view, maybe a very low-volume production run. All this was for the future, however: the first issue was whether or not to show the car to the general public.

There was much debate both for and against; some of the corporate suits were firmly against the idea of showing the MG to the public, from the point of view that the car could become yet another means of criticizing the company for failing to deliver on an exciting promise. Sales and Marketing were far from convinced that a supercar would lift sales of Metros, Maestros and Montegos, while some in senior management were undoubtedly nervous of the

THE MODERN MG LEGACY

The MG EX-E caused a sensation when it first appeared in public, initially at the Frankfurt Motor Show in September 1985 and then a month later at London's Motorfair.

view that some politicians (and commentators) might take of a publicly accountable company dallying with the frivolous exotic sports car market. It was true that similar false promises had happened before – the 1966 Rover P6BS still excited debate in enthusiast circles – but the people at Austin Rover knew well that, this time around, some genuinely impressive new product was on the way in the form of the Rover XX, and who knew what success with XX could lead to in the future?

Of course, if the MG supercar was going to be shown to the public, it needed a name and 'MG SCV' didn't really cut the mustard. Following the long tradition of MG, 'EX' naming was perhaps a no-brainer, but there seems to have been little enthusiasm for following on from the last 'EX' number: the 'EX253' name would appear some years later (see Chapter Four), but perhaps it didn't have the right cachet in 1985. In the end, the idea came from Austin Rover PR man Ian Elliott, working on what would become the publicity poster for the MG supercar concept, who remembered seeing Paul Hughes's sketches of ADO21 (the earlier idea for a mid-engined MG) with their 'MGD' badges, and suggested that it did not take much of a leap of imagination to see this latest 'future MG' as an 'experimental MG-E', which soon became the euphonious EX-E.

Despite the effort that had been put into providing EX-E with the illusory appearance of a fully functioning, production-ready sports car, and the design and manufacture of a dedicated red and grey motor show display stand, the debate on whether or not EX-E should be shown to the public raged on from July 1985 into September. According to Roy Axe, Musgrove had even been reluctant to come and see EX-E: 'in the end I said he had to come down and have a look at the finished article; the Frankfurt show was about three weeks away'.

Musgrove relented and told Axe, 'I'll look at it – but I'm not going to decide on whether or not we're going to show it until two days before

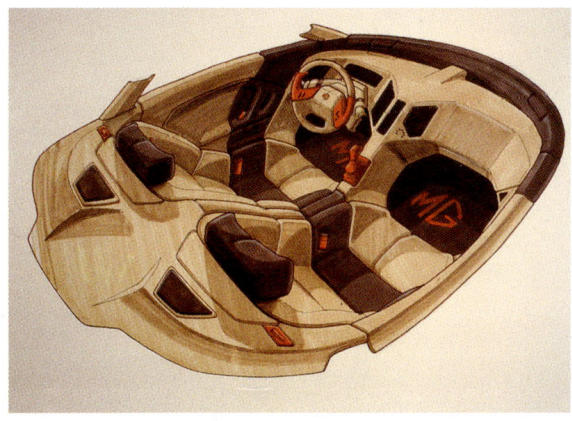

The layout of the EX-E interior was loosely inspired by the traditional MG octagon shape. (Richard Hamblin)

the show'. When Musgrove saw the car he was, according to Axe, 'really knocked out by it', but he had brought along some marketing colleagues, explaining 'I don't know if we can do this, because Marketing aren't really behind it'. In the end, it was only a few days before the Frankfurt Motor Show that Harold Musgrove finally, and reluctantly, came round and agreed that the model could be crated up and shipped out to Germany.

Press Day at Frankfurt was a remarkable occasion, not only for the folk from Austin Rover but for the motoring and press world in general: the reception accorded the EX-E was little short of rapturous, with accolades heaped upon the car – and a beaming Roy Axe – from design professionals and journalists alike. That evening, BBC television's main news bulletin at nine o'clock featured a prominent report by their leading motoring correspondent, William Woollard, which heralded (with typical journalistic hyperbole) the rebirth of the MG sports car.

Back home in England, some of the Austin Rover management were probably as much thrilled as nervous at the publicity their design study had created, although according to Roy Axe, 'after the Frankfurt Show, you couldn't find anyone who wasn't all for it!' The ever cautious Harold Musgrove refused to be drawn beyond a statement that the EX-E was 'a superb illustration of the talent and technology within Austin Rover', although he conceded that the design warranted further study: 'we must consider whether to make some prototype runners', he concluded.

EX-E again proved a smash hit a month later at London's Motorfair show, and excited further debate about the prospect of a functional prototype that one could drive or maybe even buy. 'The MG EX-E explores many new styling ideas and a wide range of new and innovative research and development technologies which Austin Rover is evaluating', the Motorfair press release stated, adding:

> but this is much more than a design exercise, for this advanced MG has been designed from the outset to be compatible with possible future production and also to provide the basis for a potential competition car.

Sadly, those running prototypes were never built, although EX-E became a much-travelled ambassador for the Austin Rover design talents of which Musgrove was now so obviously proud. Normally finished in the designers' eternal favourite metallic silver, a colour that generally shows off designs to their best advantage in any kind of light, EX-E ended up as part of the Heritage Collection at Gaydon, but along the way it was temporarily refinished in Ferrari red (as seen in some of the accompanying photographs) especially for a high-level delegation from the United States associated with the Sterling business.

EX-E may never have driven under its own power (nor served as the basis of a possible Group-S successor to the 6R4), but it had raised expectations ahead of the definitive Rover XX launch and pointed the way for a possible MG sports car some way down the road.

chapter two

Return of the MG Sports Car

IN THE WAKE OF THE NEW ROVER: WHERE WAS THE NEW MG?

In the early part of 1986, with the rapturous reception accorded the MG EX-E still fresh in the memory, the key focus at Austin Rover was on getting the Honda-Rover XX ready for launch that summer. By the time that the production car was unveiled as the Rover 800, thoughts about MG sports cars had been pushed into the corner for the time being while attention turned to the latest 'make or break' product for the company that had until only recently still been known as British Leyland. Along with closer ties with Honda, the success of the Rover 800 would form the basis of yet another return to the North American market and many more potential products aimed at a world market.

In the spring of 1986, the Austin Rover design studios were shaken up, with two new teams reconstituted from the old 'exterior' and 'interior' studios as 'current car design' and 'concept design'. According to Richard Hamblin, who took over the concept studio, the idea was that current car design worked on cars that were about to be launched, but the task then for Concept Design was to look ahead of that, conceiving styles that would fit into a market after the current cars were discontinued. Concept Design was set up at Rover in April 1986 – amidst the blaze of publicity for EXE and CCV.

Hamblin's design team was managed by Graham Lewis and included David Saddington, Jeremy Newman, Richard Carter, Ian Beech and Gerry McGovern, many of whom would go on to greater things: 'Derek Anderson led my Engineering team and Vic Horner led my Modelling team. We also had access to Workshops and Build areas that contained some exceptional skills'. It would not be very long before this talented group would be working hard on their first all-new project.

It did not take long for the debate to return to the subject of MG: if Rover 800 sales in the USA and Canada were being planned, many observers thought a new MG sports car would inevitably form part of the grand plan in the medium term. The repeated use of the MG EX-E model in corporate events only exacerbated this kind of debate. As it happens, Austin Rover created an all-new brand name for the 800 exclusively for North American sales – eschewing the 'Rover' name in favour of 'Sterling'. At the time we were told that this

RETURN OF THE MG SPORTS CAR

Although the EX-E was shown to public in silver (and that is how it survives in the Heritage Motor Museum), it was also finished at one stage in Ferrari red for viewing by a US dealer delegation. (Rover Group)

was because the Rover name 'was not well known' in the USA, but nobody really believed the story given in the Rover 800 press pack issued by Austin Rover in July 1986:

> A number of names were selected and given rigorous consumer research in New York, California and Florida ... The name Sterling was a runaway winner. People readily associated it with hallmark silver quality and a prestigious British luxury car.

The truth was more prosaic; Rover's last foray into the USA had been with the Rover SD1, which had clocked up pitiful sales numbers before the programme was cancelled. Withdrawal – followed by the abandonment of Triumph sports car sales – had been a painful, costly and perhaps clumsily handled business, leaving various brand liabilities inadequately resolved. Coupled with the potential for confusion between 'Rover' and 'Land Rover', Austin Rover resolved to avoid legal battles in a litigious market and so created a new name rather than use one of their old ones.

It was a curious situation, and had militated against the 800 simply being badged as a Triumph or even an MG, but one is tempted to wonder even now why the choice of a fabricated name like Sterling was so much better than even a well-worn name like Wolseley or Vanden Plas, both little known in the USA at the time but possessed of heritage ripe for clever exploitation (a philosophy later adopted extremely successfully by BMW with the Mini name).

Following on from EX-E, which started life as the SCV, came the Rover Coupé Concept Vehicle (CCV), which once more wowed the public and design professionals alike. But it was to be the last of Roy Axe's Austin Rover design studies to be shown at a motor show. (Rover Group)

A NEW MG DIRECTION: THE BEGINNINGS OF THE MG*F*

Even the possibility of legal battles, however, including suits from any former dealers who might have been tempted to claim sales rights, did not prevent much lively debate about the idea of MG one day returning to the US market via the doorway opened by the Sterling, launched there in 1987.

In the meantime, however, as the Rover 800 edged closer towards launch, there were some tentative thoughts about what role MG might play, especially now that EX-E had dramatically raised expectations that there would be a new sports car somewhere not too far in Austin Rover's future.

In the wake of the ECV3 studies (*see* Chapter One), Austin Rover, as we saw earlier, created an all-new engine range to replace the A-Series; originally envisaged, like the B-Series of thirty years before, as a 'small' engine of around 1200cc, this new engine – the K-Series – would eventually, rather like its forebear, span capacities of 1.1, 1.4, 1.6 and 1.8 litres. As part of this programme, there was some thought about the kind of projects that the new engine could be used for, and semi-serious consideration was given to a fresh sports car study.

With the EX-E concept under their belt, and given the enthusiasm for the F-16 fighter plan, the concept (first to be looked at by the new Concept Studio) was dubbed the MG F-16;

RETURN OF THE MG SPORTS CAR

This rear view of the early F-16 model shows a simple if rather bulky rear light treatment, with lenses that wrap across the whole of the rear bodywork – a feature that dates the style. (Rover Group)

the fact that the K-Series would be available as a 16-valve engine was part of the logic too. Wheelbase was set at around that of the contemporary MG Maestro.

According to Richard Hamblin, the basic tenet was the creation of a 'new MGB' for the next decade: 'the aim of the new project was to start with a clean sheet of paper and produce a design that would convince the Company to consider an all-new MG Sports Car'.

Several members of the design team became involved, with Gerry McGovern taking the

A contemporary sketch of the MG F-16 concept shows neat, compact proportions which would serve later prototypes very well. (Rover Group)

The F-16 was not Rover Group's only foray into open-topped concepts: the silver-finished full-size model is seen here in a studio with a larger open-topped concept built by a US company. (Rover Group)

effective lead but with key input from colleague Richard Carter and an overview from Graham Lewis; the concept decided upon was a modern front-wheel drive sports car, but no definite decision was made regarding the intended engine: the K-Series was one potential option, but it was also feasible that the O-Series, S-Series and various developments, such as the M16 engine for the Rover 800, would have been in the pipeline.

A composite-bodied prototype was built, à la EX-E, and finished in the designer's perennial favourite silver, although a later more detailed version was finished in the obligatory red. Some limited concept engineering ensued up to the early part of 1986, by which stage it was assumed that the K-Series would be the engine of choice. By the summer of that year, the project had reached a point where it would need corporate approval to take it any further.

Roy Axe and his team were pleased with the outcome, and they hoped that Harold Musgrove and the Austin Rover directors would be too, but if they thought the project had a chance of a 'green light' they would be sadly disappointed. Also in due course, the silver prototype would be shown alongside a concept for a two-door convertible, based on the Rover 800, that was built by American Sunroof Company. Although the idea of a sports car was attractive, the Americans who saw the silver 'MG' generally thought it was too small. 'Not everyone agreed with the analysis that Americans would not buy a small sports car, especially a certain Japanese company', Richard Hamblin points out.

Even though the size issue could arguably have been addressed, the main problem was that by this stage the AR6 new Metro project had been cancelled in favour of a major facelift of the original Metro so that it could take the new K-Series engine. Also at this time, a planned facelift for the Maestro was abandoned in favour of the 'YY' project. With the death or dethronement of the obvious donor vehicles, one of which might have been used as the platform for the new sports car, the concept gathered dust just like the earlier Midget.

RETURN OF THE MG SPORTS CAR

Interlude: An Attempted Arranged Marriage to Ford

In February 1986 a remarkable story was leaked to the media by Roy Hattersley, a member of the Labour opposition, claiming that the government had been courted by the Ford Motor Company with a view to buying the cars division of BL. In the event, public outcries over similar deals led to the talks being cancelled, but not before some of the thinking behind Ford's approach had become known. Ford was understood to be interested in the forthcoming K-Series engine, perhaps for use in its own Fiesta, but there was a lot more besides.

Speaking at the Geneva Motor Show that March, Ford of Europe Chairman Bob Lutz told Daniel Ward, who was now writing for *Autocar*, that he thought a great opportunity had been lost. With an obvious dig at Austin Rover's Japanese connection, Lutz said 'we were committed to retaining the Britishness of the MG, Austin and Rover marques, and what we would have produced down the road would have been more British than the current Rover 200'. An avowed MG fan, Lutz saw particular scope for selling Rover and MG cars through Ford's established European outlets, and he told Ward that 'one of the fascinating things for me is to take the MG marque, now nothing but a badge, and return to its past glory with a popular-priced sports car'. In the event, this all proved academic, although the fact that the Ford Motor Company had said such public things about the potential for an MG sports car struck a chord with some inside Austin Rover.

By March 1986, however, with the Ford interlude behind them, Harold Musgrove and senior colleagues were in Japan agreeing the terms of a deal that would see them work on the second true joint venture after 'XX', the so-called 'YY' mid-range car, seen at that stage primarily as a replacement for the Maestro but with the potential to generate other models too. Part of the deal would also see the Longbridge factory building versions of the new car with the Honda name, mainly for sales in mainland Europe.

A month later, and Musgrove and Axe were at the Turin Motor Show, the heartland of Italian car designers, to show off another design concept, the finalized version of the elegant Rover CCV (Coupé Concept Vehicle). It was very impressive, but still left the MG questions unanswered.

CANADA DRY: THE ARRIVAL OF GRAHAM DAY

Graham Day, who had been appointed by Prime Minister Margaret Thatcher to take charge of BL after the abortive Ford deal, and Austin Rover Chairman Harold Musgrove were as different as chalk and cheese.

Day was a high-flying, politically astute, Canadian industrial magnate skilled in either dismantling or reconstructing major industrial combines; he readily acknowledged his lack of detailed product knowledge wherever he worked, but always held to the maxim that he should love his customer to death. Musgrove for his part was a hard-grafting British Leyland-trained man who had learned his skills through the school of hard knocks and knew a great deal – perhaps too much – about the detailed machinations of his corner of the industry. Musgrove, who had won crucial battles with the unions, knew that the customer and his workforce were vital cogs; while he thought that sometimes 'tough love' was needed to get things done, it is unlikely that he ever thought of loving anyone to death.

'The two of them never gelled', Axe believes:

> they were totally and utterly different people. Graham was a strange man – he was very supportive of what I was doing – very enthusiastic – and when we looked at variations of themes he was only too pleased to show them to the government to let them know what we were doing.

Day was ever the political animal, adept at

handling politicians and the press alike, whereas Musgrove (passion and determination notwithstanding) never seemed especially comfortable in his dealings with either group.

It was also said by many that Musgrove had a blind spot when it came to the manufacturing and production engineering talents inside the company: when Roy Axe arrived, Musgrove had told the designer that all of the company's problems could be fixed by good styling, whereas Axe's view, in contrast, was that styling was arguably the least of BL's problems. With the new joint venture project, Musgrove's faith in his engineers would be severely put to the test.

Day's brief from Margaret Thatcher was simple: rid the government of financial responsibility for British Leyland as soon as humanly possible, preferably by making a lean and attractive company that someone in the private sector would want to buy. The first indicator of how this plan was progressing would be the new Rover 800, due for launch in July 1986, just two months after Day arrived. That summer the omens should have been good, but not everything with the Rover 800 launch went well enough for Day's taste.

For one thing, a great deal of emphasis had been placed on the technology-laden 'Sterling' top-of-the-range 800 models, but these were priced at a level that made them more expensive than the lowest price versions of Jaguar's new 'XJ40' XJ6 saloon. This was not lost on the press, and BL (or 'Rover Group', as Day renamed the company in July) suffered in the comparisons, unfair or otherwise. Delays with various model variants and a questionable relationship with the projected North American ARCONA group did not help either, but above all Day's and Musgrove's styles of management were simply poles apart.

A much-criticized press launch of the Rover 800 did not help matters, with Harold Musgrove trying to sell the product to bemused journalists with the kind of evangelical zeal that would have been more appropriate at a dealer conference. Even allowing for the fact that the cars were pre-production, and therefore not necessarily of the highest quality, the criticism of some aspects of build quality was a harsh message about a car that Austin Rover had clearly pitched as an executive car more sophisticated than Ford's big-selling Granada. External Affairs Director Jean Denton (later Baroness Denton) left soon afterwards.

In September 1986 it was announced that Harold Musgrove and a couple of senior colleagues, Peter Regnier and Mark Snowdon, were 'retiring' from the company (a contemporary from the time puts it more bluntly, 'all three were blown out the door one morning'). So, despite all the work he had overseen, Musgrove would no longer be at the helm when 'Sterling' returned to North America the following year. For some at the newly renamed company, however, the arrival of the Graham Day era signalled a breath of fresh air: like Musgrove, the Canadian suffered no fools, but he was prepared to listen to the more off-the-wall ideas and cut some slack in developing them. Day sanctioned an £8 million further investment in Roy Axe's design studios, and began to ask questions about such ideas as MG sports cars.

Day brought a new way of dealing with the press that was quite unlike previous years. It is very enlightening to look back on some of his interviews from the time. A good example is the discussion he had with Steve Cropley that featured in the April 1987 issue of CAR magazine. 'I think that MG is the second of two valuable brands we own', he said, without even a cursory reference to Austin, 'I think [MG has] been under exploited over the last five to eight years. I think that's a shame, and would like progressively to change things back'.

Day did not go as far as to undermine the Metro, Maestro and Montegos with MG badges (still on sale, with an MG Maestro Turbo yet to be launched, although none of these cars were destined for a long-term future), but he acknowledged what the outside world had been thinking for some time: 'What we haven't done is to put MG in its traditional role as a responsive, handy, two-seater roadster; a

RETURN OF THE MG SPORTS CAR

separate car from the rest of the range'.

One could hardly have imagined Harold Musgrove expounding this train of thought to a journalist (especially in light of Musgrove's words just two years beforehand, referred to above), but Day went even further by admitting, 'we're looking at it now ... I'm making no commitment about it, but it's one of those specialised sectors like the 800 coupé'. Day drew a possible parallel to the Honda CRX as a possible role model: 'we've got a couple of models we're looking at. But I'd be a bloody fool to focus attention on fringe products before the mainstream of our range is lined up.'

By this stage, Graham Day had brought in a new sales and marketing chief, Kevin Morley, a Ford high-flyer who was looking at opening up new markets for the company. Since the next big Honda-Rover joint venture, the 'YY' project, was under development, it appeared that Day was hinting at a sports car spun off this platform. Behind the scenes, however, some of the Austin Rover designers were taking Day's enthusiasm as a cue to find some way to make such a car a reality. As Richard Hamblin recalls,

Harold Musgrove had run the company with a rod of iron. Some things that happened later would never have got off the starting blocks in his day. I can just imagine trying to get a 'skunk' project up and off the ground, with no approvals and no approved budget whatsoever – as I did later; I would have been on the carpet in Harold's office just for thinking about it.

With Graham Day overseeing matters, and with Les Wharton effectively filling Musgrove's shoes, there was clearly more of an open mind to 'what if?' exercises.

A VIABLE MG SPORTS CAR: THE F-16 CONCEPT SHOWS THE WAY

From the perspective of 1987, the key priority for Rover Group, as the company was now known, was clearly the Honda-Rover 'YY' replacement for the Rover 200 then on sale. 'YY', which, for fairly obvious reasons, was swiftly renamed 'AR8' (and then, as Austin

As the MG F-16 project evolved, it became more believable – and the red paintwork probably did it no harm. This side view taken in the outside viewing garden at Canley shows the pert proportions and a proposed new style of alloy wheel that was being investigated. (Rover Group)

RETURN OF THE MG SPORTS CAR

Like many contemporary full-size styling models, the F-16 was fitted with fake number plates in the contemporary UK style of white front and yellow rear. (Rover Group)

fell from grace, simply 'R8'), was another joint exercise between the two partners.

Eventually, what would become the new Rover 200 series in 1989 would spawn a cleverly contrived range of models on a common 2,550mm wheelbase including a three-door hatchback, four-door saloon, estate car, cabriolet and coupé (a far more varied portfolio than Honda would ever extract from the venture), and any serious thoughts about 'MG' variants were initially tied to what was being planned for R8.

However, with Graham Day's endorsement of the possibility of an MG sports car ringing

Compare this shot of the rear of the red version of F-16 with the earlier iteration shown at the top of page 30: this is definitely a better posterior! (Rover Group)

in their ears, Roy Axe's designers began to plan what a proper MG sports car could be like. They were undoubtedly helped in this endeavour by an £8 million investment in the design studios, accompanied by a trebling of staff to 300. In a statement to the media in July 1987, Graham Day acknowledged the role that the design studio played, saying, 'they are not just responsible for styling and design, but the whole process right through to engineering resources. What they are doing is vital to our short-term survival and long-term success.'

As we saw earlier, even before Day's arrival, the Concept Design Team, with major inputs from Gerry McGovern and Richard Carter, had worked up a fresh MG sports car concept (the silver car referred to above), although initially with no serious thought given to engineering practicalities other than that it would have been front-wheel drive – logical in terms of contemporary Rover powertrains, but potentially controversial as Lotus would find with their new Elan. The result of this exercise had been a pretty sports car with pop-up lights, with many styling cues drawn from the successful EX-E.

With Day's arrival, a new approach ensued, also spurred on by ramping up of US sales of the Sterling; accordingly, the McGovern/Carter car was spruced up and an engineering feasibility exercise undertaken by Derek Anderson with a view to equipping the car with the new K-Series engine. In the end, marketing and corporate finances got in the way of F-16, and it never made the leap to a proper prototype, as Richard Hamblin explains:

> The killer blow came when Marketing 'proved conclusively' that there was no market for sports cars and that therefore the programme would never pay for itself, let alone make a profit! They had added up the numbers of sports cars sold that year – not many, as there was so little credible product available then – and they ignored – or would not accept – any latent demand.

Thankfully, Graham Day at least was more open to the idea. First, however, Day had to get Rover Group off the public books and back into the private sector.

BRITISH AEROSPACE

At the beginning of 1988, Graham Day met Professor Sir Roland Smith of British Aerospace (BAe) at a dinner function. The conversation turned to the possibility of BAe acquiring Rover Group and the discussion led, before long, to more detailed negotiations and ultimately, in March 1988, to a formal bid for the company.

The terms seemed very beneficial to BAe, which would pay £150 million, but at the same time Rover Group's bank debts of around £400 million would be written off. To sweeten the pill even more, the government would include a bonus of £547 million as working capital. There was speculation that Honda, Ford or even VW could be tempted into a bidding war, but in fact Honda was not interested and the British government made it known that it preferred the idea of a British owner for Rover Group, thereby setting the seal on the BAe deal.

BAe gave assurances that it wanted to build up the Rover Group business, and the government's only requirement was that BAe should hold on to the company for at least five years. Nobody was naïve enough to imagine that the future was going to be problem-free, but at last, after thirteen years, the direction of the company would be entirely overseen by private rather than political eyes.

According to Richard Hamblin, despite the fact that people from Graham Day downwards had expressed enthusiasm for the idea of an MG sports car, the fact remained that there were no definite plans in place:

> In that period, there were detailed, thorough and approved product plans for the company – but an all-new, viable and realistic MG sports car featured on none of them, could not be

RETURN OF THE MG SPORTS CAR

Another day, another body kit – only this one is rather special. Photographed at Canley, this is an MG Maestro sporting the body kit that would become standard fitment on the low-volume 'MG Turbo'. Note those F-16 style wheels, which would not make it to production on any Rover Group products. (Rover Group)

funded, and was the least of the 'main line' problems.

Product plans went through an annual cycle, starting with a giant wish list and ending with a minimum position; the main line strategies for new small, medium and large cars were hard enough to fund and resource, without the distraction of sports cars. Honda's own developments were also heavily influencing Rover, although the MG name kept cropping up, as Richard Hamblin explains:

> It is for this reason that MG versions of Austins, Rovers and even Hondas kept being mooted and I was obliged to work on a number of these – most of which no real 'product man' would have had anything to do with.

Around the same time that the British Aerospace deal was being finalized, a small offshoot of the Rover Group business, known by the name of British Motor Heritage, was also in the process of bringing to fruition a project that was almost unprecedented in the industry: to bring back into production the bodyshell of a car that had been discontinued for the best part of a decade.

The classic car industry was booming in the 1980s, an interest partly fuelled by the simple fact that so many of the really interesting cars of the past were so different from the modern mainstream. When it became apparent that most of the original body press tools and many of the jigs that had been used to build MGB bodies were still in existence, a plan had been hatched to bring all the equipment together, refurbish, substitute or replace as necessary, and begin limited production of new bodies effectively as 'service replacements' to enable owners of rusting MGBs to refurbish them properly, safely and economically.

The Concept studio also came up with a proposal to offer a multi-purpose sporting version of the forthcoming Rover 'R8' 200 range, with a removable coupé roof, seen here wearing MG badges and those telephone dial alloy wheels again. (Rover Group)

You did not have to be a rocket scientist to work out that by keeping these cars roadworthy in this way, the whole spare parts business supporting the classic MGB scene would benefit too. The British Motor Heritage MGB bodyshell was launched in London in April 1988, just weeks after the BAe deal: the project may have been pretty far removed from the production of entire state-of-the-art motor cars, but the omen of a project that gained worldwide coverage on the back of the MG badge was surely a good one.

The first priority for the newly privatized Rover Group, however, was to move the R8 (all references to YY and AR8 had been long forgotten) towards a launch in 1989. In October 1988 a limited-production MG Maestro Turbo was launched. Behind the scenes, a concept for a cabriolet/coupé version of R8, envisioned as a convertible with a removable fastback hardtop, was photographed in the design studio wearing MG badges – even if there were mixed feelings about providing fresh scope for allegations of 'badge engineering'.

In the case of the MG Maestro Turbo, this project came off the back of a lot of work that the Concept Studio had been doing to develop aerodynamic body kits as a means of compensating for the lack of much really new product. According to Richard Hamblin,

> As much as anyone, I guess I can be blamed for the Maestro Turbo. I encouraged John Thurston of Tickfords to build such a car for us. We designed the form and he produced around 1,500 kits or so, and these were used for around 500 cars by marrying the MG Maestro to the MG Montego Turbo drive-train.

Similarly, the concept studies that led to the

coupé and convertible versions of the Rover R8 200 (coded ultimately as 'Tomcat' and 'Tracer') actually started in the Concept Design studio as the second project after the F-16, purely as an experiment, in Richard Hamblin's words, 'in the hope of bringing a bit of excitement into Auntie Rover's range'. The initial concept was effectively one highly versatile car, with removable roof sections and other demountable parts, although what eventually emerged in production would be two separate cars:

> A final twist in this project was that we seemed to have produced a model so sporty in looks that the Board insisted on seeing it with MG badges. Moreover there was a body of opinion that this could be an MG for America – due to its Honda underpinnings. In Concept Design, we were aghast at this idea as the car was clearly a modified Rover – no matter how sporty it looked – and furthermore it would threaten any future MG programme.

Hamblin's point was that an MG R8 might dilute the case for a proper MG sports car; eventually the point became academic as the two models would be launched as Rovers, although, as he also points out, the car that did eventually appear, the MG*F*, unfortunately formed a single-model marque – something that would remain the case right up to the end of the following decade.

Ian Pogson was the Competitor Analysis Manager for Rover Group at the time:

> The R8 coupé was shown to me; I walked into the Styling Review garden at the front of Canley 'Building 50/51' and saw it. One word came from my lips – 'Spunky'! The lads were pleased at the response. I never gave the badge a thought, but in hindsight it should have been an MG.

Before long, however, something would happen that would really focus attention on the idea of an MG sports car once more.

MAZDA'S MGB: THE MIATA

Visitors to the Chicago Auto Show in February 1989 thronged to the Mazda stand, where the Japanese company displayed a new production sports car with obvious visual similarities to the classic Lotus Elan, with which it shared the concept of an in-line twin-cam front engine, mounted well back for good balance, and rear-wheel drive.

First 'leaked' by *Autoweek* magazine two months earlier, in December 1988, the new small Mazda was in essence the classic British sports car, lovingly created in a new form by a Japanese manufacturer who had nevertheless worked with Americans and Britons in arriving at the end result (many inside Mazda had initially preferred the idea of a front-wheel drive or a mid-engined configuration, both of which could have been easier and cheaper to achieve but arguably less pure).

MG enthusiasts worldwide bemoaned yet another example where it had taken an overseas company to recreate something that the British car makers talked about but never delivered. Of course, little known to most of us at the time, the arrival of the Miata (or MX-5 as it was known in other markets) was also a source of much wailing and gnashing of teeth inside Rover Group. Roy Axe was especially frustrated:

> The MG F-16 could have been in production eighteen months ahead of Mazda's Miata: everything was there – all the data was available that the Mazda people were looking at – and I'm sure that our market research people said 'it'll be a hard battle – very difficult ...' and so on, and of course the argument over here in England was 'well, very nice – but the only market we've got is England, because the Americans will never buy an MG, so there's no point in putting it over there'.

In the wake of the Mazda sports car, however, the idea of the MG F-16 becoming a Mazda MX-5 rival kept coming up. Matters came to a head at a management meeting in September

1989, when Graham Day threw down a gauntlet, saying that if someone could show him a way to make an MG sports car for £40 million, he could find the money. Richard Hamblin quietly took this as an invitation to do just that, although Day had said that he doubted that it could be done.

In the meantime, Ian Pogson recalls that Graham Day also asked his team to source a Miata:

> My colleague Tim Davis did this, obtaining it from the US. It was blue and hung around the studio annoying us something rotten for ages. Sir Graham eventually bought it for his son, I think. I liked Sir G, he was cool!

Within a few weeks following the September meeting with Sir Graham, Hamblin managed to get an introduction to Takado Kogyo, a company in Japan that had been responsible for some of the low-volume weird and wacky Nissan Micra-based cars, such as the Be-1, Pao, Figaro and S-Cargo, to see how limited edition cars could be spun off mainstream platforms. 'Takada were producing the first of these cars at a rate of 50 a day in up to 20,000 volume runs per car in a highly professional manner', Hamblin recalls; he found that the Japanese company was doing 'nothing particularly different, but everything particularly well'.

Upon his return to the UK, Hamblin met with Nick Stephenson (then Rover Group's Director of Small Cars), Fred Coultas and Mike Donovan to share what he had discovered. He also met with some of his contacts amongst suppliers: 'my thoughts went back to my time working in the supplier industry, where if one wanted to stay in business, one had to find a way to deliver, or go broke (having no manufacturing to fill the bank balance)'.

To investigate this approach, Hamblin visited Merrick Taylor at Motor Panels, with whom Hamblin had worked on the Leyland Truck range while still at Ogle, and Patrick Twemlow at ADC, whose facilities had been left over by GM when they withdrew the function from the UK; both firms had extensive and somewhat underutilized facilities at their disposal. According to Hamblin, 'They both felt that building a running prototype of the F-16 could be done and they were prepared to accept the challenge – but they were very shocked to hear the time and budget that I was proposing!' Thus it was not long afterwards that the 'Phoenix' project, born in 1989, gained momentum, with the objective of finding a way to produce a practical sports car.

One thing seemed certain in the eyes of the Rover people; it would be no good producing a 'me too' sports car like the Miata ('which could be said to have now stolen the clothes of the traditional British Roadster', Hamblin says). Any new MG would have to win sales from Miata customers or drivers attracted to the general concept, but the British offering would have to be different in some significant way. One possible route had already been shown by Toyota, who had shown a prototype of a small mid-engined sports car as the 'SV-3' at the 1983 Tokyo Motor Show; this translated the following year into the MR-2, which married a Toyota Corolla 1.6-litre transverse twin-cam powertrain with a mid-engine configuration.

ROVER'S THINK TANK: DESIGN RESEARCH ASSOCIATES

In October 1989 Roy Axe stepped aside from the mainstream studios, by now under the control of Gordon Sked and Richard Hamblin, and established a stand-alone studio a few miles down the road from Canley at Tachbrook Park, Leamington Spa. The small, relatively anonymous complex was ideal to allow various advanced studies to be undertaken, not only for Rover Group but also increasingly for other corporate clients, such as BAe's mainstream aircraft business. 'The first two vehicles we produced for Rover Group were DR1 and DR2;

Roy Axe's Design Research Associates studio, based off-site at Leamington, was tasked with exploring facets of 'Britishness' and came up with two full-size models. DR1 was a large Rover saloon but this one was DR2, a rather lovely large sports car. (Rover Group)

Roy Axe owned an Austin Healey 3000 and its influence could be seen in the flowing, curvaceous lines of DR2. (Rover Group)

Graham Lewis was one of the designers who worked at Design Research Associates; his two sketches here show how ideas about advanced construction concepts were being looked at in 1989. (G. Lewis)

Nothing was too weird or way-out when exploring futuristic sports car concepts intended to embrace new polymer body ideas. (G. Lewis)

DR1 was a kind of Rover 800 replacement, but DR2 was a sports car', Axe explains.

'DR2 was a much bigger sports car than we had shown before', according to Axe, who cites the Mercedes SL that he owned at the time as a source of inspiration. 'I thought there was no reason why Rover shouldn't make a car like that; and I designed it in such a way that it could have been an MG or an Austin Healey'. In fact, all the time that DR2 was being worked on in the studio, Axe's own Austin Healey 3000 was on hand to serve as a classic inspiration.

Neither DR1 nor DR2 was intended to be an actual production car; like F-16 before them, they were exercises in exploring a theme, in this case 'Britishness', which was something that Rover Group needed to rediscover if it was going to carve out a niche – especially in the tough North American market, where the Sterling was struggling to keep afloat. Everyone who saw DR2 loved it. The smooth, flowing lines were arguably some of the most attractive since the Jaguar E-Type, and it was perhaps inevitable that, when further MG sports car studies began to take shape in 1990, DR2 should form part of the exercise.

PHOENIX

Not to be confused with the corporate name used by the group who would acquire the Rover Group business in 2000, what was to become the 'Phoenix' project nevertheless involved some of the same people as that later venture. Starting with Richard Hamblin's original October 1989 report, five possible routes were set out for delivery of a new MG sports car. For all these and any routes, designers had to consider how to achieve maximum carry-over from an existing platform, and how to incorporate as many systems as possible from the Rover 'parts bin' to achieve the necessary low-cost programme. Soon known as the 'Phoenix Routes', these paper exercises were later dubbed PR1 to PR5 inclusive. The options were envisaged as follows:

- Route 1: Front engine, front-wheel drive;
- Route 2: Front engine, rear-wheel drive with a polymer body and separate chassis;
- Route 3: Mid-engined, rear-wheel drive;
- Route 4: Like Route 2, but with a steel or alloy body;
- Route 5: Exotic sports car, possibly in the mould of EX-E.

Of these, arguably the most obvious was the first one, which could well have been spun off the new R8 Rover 200, then just about to be launched, complete with K-Series engine. However, despite the fact that Lotus was just in the throes of launching their all-new front-wheel drive Lotus Elan (with an Isuzu engine) there remained some nervousness about a front-wheel drive sports car and also there was clearly a risk that such a car could quite easily fall victim to rationalization by the cost accountants, leaving an end result hardly different from the mainstream R8.

At that stage, however, the K-Series was limited to 1.4 litres and so there was a better prospect of using something loosely based on the Maestro O-Series platform but with the Rover M-16 or forthcoming T-Series engine in order to open up what were seen as essential US sales. Hamblin explains that some of the initial thinking extrapolated from the F-16 study informed Route 1:

> I personally favoured this route because of the good engine options, the similarity of size to the base Maestro platform, the fact that all parts and systems would have been Rover owned and finally the conventional engineering and body route.

Route 2 and the essentially similar Route 4 were the ones for the hard-core enthusiast. The only drivetrain in the Rover Group range that appeared to fit this model was the classic Rover V8, most recently used in a mainstream car in the SD1 of 1976–86, but still a key cornerstone of the Land Rover portfolio. US sales of the Range Rover clearly provided an emissions and service infrastructure basis for a similarly powered sports car, but the fact that the chassis would need to be all-new and low-volume would have made this route quite a challenging one, albeit potentially a very exciting one.

Route 3 was technically the most intriguing, as it followed the principle of MG's old ADO21 concept as well as, more recently, Toyota's MR2. Envisaged as a kind of modern Midget, Route 3 would have used the K-Series engine and was thought more ambitious than the front-running Route 1, 2 and 4 options. Richard Hamblin elaborates:

> We didn't just think 'let's copy the MR2' – rather we thought 'can we create a low-investment carry-over route from the Metro?' and at the same time do something different from Route 1 – and that's the solution that eventually came out!

At first, the concept of Route 3 even envisaged using the Metro floorpan, suitably modified for the runner, but with polymer skin panels, in the hope that more investment could be saved; this is evident in the photos of the PR3 running prototype under construction, about which Hamblin jests, 'note the crumple zones!' According to Hamblin, the idea of using polymer skin panels was swiftly dropped ('this despite the work done on SMC and VARI – vacuum assisted resin injection – with the help of BASF and GE Plastics, Eddie Adams of Lotus and Foden'), and PR3 briefly spawned a PR4 variant with steel panels, although PR4 swiftly switched to being a variant of PR2.

Route 5 was something of a wild card; there were still a number inside the company who bemoaned the fact that EX-E had never been built and, given the links with BAe, there was a thought that a car built using some technologies borrowed from the aerospace industry could serve as a platform to justify the supposed synergies between the different parts of the BAe business. Route 5 as envisaged in that form would never have been a high-volume seller, but it was argued that it could provide marketing benefits of the kind that Fiat gained from associations with Ferrari.

Richard Hamblin did look at finding a way to make EX-E viable:

> I had a number of meetings with the British Aerospace boffins at the Factory at Manchester (where they were making the prototype Eurofighter wings) to consider this question of 'Synergy'. Could an EX-E body be built with aircraft technology, or was there any other process or techniques they held that could apply? It soon became apparent (not surprisingly perhaps) that whilst they very well understood Mass and Performance they did not spend too much time worrying about Low Cost, Volume Production, or many of the other factors we had to struggle with in the Car World.

Of these various 'routes', Richard Hamblin admits that Route 1 was not necessarily the most exciting but was certainly in his view the most deliverable – and would have been the most conventional in contemporary body structure terms of all five options shortlisted; both Routes 2 and 3 were seen as testbeds for composite body panels over steel structures, although Route 4 was a more conventional fallback but still with a separate chassis structure.

Not everybody at Rover Group, where they had only just got to grips with the material used for Maestro and Montego bumpers, was overly convinced about making whole body panels in plastic. Hamblin brought in a selection of composite-bodied cars from other car makers (the Mazda Miata, for example, had a composite bonnet panel), but the conventional view at Rover Group at that point was to stick with the tried and tested formula with which they had the most experience.

Having briefly debated the options available, the next task was to get some prototypes up and running – and quickly if the momentum behind Graham Day's challenge was not to be lost. In Hamblin's view, the time-honoured approach of seeking pre-qualification expressions of interest and then going out to tender would only drag the process out interminably; he argued that the company needed to move more quickly.

With Nick Stephenson on board, the case was put to Rover Cars Chairman John Towers to offer simple three-month contracts to three companies, each of which would build a running prototype for one of the key 'Routes' (1 to 3). Towers agreed and so in October 1989, after narrowing down a shortlist of five companies to a final three, identical copies of the MG F-16 bodyshell were made ready and shipped out with kits of appropriate mechanical parts to Motor Panels (Route 1), Reliant (Route 2) and ADC (Route 3). In return for payments of £250,000 and an outline brief, each company would commit to deliver a working prototype to Gaydon in 27 weeks time, ready for a management ride and drive early in the spring or summer of 1990.

Each brief was slightly different, according to the philosophy behind the respective 'Route' (swiftly shortened to 'Phoenix Route' and then simply to 'PR'). For PR1, Motor Panels received a Maestro floorpan and a Rover 800 'M16' two-litre engine: Hamblin and Stephenson knew and respected Motor Panels' great skill in hand-building steel prototypes, and so the brief was to make effectively a steel-bodied 'clone' of F-16 built over the Maestro floorpan, adapted to suit.

In the case of PR2, Rover Group was interested not only in Reliant's well-known skills in composite body construction but also the potential of the chassis that the Tamworth company had already engineered for their quirkily styled but dynamically very competent Scimitar roadster. Stretching the potential of the chassis, Reliant was sent a 3.9-litre fuel-injected Rover V8 engine and gearbox and asked to stretch the F-16 body over a longer wheelbase.

Finally, for PR3, the Luton-based ADC (Automotive Development Centre, once part of GM Vauxhall) was probably faced with the most interesting challenge of all: they had to shorten and narrow down the F-16 body envelope and marry it to a steel substructure adapted from various Metro sections and with a 1.4-litre K-Series engine and subframe mounted amidships. If PR1 was a sort of front-wheel drive 'new MGB' and PR2 was a testbed for something along the lines of Roy Axe's DR2, then PR3 was unquestionably intended as an MG Midget. If US sales remained a key goal, it was already obvious that PR1 and PR2 had some realistic prospects but PR3 seemed more likely to be an interesting dead-end.

By July 1990, all three prototypes had been duly delivered to Gaydon under great secrecy (PR2 had arrived first, in February); hardly anyone other than a select few inside Rover Group even knew what was happening. In the meantime, however, the company had set up Rover Special Products (RSP), a special task force reporting to sales director Kevin Morley and overseen by four senior directors, of whom Richard Hamblin was one. As he recalls:

> RSP was set up in April 1990 – initially under three directors, one each from Engineering, Product Planning and Design, reporting through Marketing to Board level [the fourth director joined later from Finance]. It was an idea that altogether proved to have been misconceived from birth ... it could have been 'the MG Car Company', it could have been 'the really interesting cars company', producing desirable niche product, or it could have been just a department fiddling around at the edges of the mainline product range. No one, in fact, could agree on *what* exactly it was.

Furthermore, Hamblin points out that nobody within RSP was in overall charge:

> Naturally everyone had their own ideas and approach. The budget may have supported one good product or a number of minor actions, but it was always going to be hard to reach agreement on how to spend it.

RETURN OF THE MG SPORTS CAR

Hamblin at first struggled even to get the Phoenix programme adopted into RSP's Product Plan.

Misconceived or not, however, what RSP became in practice was a vehicle to short-circuit the design and production process for niche products that could be cleverly created to add value to the Rover Group portfolio, extending rights across the range from the Mini (RSP helped recreate the Mini Cooper and convertible), via the Metro (a cabriolet version of which was created) and even to a limited edition Range Rover – and also the MG RV8 (see Chapter Three). Once accepted within the RSP brief, the Phoenix project sat in a rather dominant position, and Richard Hamblin says he sometimes felt that he was seen as too close to this project as he had championed it through to the first prototypes.

FIRST SIGHT: APPRAISAL OF PR1, 2 AND 3

The purpose of the contracts with the three specialists had not been to create a fully 'styled' sports car with something resembling a production-ready finish; after all, although the F-16 shape was still seen as very attractive, it was no longer necessarily what the designers would have wanted nearly four years on from its creation. However it was clear that all three companies wanted to make a good impression with their client, and it is true to say that in that regard they all succeeded admirably.

According to Richard Hamblin, when the original F-16 body had been dropped over a Maestro floorpan, 'the wheels fell exactly into the wheelarches, as if by intent; even the scuttle matched!' However, for its PR1 prototype, Motor Panels nevertheless chopped 70mm (nearly 3in) out of the Maestro floorpan and engineered and hand-formed new steel bodywork with such neat features as specially engineered electric pop-up headlamps, a flush steel hood tonneau and a battery relocated to the boot for better weight balance. Inside the cockpit, a new Rover R8 facia had been fitted and the rest of the interior had been neatly trimmed to match. To all intents and purposes, the car looked as though it had just been delivered straight from a dealer. 'With the MG Maestro Turbo set-up, this could have been faster in a straight line than some supercars', Hamblin believes, noting that this was already the case with the five-door Maestro bodyshell.

Reliant, who had finished PR2 well ahead of schedule, used their impeccable composite

In many ways, Motor Panels' 'PR1' prototype seemed to have everything going for it: it had good looks, a deliverable platform, exquisite build quality and the right proportions. However, it just didn't excite the emotions as much as the other two ...

RETURN OF THE MG SPORTS CAR

Reliant's PR2 was the gruff he-man sports car with the rough edges and a hunking V8. Actually 'rough edges' isn't fair, for Reliant built it really well, and the prototype was an early favourite for those who drove it. The question was, though – was it too outré for Rover Group? (Rover Group)

body skills to neatly stretch the F-16 forward of the windscreen and wrap the longer shell over a modified version of their Scimitar SS1 chassis, into which the V8 drivetrain had been slotted and Maestro-based front suspension fitted. Inside the cockpit it was nearly all pure Scimitar SS1 – but very neatly done and impeccably finished, while the pop-up lamps used SS1 motors.

With the fabulous sound that the engine made, and the way that the chassis rocked with every blip of the throttle, PR2 was the one that most of the enthusiasts at Rover Group lusted after (it regularly overheated, according to RSP engineer Robin Nickless, a testament as much to its popularity as to a lack of adequate cooling). 'The body was an issue', Hamblin maintains, thinking of the task of matching a composite body to the backbone chassis:

Others had solved this by the use of SMC Polymer panels – cars such as Corvette, for instance, or by the use of a basic GRP body, like TVR: but the first was complex and expensive, and the latter not acceptable to the MG marque.

Definitely the most special of the trio was ADC's PR3 – beautifully finished like the other two, but with a number of extra surprises that undoubtedly made the little sports car (soon dubbed the 'Pocket Rocket' by RSP's John Stephenson) even more special. Narrower than F-16 by 100mm and shortened by 150mm, PR3 was truly compact and somehow the trick had worked, even though the exercise had not been style-focused. Fitting clever drop-down rather than pop-up headlamps, ADC had styled and created a removable hardtop, squeezed in the Metro subframe with a 1.4-litre engine just behind the cockpit and trimmed the latter with the latest Rover Metro dashboard and matching trim. If PR1 and PR2 were the sensible options, PR3 was the most intriguing, and with its entertaining combination of mini-Ferrari layout

RETURN OF THE MG SPORTS CAR

ADC at Luton worked hard to ensure that their little mid-engined prototype looked good and was built well, even if the packaging was marginal; uniquely it had drop-down (rather than pop-up) headlamps. (ADC)

The PR3 running prototype under construction at ADC, early in 1990. (ADC)

and handling, it soon became something of a favourite.

Before the project could go much further, however, the three cars would need a senior management review. This took place in August 1990, still under a great cloak of secrecy. Meanwhile, however, the media had been engaging in further speculation, and *CAR* magazine had been talking to Sterling's Graham Morris, who admitted that Rover Group was looking at the idea of a new MG sports car, but that 'whatever we do, it will be a niche car – it won't be another Miata'. The magazine's April 1990 issue had even featured a cut-out coupon for readers to post to George Simpson, Rover Group Chairman, to ask him to build this new MG. When I interviewed Brian Griffin in 1995, he remembered how:

RETURN OF THE MG SPORTS CAR

PR3 soon became a firm favourite, even if it was not seen as the leading contender for the time being. It was nevertheless dubbed the 'Pocket Rocket'.

AUGUST 1990: DECISION TIME APPROACHES

By the time that Richard Hamblin submitted his own report in July, a further part of the MG sports car equation had slipped on from stage left. The launch of the Heritage MGB bodyshell had led to some debate about whether BMH could take the logical next step and build a low-volume turnkey 'new MGB', perhaps with either the Rover M-16 or the V8 engine under the bonnet. If Morgan made a good fist of building new retro-styled sports cars, why shouldn't Rover Group?

In fact the first person within Rover Group to explore this thought process was Richard Hamblin, who started the ball rolling:

> The Board at that time thought they ought to do the V8 one first for the North American market; Graham Morris definitely wanted that! They loved the mid-engined car, but simply felt they needed a larger one more urgently.

> I produced the first concept board for what became the MG RV8 in August 1987 – long before I met anyone from British Motor Heritage or knew about any V8 powered MGBs – and well before I had even spoken to David Bishop of Heritage. The concept came from

A neat, sporting and compact two-seat sports car – surely the very epitome of what a modern MG Midget should be? (Rover Group)

realizing that the Porsche 911 and MGB had both been launched around the same time, and yet the Porsche was still in production. What then would the MG have looked liked if it had followed the same path?

A sketch that answered this question was produced by Jeremy Newman, and it was this sketch that was resurrected three years later as the basis of Project Adder within RSP. Meanwhile, however, an early home-built MGB with a fuel-injected Rover V8 had been built by policeman Roger Parker (nowadays a consultant to the MG Owners' Club), who had been invited by BMH's David Bishop to bring his MGB V8 along as a sort of 'show and tell' session at the end of a product planning meeting at Longbridge in the summer of 1989, just before the Phoenix project got off the ground. Parker's V8 proved a great hit with the Rover Group directors, who took turns in driving it round the factory roads. Sharing their enthusiasm, David Bishop then took the idea a step further by the spring of 1990 by having a prototype built.

Despite enthusiasm for what was a great concept, however, it was soon realized that BMH had neither the resources nor the capital to build complete cars for sale complete with all the guarantees and dealer backup that new car customers took for granted, and so the project fell back to RSP and Richard Hamblin for further development.

By July 1990 Hamblin had secured a clay model, built by Styling International, taking inspiration from Jeremy Newman's 1987 sketch. The model was worked on under the direction of Styling International's Jonathan Gould, on the basis of an old MGB shell with what amounted to a modest RSP styling makeover, with red 'Di-Noc' to simulate paintwork. Hamblin showed the car to Kevin Morley, who said that he could see the appeal but not the commercial case for making the car; for the time being, the 'new MGB' had to make way for the main event – the three PR prototypes.

One of the first people to actually drive the ADC-built prototype was Rob Oldaker, at the time Rover Group's Chief Chassis Engineer. 'PR3 came in to Gaydon at three in the morning in a box trailer', he remembers, noting the cloak and dagger secrecy. However, pretty and petite though it undoubtedly was, the prototype was obviously not a fully developed piece of work, and Oldaker bluntly observes that:

> it was a bit of a disaster, actually ... the control systems didn't really work properly and because of the way the exhaust was routed it kept overheating: in fact the guys from ADC

The cockpit of PR1 was highly professional, and featured a neat amalgam of R8 Rover 200 facia and other parts from contemporary parts bins. It looked almost as though it had emerged from a showroom – praise indeed for a concept.

RETURN OF THE MG SPORTS CAR

Reliant's PR2 retained most of the interior of the Scimitar SS1 donor vehicle. Clearly a production car would have needed something different entirely, but it was a reasonable starting point and in any case a complete design package was never the raison d'être of this prototype.

were having kittens about their car when I took it out on the ride and handling circuit – not that I really could exercise the car.

Even so, Oldaker says, PR3 was the car for him: 'PR1 was faster and better made as a prototype, but the mid-engined car looked the part'. PR2 was assessed separately a week or two later by Oldaker's colleague Andy Smith.

In fact the ADC PR3 running prototype was loved by just about everyone who drove it, but at the same time they all recognized that it just couldn't be a practical production proposition in quite that form. For a start, the little 'Pocket Rocket' had virtually zero luggage space, a tiny and impractical fuel tank of around 27 litres capacity and hardly much more in the way of crush-space: it had been engineered on a shoestring to see if the concept worked, but a production car would have needed a lot more work and would almost inevitably have grown bigger in the process. ('That was the general view then, although other cars like the Smart Roadster would later solve the packaging issues in an equally small size', Hamblin comments.)

After Oldaker and Smith, the next group to assess the prototypes was a cadre of Rover Group Directors who arrived at Gaydon to look over and drive all three 'Phoenix' sports cars; as before, they felt each had its merits but by all accounts the one that most commonly inspired wide grins was PR3, arguably the least feasible for US sales but the most fun on Gaydon's circuit; indeed Rover Japan's David Blume felt that PR3 was for him the only game in town. Realism seemed to point towards PR2, but John Towers wanted more work done to see if PR3 could be made to work.

Inside the PR3, ADC had neatly shoehorned the facia and seats and much of the other interior furnishings of a Metro, which was quite fitting for a budget sports car derived from that car. It was well finished and surprisingly effective.

RETURN OF THE MG SPORTS CAR

The first iteration of 'Adder' was developed by Styling International in clay over the MGB shell. The case for taking it further was initially not thought strong enough by Kevin Morley of Rover Group Marketing. (Richard Hamblin)

At the Motor Show in September 1990, Graham Day gave a hint of what had been going on behind closed doors – 'we're going to do a proper MG', as he told journalists on Press Day – despite the fact that the Phoenix project was still not on any formal programme. The Chairman, however, had given the clearest public indication yet of what was coming. Shortly afterwards, Day was equally forthcoming in a conversation with *CAR* magazine: 'We are going to do another MG, but we'll be doing what MG was, not what people thought it was'. Hinting that the idea of an exotic MG supercar was less likely, Day added: 'MG was not a lesson in high-tech, it was badge engineering at its best'.

Then, with slightly bizarre humour, Day went on to say 'Remember, MG TD stands for Morris Garages Test Division. Even in the future, MG will be a relatively basic vehicle. And it's not one that is on the very top of our priority list.' Hinting at Rover Group priorities for the near future, Day added, 'first of all we have got to get the base products right. Then we can look at the derivatives of those base products. Only in a third step can we consider low-volume niche products – cars such as the next MG.'

The mid-engine layout of PR3 held great appeal and offered an exciting driving package. As built by ADC, however, the packaging was not really resolved and was unfeasibly tight: a production version would clearly have to grow slightly.

chapter three

Route of Destiny

THE THIRD WAY: THE DEVELOPMENT OF PR3

After the ride and drive assessments, RSP, which was still in charge of the sports car studies, decided to send out design study contracts in the New Year of 1991 to ADC, while meanwhile main-line product engineer Brian Griffin and manufacturing engineer John Doyle began to undertake engineering feasibility studies.

For the design studies, part of the brief was to explore a mid-engined car along the lines of ADC's PR3 'Pocket Rocket', but with a 100mm longer wheelbase, bringing the size more up to MGB than Midget class (or, more relevant perhaps, nearer in size to the Mazda Miata). RSP designer Richard Bartlam had done some exploratory work on this larger PR3 and so Richard Hamblin sent Bartlam's (and his own) sketches to ADC at Luton to work with John Sowden (ADC's Design Chief) with a brief to create an updated clay model:

We wanted an updated style/design over the package, as F-16 was four years old by now, and was never designed as a mid-engined car. RSP also wanted our potential customers

Some sketches were produced by Richard Bartlam of Rover Special Products and used as part of the thinking process behind the task of 'growing' PR3 from the slightly impractical dimensions of ADC's Pocket Rocket. (Rover Group)

Another sketch from Rover Special Products intended to help inform the development of a feasible style for PR3. (Rover Group)

to tell us exactly how they wanted that design tuned and adjusted: i.e. more aggressive or less; more masculine or less; bigger or smaller – and as a consequence an interesting discussion ensued involving the experts who ran the Clinic. As a result we decided not to make the model too definitive at this stage.

Hamblin notes wryly that 'a number of people would later – not knowing all this – be quick to be critics of these models as *not* being definitive!'

In the midst of this, another company, MGA (Michael Gibbs Associates) Developments at Coventry, contacted Hamblin and volunteered their services at a knockdown price. Hamblin then sent MGA a similar brief to the one for ADC, but looking for a slightly more aggressive design approach compared to that taken by ADC. This was due to the fact that

> at that time we had to work with what was available to us, and the Metro then only offered us its 1.4-litre engine. I was clear that the look of the car should not visually 'offer' performance it could 'not deliver'. To avoid this happening we took this opportunity to test the boundaries of this issue by asking ADC to produce a softer design, and MGA to test how far we could push it towards the slightly more aggressive.

ADC, which had been responsible for building the 'Pocket Rocket' running PR3 prototype, took Richard Hamblin's brief and created a full-size clay with slightly larger proportions. Note the deliberate use of anonymous badging. (Richard Hamblin)

The designer in charge at MGA at that stage was one Peter Horbury, more recently better known

ROUTE OF DESTINY

A low sleek nose, the then-fashionable pop-up headlamps and side air intakes are hallmarks of the neat ADC clay, known as 'Project 8300'. (Richard Hamblin)

as the Director of Design at Volvo. Meanwhile, John Sowden at ADC was responsible for that company's effort, which included an interior model.

'To fully appreciate the position here, one has to understand that there had been months of discussions, energetic debate and "position taking"', Hamblin maintains; already at this stage (1991), the larger K-Series engine variants were under development, and this became another impetus to increase the size of the PR3 ('although all this really achieved was the Clinic saying it needed an even bigger engine!'). At the time, Hamblin was keen to keep the ADC clay model the same size as their original PR3 running prototype, and to make only the MGA model larger by 100mm, while waiting to see what came back from the clinic. He states, however, that he had to let this position go, in order to keep the project moving forward:

> A moot point here is did we lose the chance of producing a really great Midget? Indeed, was much of the charm of the PR3 Prototype derived from its 'great performance set against its tiny size' – in other words, its very 'pocket rocket ness'? Indeed, wasn't *that* what had attracted everyone to it in the first place (and what had dumped the other two credible solutions into the shade)?

The high rear deck and longitudinal wedge stance of the ADC clearly hark back to the EX-E design. The lights, bumper and exhaust details are especially nice aspects. (Richard Hamblin)

55

ROUTE OF DESTINY

While ADC worked on their clay, another team at MGA developments, led by Peter Horbury (later to be known as an influential chief designer at Volvo), were also working on a slightly different brief. These are sketches from February 1991 by designer Steve Harper, who was leading on the MGA team. (Steve Harper)

Echoes of similar thoughts would come back many years later, as the story of the X120 was to show (see Chapter Five):

> The Clinic respondents of course, never saw and certainly never drove the PR3, so had no idea if it needed a bigger engine or not. They were just shown a bigger car and asked what size engine did they think it would have! (That's how Clinics work.)

Of course, Hamblin maintains, a richer company could have done PR3 (a 'Midget') and PR1 (an R8-based 'MGB') – and added a PR5/DR2 (designed down below a £30,000 price point) to make a full range – an idea that would resonate more than once in future years:

> But, we were going to be lucky to do one! And I know that a lot of the thinking around at that time was to span as much opportunity/pricing as possible, and/or be head-on with MX5/MR2 in terms of Market Positioning.

One of the designers working at MGA at the

Steve Harper says he drew upon some contemporary iconic sports car designs, and you can see hints of such near contemporaries of these 1991 sketches as the Jaguar XKR15 and front-wheel drive Lotus Elan, both the work of Peter Stevens, who will feature in the MG story a few years hence. (Steve Harper)

ROUTE OF DESTINY

The grille shape of this sketch, dated 6 February 1991, is echoed on the nose of the red Di-Noc finished clay shown on page 58. (Steve Harper)

time was Steve Harper, who had left Austin Rover in 1984 and then moved around the industry (working at Volvo for a while on the 480ES sports estate car) before joining MGA in 1987. When the PR3 clay job came in, it was Harper who led on the sketches in January and February 1991, using Peter Stevens's Jaguar XJR15 as partial inspiration. Full-size clay modelling began in March 1991, and a car finished in 'Di-Noc' film to simulate a painted

Work under way at MGA on the clay; in the foreground is a clay for the Rolls-Royce Silver Seraph, another MGA project at the time. Notice how the nose in this viewing bears some resemblance to the treatment of the 'Adder' project, the basis of the MG RV8. (Steve Harper)

The MGA clay, finished in Di-Noc film, is ready for a viewing by the Rover Special Products client. Contrast this grille treatment with the previous image; at this stage, it is closer to Steve Harper's red sketch at the top of page 57. (Steve Harper)

finish was first shown to Rover management that same month.

Richard Hamblin visited frequently and, according to Harper, suggested that, while the style was promising, the front end lacked character; as the V8 MGB 'retro' project (see below) was being developed, the nose of the MGA clay was modified to use some of that car's styling cues. 'I was there at least three to four times a week', Hamblin says, adding that his designers 'almost lived there'. Meanwhile, ADC was also asked to develop an interior style:

> Our designers worked alongside theirs. Major carryover was the order of the day and so controls, vents, switches, column stalks, seats and so forth from the overall Rover Group parts bin were incorporated. Notwithstanding this, the result was highly credible and in fact photographs show that this design, with relatively few changes, went forward to production.

The final, finished MGA clay bears some resemblance to the corresponding ADC offering, although the shape seems lighter and more compact. (Richard Hamblin)

ROUTE OF DESTINY

From the side, there are aspects of the MGA clay that can be seen to form some resemblance to the later definitive MG*F*. (Richard Hamblin)

By May 1991, there were two clays (ADC and MGA, which together tested the boundaries of the design appearance), where only one had been planned, and both had been delivered.

After a review report by Nick Stephenson, it was decided to show them both alongside the other larger sports cars (DR2 and Adder) at a customer clinic in Manchester. The outcome of

Compare this sketch by Steve Harper with the photo of the rear of the final clay. Is there perhaps here something of a similar theme to that of the final MG*F*? (Steve Harper)

ROUTE OF DESTINY

The unusual rear lamp treatment of the ADC clay is more or less as shown in Steve Harper's sketches: simpler but not entirely dissimilar lamp shapes would appear on the MG*F*. (Richard Hamblin)

that clinic is discussed later, but first we need to catch up with the story of those larger MG studies.

TEMPORARY DIVERSION: AN ADDER WITH BITE

When we last left the story of the retro sports car, based on an MGB, it had just been rejected by Kevin Morley in July 1990. Undaunted, however, the RSP team went back to the drawing board and sent a second car down to ADC, where they were soon also destined to work on the new PR3 clay.

Working with slightly different themes on either side, before resolving the shape that would later become familiar, 'Project Adder' (a play on the Cobra name) began to take shape with a reworked style, and further work on predicted sales volumes and 'return on investment' was now complete. Kevin Morley was coming back round to the idea and so a GRP model was cast using the styling clay. Finished in classic British Racing Green rather than the red of the previous Styling International model, the new Adder would be ready to form part of the styling clinic alongside other models.

However, 'Adder' was always going to be something of a sideshow: the big story was supposedly the larger sports car. PR2 had never been more than a broad concept, and styling of the Reliant-built car was no more relevant than that of the other two original running prototypes. Everyone who saw DR2 loved it, although even then some doubted that it quite fit the 'affordable sports car' MG tag. There were also worries that the rear-wheel drive V8 chassis might be hard to deliver, sell and service in practice, and so behind the scenes there were further studies looking at alternative ways to deliver the big sports car. A commercially obvious, if dynamically questionable, solution would be to use the Sterling platform and its front-wheel drive Honda powertrain (although a new Rover KV6 was in the programme).

Thus the front-wheel drive philosophy of PR1 had come back and been married to the larger format of PR5/DR2, but with a Rover 800 base instead of Maestro. From here, there were two paper exercises in October 1990 looking at either a conventional Sterling wheelbase (PX1) or a shorter wheelbase (PX2), the latter swiftly gaining favour. Then there were two further schemes, 'Adventurer 1' and 'Adventurer 2', both following the shorter wheelbase of PX2

ROUTE OF DESTINY

The nose of the new ADC Adder clay was carefully evolved further from the slightly bland version on the earlier model, with bolder front lamp treatments. (Rover Group)

The designers experimented (with rather limited success, it must be said) with attempts to graft on Metro and, in this case, Porsche 911 tail-lamp units. Thankfully the taste police stepped in and quashed this particular aberration. (Rover Group)

ROUTE OF DESTINY

The final Di-Noc finished clay was a very attractive specimen and was given a 'British Racing Green light' to proceed towards limited series production. (Rover Group)

but with different cockpit layouts and positions within the length of the car.

'Adventurer 1' was conceived as a more modern style, with the potential for proper two-plus-two seating and a nose that was the same length as the Sterling; 'Adventurer 2' was schemed with more 'classic' styling (broadly aligned to DR2), but with a clever secondary firewall that allowed the windscreen, dashboard and the whole of the cockpit to be moved rearward to give more traditional longer-nose proportions.

Wire-frame models of both concepts were made by Motor Panels (Hamblin explains that 'this was an idea I had used on a project back in my Ogle days for a project to produce a

Using an idea from his days at Ogle Design, Richard Hamblin hit upon a way of creating wire-frame packaging models to explore different options for the evolution of PR5. 'Adventurer 1', shown here, had modern styling and the same platform proportions as the Rover 800/Sterling base. (Rover Group)

ROUTE OF DESTINY

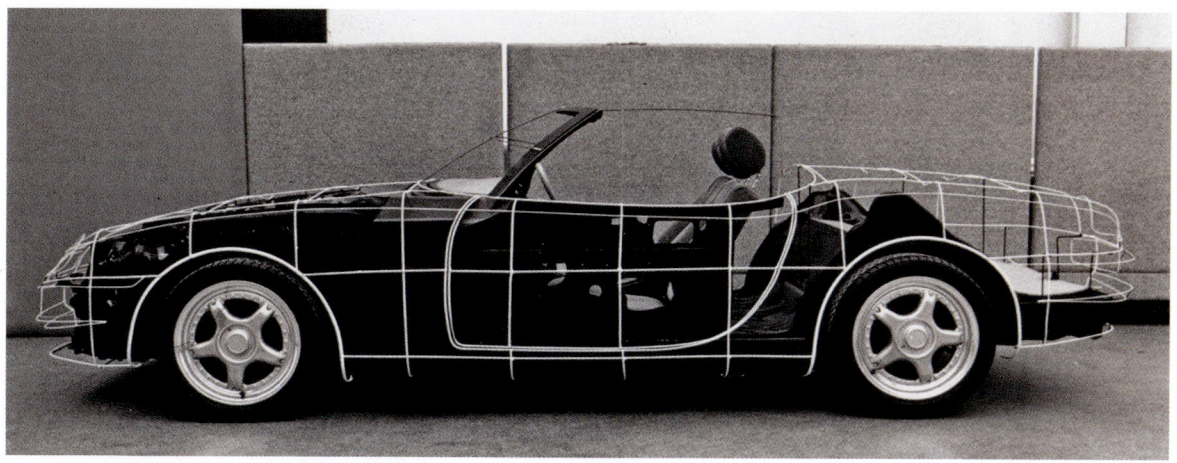

'Adventurer 2' had more traditional styling and a secondary bulkhead 'firewall', which allowed the facia and cockpit to be set back to classic roadster proportions. (Rover Group)

generic wire-frame car for use by DuPont to display their wares'), but no work at this stage was done on a clay or a studio model – money associated with the by now under-performing Sterling business was hardly flowing like water, and so the project proceeded slowly. DR2 was still seen as a more than adequate litmus test for the concept, however, and so before embarking on more detailed studies, it was felt that some kind of running prototype based on the DR2 design over the PR2 layout would be worth looking at.

Both the 'Adventurer' wire-frame models were made by Motor Panels (part of the Mayflower group, whose significance will become apparent). In this view, it can be seen that 'Adventurer 2' was not far removed from the DR2 style, even if the idea of front-wheel drive might have been a turn-off in such a car. (Rover Group)

We saw Roy Axe's rather lovely DR2 styling model earlier. It made sufficient impression that is was decided to marry the model to the running gear of a TVR to provide a further running prototype known as PR5/DR2.

Consequently, a copy of the DR2 body was made and a secondhand TVR purchased from an unsuspecting dealer: once back at Gaydon, the outer panels of the TVR body were unceremoniously cut off and the DR2 body sections were grafted on. The end result, finished in red rather than the green of the original DR2 studio car, was known as PR5/DR2; just as PR2 had retained an untouched Reliant cockpit, so PR5/DR2 retained the TVR interior. By the summer of 1991, PR5/DR2 was ready to take its place alongside 'Adder' and the two PR3 styling clays.

Just like the Reliant-built PR2, the interior of PR5/DR2 was almost entirely borrowed from the donor car.

ROUTE OF DESTINY

THE END OF STERLING – AND THE RISE OF PR3

In the same time that the MG sports car project had been gathering momentum, the Sterling business in North America was doing just the opposite. By the end of 1989, Sterling had already chewed through two presidents, Rover Group had bought out their partner Norman Braman, and ARCONA had become Sterling Motor Cars Inc. The third president was Graham Morris, who arrived at the US arm's Miami headquarters in February 1989 with the task of making or breaking the franchise, whose sales and image had been in a downward spiral almost as soon as the initial launch euphoria had died down.

The biggest issue, unfortunately, was quality. This was part of the reason why Honda was able to outsell the Sterling by a factor of ten, despite the Rover Group product being far more visually appealing: Honda had cleverly established a stand-alone 'Acura' franchise in the USA, whereas Sterlings often shared showroom floor space with Buicks, Pontiacs and Cadillacs. Added to that was a weak dollar, which by 1989 was severely constraining profit margins, but Morris was already badgering the people back in Britain about a sports car in order to give the beleaguered Sterling dealers something to sell beyond the 800.

Speaking to Richard Truett for an article about Sterling in the 6 December 1989 issue of *Autocar & Motor* magazine (the two former rivals had now combined), Morris said, 'we're going to give it our best shot. It's going to be hard, but it's going to be hard for everybody.' With Morris at the helm, the business was kept alive, but its pulse never grew any stronger during 1990 and the early part of 1991; it was obvious that tough decisions would have to made at some time.

During the Manchester clinic of June 1991 (see above), the 'Adder', PR5/DR2 and both PR3 styling clays were shown to an invited audience. Their views were illuminating. While most people could see the point of 'Adder' as a kind of bridge between the old MG sports cars and the new, they saw the beautiful PR5/DR2 as something in the Jaguar or even

The Sterling Coupé never actually came to pass, even though this teaser sketch was issued by Graham Morris. In the end, the Rover 800 Coupé would struggle with mainly European sales. (Sterling Motors)

ROUTE OF DESTINY

Another 'might have been'. RSP's Don Wyatt produced this retro-inspired sketch as part of the evolutionary process of marrying some of PR5/DR2's style to the modified Sterling platform. (Don Wyatt)

Aston Martin class: credibility might have been stretched as an MG and no one really saw it as a Rover – or, presumably, a Sterling.

On the ADC and MGA PR3 clays, however, the size meant that clinic visitors saw them more as 2–2.5 litre cars. Although, as we saw earlier, recognition as MG was not a prerequisite, it was perhaps disappointing that nobody saw either as having any MG design cues (although, as Richard Hamblin points out, 'in clinic tests, 64 per cent of people can't recognize their own car in a different colour with the badges removed').

In the summary report of the clinic, it was concluded that:

> PR3 is all about positioning and credibility. 1.4-litres would be a major threat to competency, and 1.6 was seen as a minimum. The 'MGA' clay is a potential product of the future but it needs more engine performance to be credible for a wide enough market. The 'ADC' clay is more mainstream, more a 'car of today' and more closely positioned to the MX-5.

Even before the review of May 1991 and the following month's clinic, there was pressure for further work on PR3 to be done in-house by the main studio, while some soul searching continued over PR5. By August, however, a major decision was taken that finally sealed PR5's fate: Rover Group decided that it was going to pull the Sterling out of North America, and without a primary product or a dealer network, any MG sports car aimed at that market was dead in the water.

The Adder – in running prototype form as well as styling clay – was fairly safe, as US sales had never been a realistic prospect, but the Sterling withdrawal suddenly meant that the only serious MG game in town was PR3.

PR3 JOINS THE MAINSTREAM: FROM RSP TO ROVER GROUP

Two months after the Manchester clinic, there was a major change at Rover Special Products: Richard Hamblin, David Wiseman and John Stephenson all left the company and their respective roles were filled by Don Wyatt, John Yea and Mike O'Hara. Richard Hamblin

ROUTE OF DESTINY

went on to set up his own OMNI Design practice (founded in October 1991), and later to undertake work for Rover Group, while Wyatt and Yea in particular would help see 'Adder' through to what would eventually become the MG RV8 of 1992.

PR3 had by now already been taken back under the wing of Rover Group's main studio, by this stage under the overall management of Gordon Sked, previously mentioned here with regard to his role on the EX-E. Working with Gerry McGovern, Sked was determined to inject some proper MG character into the design, and so they set about creating their own interpretation, drawing on the efforts of the outside consultants. It would be fair to say that, of the two different full-size models, the MGA version was closer to what eventually emerged, and comparison of the two is quite interesting.

Even so, it would be wrong to imply that the two were identical; yes, they had many features in common – including the layout, package, proportions, front and rear overhangs, the side air intakes, the curved shape of the doors (a design cue taken from the EX-E), the general proportions of the rear of the car and the rounded nature of the tail lights – but other aspects, such as the front cowl, nose, the height of the rear deck and the careful MG detailing, are quite different. Gerry McGovern, who recalls that work on the definitive clay got under way in September 1991, readily admits that the creation of this final design was a team effort, although Gordon Sked credits Gerry as the inspiration behind that team.

The autumn and winter of 1991 saw the last of the Musgrove-era MG-badged saloons, with the end of the MG Maestro and Montego (the MG Metro had already gone in May 1990), as well as the retirement of Roy Axe. By January 1992 the clay of the definitive PR3 was ready for management review, and was approved on 22 January. That same month, the Adder prototype was displayed at a dealers' conference. The two surviving MG sports car projects were by now running separate evolutionary paths, with the 'retro' car still under the wing of RSP but the all-important new car firmly under the main design studio and engineering teams.

March 1992 saw the launch at Geneva of a cabriolet version of the R8 200 (but as a Rover, rather than an MG), as well as the much-delayed coupé version of the R17 Rover 800, somewhat bereft now that the Sterling franchise had been cancelled. Also that month, the styling of PR3 was formally agreed, allowing the next stage of 'style ratification' comprising engineering of the 'body-in-white', including packaging all the components into the body structure.

One of the team involved in the original concept work on PR3, once it was brought back to the mainstream Rover Group design studio, was Oliver Le Grice, who moved on to Land Rover. This is one of his sketches from the spring of 1991. (Rover Group)

ROUTE OF DESTINY

Tony Hunter was another member of the design team; this concept sketch of his shows a slightly more traditional approach with round headlamps. (Rover Group)

One of the more interesting events that month was an MG Awareness Day, to which about 450 Rover Group employees were invited in order to contribute to the thinking process and ensure that the new car would have the right detailing. The idea was thought up by Graham Morris, who had wound up the Sterling operation and was now running Rover Group Europe. It was his suggestion that an event like this would be a good litmus test and would ensure that no important MG 'cues' had been missed.

Examples of older MG sports cars were on show, but McGovern and his colleagues deliberately avoided showing any of the more recent studies, other than EX-E, in case they distorted the picture. Alongside some of the obvious but less feasible ideas – such things

Gerry McGovern was the lead designer on the project to create the definitive MGF; this is one of his sketches from the early stages of the project. (Rover Group)

ROUTE OF DESTINY

Julian Quincey was one of the key members of the design team working under Gerry McGovern to develop what became the definitive MG*F*; this is one of his sketches from the spring of 1991. According to Quincey, 'I worked on the MG*F* all the way through with Gerry but initially Tony Hunter produced sketches and worked on one side of the initial model. Oliver Le Grice also contributed some great sketches, as did Phil Simmons.' (Julian Quincey)

as wire wheels and massive chrome grilles – there were some simple but effective ideas such as mounting the MG badge on a shield at the front. Some ideas were already part of Sked and McGovern's game plan (for example, rounded exposed headlamps and a nose loosely modelled on that of the last of the MGBs), and reassuringly the awareness day served to show that the design teams had been broadly on the right track all along.

Moving the design on from the first clay was not without some challenges, however,

Another Julian Quincey sketch from the spring of 1991, not far from the final car. Note the fancy petrol filler cap, which is like that on the production MG*F*.

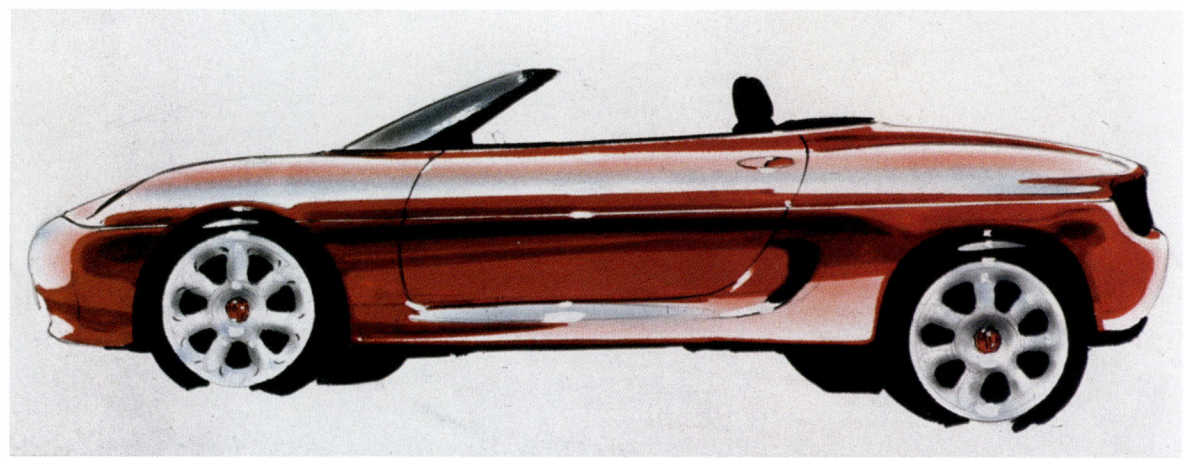

The nose on this sketch produced by Tony Hunter shows some resemblance to the Porsche 911, as per the MG RV8. (Rover Group)

for everything new and bespoke comes at a cost, and money was one thing that was never in generous supply. At one stage, McGovern was being offered a choice of either unique headlamps or tail-lamps – but not both. Brian Griffin even remembers a brief dalliance with recessed round headlamps like those on the contemporary Alfa-Romeo GTV. A similar battle was taking place over at the Adder project, where some (frankly horrible) efforts had been made to try to marry a Porsche 911 tail-lamp and even – horror of horrors – a Rover Metro tail-lamp into the basically MGB-shaped rear wings. The use of Porsche

Early stage of evolution of the Rover Group full-size PR3 clay, leading eventually to the familiar final style. (Rover Group)

ROUTE OF DESTINY

According to Julian Quincey, this 1991 sketch of a suggested long-wheelbase MGF variant for the USA was more of a 'what if?' exercise than a serious programme excursion: 'this amounted to little more than a few sketches that were taken to discuss an opportunity within the business. I don't think that the MGF got much work to make it certifiable in the US.' (Julian Quincey)

911 headlamps was rather more successful, however.

In the end, the cost accountants were finally persuaded to relent: the Adder got unique tail-lamps while the PR3 got unique lamps at both ends (the need and basic principles for the rear ones had, according to Richard Hamblin, been agreed during his time, but those eventually adopted by the Sked/McGovern team at the front were indeed all-new and very subtly

This sketch by John Gregory was produced as concept artwork to support the launch rather than to show a real evolutionary path that had been taken. (Rover Group)

Another of John Gregory's futuristic concept sketches for the interior (*see* also page 71). (Rover Group)

At an early stage in its evolution, the interior proposed would have utilized even more Rover Group parts than was eventually the case. (Rover Group)

recessed with a lower lip redolent of that of the MGB).

On the run-up to the launch, a number of slightly wild and wacky schemes for the interior were sketched by designer John Gregory, inspired in part by Ford's Ghia Focus sports car concept of 1992 (no relation to the much later Ford Focus hatchback). However, these were more for illustrative purposes and although it was deemed important to make the

A full-size clay model representing the interior of the new mid-engined MG was developed at ADC under the supervision of senior designer Gerry McGovern. Compare this view, dating from 1992, with the interior of the 2009 MG *TF* shown on page 188 in Chapter Six. (Rover Group)

The interior of what would become the first all-new MG since the MGB of 1962 takes shape. (Rover Group)

ROUTE OF DESTINY

PR3 interior somewhere special, the end result – based on the ADC concept and with its cosy 'twin cockpit' with a classic cowled instrument cluster in front of the driver – was a more subtle but elegant compromise, and one that would live with the car from its launch and right through its subsequent evolutionary phases.

PIZZA VANS AND THE VERY COMPLICATED ENGINE

One way to start the serious business of engineering feasibility was through the time-honoured method of building simulators as mobile engineering testbeds. Since the key mechanical components of PR3 were Metro based, it is hardly surprising that the first simulators were too.

The clever ruse that Brian Griffin and his colleagues adopted was to take a Metro van, remove the engine from its nose and insert the 1.4-litre K-Series engine and subframe behind the driver. The problem of engine accessibility was eventually solved on the second and subsequent simulators by making the whole rear upper section of the van body into a liftable section. The first van, Sim-1, was built in 1991 by ADC, but further examples (Sim-2, -3 and -4) were built by Rover Group in 1992. Before long, locals in the Gaydon area would occasionally see a beige Metro van, sometimes (if it was Sim-2, which survives in the Heritage collection) with the legend 'RTC' (a sly reference to 'Rover Test Centre') emblazoned on the side.

Griffin and his colleagues dubbed these cars the 'Pizza Vans'. Before long they were joined by four Toyota MR2 sports cars that had received K-Series engine transplants – great for popping down to the local shops without anyone batting an eyelid. Once the styling of PR3 had been approved, the engineers could work towards more representative simulators, but as the full body-in-white engineering was some way off, and would be dependent on the supply arrangements, the Pizza Vans and the MG MR2 simulators were essential tools. Eventually, there would be sixteen simulators overall, of which four were effectively mock-ups of the definitive PR3. 'One of those was used for a 30mph rear, offset front impact, side impact, roof crush *and* pavé test – all on the one car!', Brian Griffin told me, adding that the roof crush test came first, and then the pavé.

One of the clever ruses to allow early testing of the PR3 running gear was to use specially modified Metro vans. Some of them, like this one, had an arrangement whereby the entire rear bodywork could be opened up. (Rover Group)

ROUTE OF DESTINY

One of the key issues to resolve was the engine size and specification; a 1.4-litre engine as originally envisaged when PR3 had been a modest Midget type car was clearly no longer an option, and yet as originally conceived, the K-Series engine was only intended to span the 1.1- to 1.4-litre capacity range. However, as had been the case in MG's past, demand elsewhere within the company at large meant that there was a case for a 1.6-litre K-Series (which would save Rover Group the cost of buying in Honda engines of that size) and it was found that, with some clever engineering, it would be possible to stretch to a 1.8-litre capacity.

As of July 1991 it had been envisaged that the new car would feature a 1.6-litre unit with an optional supercharger (the team looked at VW G-Lader and Sprintex units), but doubts about the performance and risk of overheating eventually ruled out the latter option. Experiments with forced-induction K-Series had started with an innocuous-looking first-generation Rover 216 Vitesse, to which a supercharged 1.4-litre engine had been fitted. As Brian Griffin told me,

The chassis simply couldn't handle it. I was asked by Roger Stone to try it out on the roads – they had quietly tried the idea – with 200NM and 150 horsepower – as an 'ideas exercise'. I tried it round the Warwickshire lanes and the car couldn't cope with the power. At the north bend at Gaydon, I was getting wheelspin at 90mph in the wet. However, the engine would have had problems with reliability and emissions and had to be usable in other cars. We were also looking at the VVC concept and felt that was a better way to go.

It was something of a coincidence that the maximum capacity of the B-Series engine, as originally used in the MGB, had been 1798cc and the maximum production capacity of the K-Series, originally for the new PR3, would be 1796cc. Both engines had been stretched safely and effectively some way beyond their original designers' intentions. For a while there were still thoughts about a forced-induction version of the K-Series for PR3 using an exhaust-driven turbocharger instead of a conventional supercharger (a turbocharged K-Series would

Another group of test 'mules' was cleverly converted from first-series Toyota MR-2 sports cars, to which K-Series engines and transmissions were fitted with virtually no external clue to their special secret. (Rover Group)

ROUTE OF DESTINY

For some testing, it was obvious that eventually a 'real' PR3 would be needed, but the Rover Group engineers, as well as their sales and marketing colleagues, were nervous in case any spy photographers unleashed too much detail on the new MG before the company was ready. Accordingly, special removable GRP covers were designed and modelled using clay patterns. Some were painted white with some black tape coverings designed by Dave Ovens, while others were painted NATO camouflage green. (Rover Group)

appear a few years later for a mainstream Rover product), but a number of issues militated against the choice for the mid-engined MG.

For a start, the addition of a turbocharger in the compact engine bay, remote from the direct cooling blast of air at the nose, could have posed both a packaging problem and the risk of serious heat-soak issues, especially in some of the real world conditions that the car could be expected to have to tolerate, such as suddenly becoming stuck on a humid summer's day in a traffic jam in downtown Tokyo, with the air conditioning on full blast. Later in the life of the production car, thoughts would return to possible forced-induction versions; the stories of the Supersports and X121 are told below (see Chapters Four and Five), as is the story of one man's attempt to build a Porsche-rivalling MG.

In the meantime, however, an alternative option was variable valve timing. Rover Group had been exploring an innovative system under the project codename of 'Hawk' since 1989, using a number of semi-independent camshafts that could be tailored throughout the whole engine performance envelope, the overall effect being to lift efficiency and power across the range. Variable Valve Control (VVC) –or 'very, very complicated', as some wags at Rover Group called it – would be seen both in the production version of PR3 and a performance version of R3, the Rover 200 hatchback launched in 1995.

For the steering, there was healthy debate about whether or not power assistance was required: there was a school of thought that sports cars should have a purer steering feel without the blurring effect of a hydraulic pump or electric motor. However it also had to be recognized that many customers of the new sports car would be women and city dwellers, both of whom would have become used to power assistance. The Japanese market also virtually took power assistance for granted, and so an electric PAS system was developed that provided speed-sensitive assistance at all

ROUTE OF DESTINY

The MG*F* mule with weird GRP disguise looked like something out of a science fiction film. (Rover Group)

times, with the obvious focus on parking and similar low-speed manoeuvres.

The use of Metro subframes pointed almost inevitably to the use of Hydragas fluid suspension, but again the engineers at Rover Group cleverly adapted the Metro-derived installation by introducing three links in the lower section of the rear suspension, all anchored in different places, to provide well-controlled suspension geometry. Coupled with the fluid suspension medium, the end result would be the best-riding sports car in the business, but also with impeccable handling and road holding.

MAYFLOWER

In 1992 the PR3 sports car programme was still a project looking for funding. With US sales now out of the question (and PR3 was in any case never likely to meet Federal standards, nor meet customer requirements in North America), the kind of volumes normally needed to make the investment sums add up simply weren't there.

Some car makers had contracted out lower volume products to specialists like Pininfarina and Bertone, but in general these were convertibles or other derivatives closely related to a volume car already in production; building a sports car would have been costlier and this could either have pushed the price of the MG out of reach of some of the core customers, or

The ultimate evolution of the K-Series, as far as the MG*F* was concerned, was the VVC unit with a very advanced variable valve camshaft unit, arguably more advanced than some of the contemporary variable valve timing units employed by Honda or BMW. (Rover Group)

ROUTE OF DESTINY

As co-investor with Rover Group in the PR3 project, Mayflower Vehicle Systems was a key partner at all stages of the programme. Here a Mayflower engineer is checking dimensional accuracy of a sample MG*F* bodyshell. (Mayflower Vehicle Systems)

reduced profit margins below the acceptable threshold.

However, the idea was suggested of entering into a joint venture whereby both Rover Group and a partner would share in the up-front investment and share the proceeds; it had worked with the MGB and Pressed Steel in 1960, so why not now? Accordingly, informal enquiries were made of a number of companies, notably Pininfarina and Mayflower

The MG*F* bodyshell production area, with colourful jigs and associated equipment, pictured at Mayflower's Holbrook Lane plant at Coventry in 1995. The company went into administration on 1 April 2004 and its assets were acquired by Stadco. (Mayflower Vehicle Systems)

(the holding company that now owned Motor Panels, whose PR1 had been so impressive and who had worked on various parts of the Phoenix programme).

By the tail end of 1992 the Rover Group Board had received proposals from both of the two short-listed candidates. In the end the decision went to the British company, not least because of its proximity to the Longbridge factory, where final assembly was likely to take place. As part of the deal, both parties had to raise finance, and for their part Mayflower achieved this through a rights issue in March 1993. Mayflower then set up a dedicated team to work on the body-in-white development, with Tim Martin at its head, working opposite Rover Group's own Project Manager, Nick Fell.

FROM ADDER TO RV8

While the new mid-engined MG sports car was still some way in the future, by 1992 the plans for the entrée, 'Project Adder', were advancing apace. As the prime mover behind the project, Richard Hamblin is keen to put the record straight on its genesis and *raison d'être*: 'Much has been said about MG RV8 – much is ill informed, or a failure to see it in context'.

The programme was never envisaged as more than a limited run of 2,000 ('all of which sold'); it was a programme with a tiny budget ('a way of drawing attention to, and benefiting from what the guys at Heritage were doing'); it was a thirtieth anniversary model (from MGB's 1962 launch) and also a method of keeping MG alive in people's minds before the company could launch PR3 ('a reaction to the question of how long would we own the name if we did not use it').

Furthermore, Adder could be seen as a response to Japanese customers' interest in niche cars at that time, something to attract attention at a number of Motor Shows when nothing much else was on offer – and a possibility that this would be the mechanical layout and engine to use if Rover Group was eventually forced down a front-engine, rear-wheel drive route for MG. 'Finally it was the dream of owning a Classic Car without

Spot the difference! The first of these two otherwise similar images of the nose of the final full-size 'Adder' model shows a grille not unlike that of the last of the so-called 'rubber bumper' MGB models of 1974–80. (Rover Group)

In this case, the centre 'block' has been removed to show a single grille 'slot'. In the end, this is the version that was chosen for what became the MG RV8. (Rover Group)

ROUTE OF DESTINY

The final Adder full-size model in the viewing studio at Canley early in 1992. This model was actually used for a photo-shoot at London's famous Ealing Film Studios for some of the launch publicity material. (Rover Group)

the nightmare, at a time when the Classic Car market was on an all-time high'. Mainly though, Hamblin feels, 'the idea [of Adder] was predicated on reminding the public of the MGB's proud history, and hence to establish a platform for the launch of MGF'.

When the MGB had been in its final stages of production, more than ten years before, the interior, particularly the dashboard, still had roots in an even earlier era and was already a cause of criticism. Clearly a new car had to move the game on. Given the nostalgia for the kind of luxury roadster that in reality never existed, coupled with a trend for expensively trimmed restorations in the classic car world, the challenge for Adder would be to find a reasonable compromise, as Hamblin agrees:

> The interior of Adder certainly seemed to be a little trickier. The original would not do, and neither would a really modern offering (nor could we afford one). This time, however, we got it right at the first attempt. The interior that evolved was perforce quite simple, though luxury in its execution. Generally it is agreed to be totally fitting with the Exterior Design. Perhaps this is the first time such a luxurious interior was ever launched into a traditional Roadster.

In hindsight, some people ask why DR2 was not done instead of RV8. According to Richard Hamblin:

> Both concepts were valid in their own right and, given unlimited resources, DR2 may have been produced. That does not mean that RV8 would then not have been, as it answered totally different questions and achieved quite specific aims. It will, however, be interesting to see which design 'dates' first, and which is the more desirable in ten years' time – but that is academic. One was good enough and could be afforded – and one was good enough and couldn't. It was purely a matter of funds (or lack of them): RV8 cost a tiny fraction of what DR2 would have cost to deliver. With RV8 we were not talking of a £500 million programme, nor even a £50 million programme, but a £5 million one.

The interior of the MG RV8 would prove to be the most luxurious of any post-war MG up to that date. (Rover Group)

Strangely, and contrary to MGF, most people in Rover were in favour of the RV8 when it was conceived – some who now dismiss it. Indeed given the situation at that time, where nothing seemed to be 'affordable' or 'do-able', it only progressed, where so many other designs had not, because the final model obtained such unanimous support at Board level.

MG RV8 was launched at the 1992 NEC Motor Show, celebrating as planned the thirtieth anniversary of the MGB. This was five years after the first idea, and only two years after the clay model – fast enough for Hamblin to comment, 'That is what was possible when people are committed!'

A common theory is that the RV8 was rescued as a project by its reception in Japan, just as the UK entered a recession. Hamblin does not hold to this version of history:

> As planned, most of the production went to Japan. Those who say Japan mopped up excess capacity were not in on the planning stage when volumes were first predicated. David Blume, Director, Rover Japan, supported MG RV8 from the start, citing Japan as a market which could easily absorb the whole limited production volume if necessary, i.e. they were committed from the start, and the programme was predicated on this knowledge. Being a 'right-hand drive' market meant RSP kept close contact with David Blume.

Despite this view, Greg Allport, MG Brand Manager from 1992, as the RV8 was coming to production, firmly believes that the Japanese angle became vitally important:

> RSP had approved the MG RV8 programme on a limited run of 1,400 units, all to be sold in the UK market. Advanced orders had stalled at around 200 cars and so I knew we had to expand the market availability. Working closely with David Blume, a Japanese programme was developed requiring few changes to the car, and the car was promoted at the 1993 Tokyo Motor Show with huge success – in total around 80 per cent of the roughly 2,000 cars built went to Japan.

This certainly rings true; the market for classic cars had been stalled by a UK recession and the Tokyo show car was finished in a special optional colour, pearlescent Woodcote Green: the vast majority of MG RV8s sold in Japan were also finished in this extra-cost paint finish.

Hamblin says he is quite happy to stand by both exterior and interior designs of the RV8 today: 'using an old body and just new wings and bumpers, we produced a good looking and relevant car to its time. *Autocar* (and other kind people) even said it was stunning from any angle'. He is convinced that in time the RV8, which has indeed held good prices in the market, will become a significant 'collector's car' and will be seen in its rightful context. It is also worth remembering, he says, that many famous car companies have existed that produced fewer than 2,000 cars, in total.

ROUTE OF DESTINY

GERMANY CALLING: THE ARRIVAL OF BMW

Even the most fervent optimist would have had to acknowledge that, when British Aerospace bought Rover Group in 1988, there could be no guarantee that the relationship would extend beyond the end of the government's requested 'golden period' in 1993. Most observers, though, would have placed their money on Honda being the suitor that rode to Rover's rescue if the need ever arose.

If anyone thought that Honda was keen on owning Rover Group outright, however, they were sadly mistaken. When BL had gone cap in hand to Honda, it was the British company that had the greater need: the Japanese could see potential benefits in collaboration, but outright ownership of BL had never been their desire. As Honda got to know BL's (and later Rover Group's) strengths and weaknesses, however, the likelihood of a fully consummated union became even less likely.

The XX project was a case in point, for while Harold Musgrove had been proud of his company's engineering capability, his Japanese counterparts were somewhat less impressed. Stories of some of the problems on this and other projects are well worth relating (and they will be, but in another book), but suffice to say that Honda expanded the facility they built at Swindon well beyond an engine plant into a full-blown car factory. From the 'YY'/R8 project onwards, the relationship between Honda and Rover Group was cordial, cooperative and effective, but it was increasingly clear who maintained the upper hand.

By 1993 BAe was in any case suffering wider problems of its own and so made it known, below the radar, that it might be receptive to good offers for the car business. In the autumn of that year, Land Rover showed its latest wares at the Frankfurt Motor Show. Among the interested bystanders during the opening days of the show were two key people from one of Europe's leading luxury car makers, BMW. BMW had already been looking at some way of expanding their product portfolio, and the Land Rover range seemed to fit the bill.

BMW Chairman Bernd Pischetsrieder and the Head of Research, Wolfgang Reitzle, knew that the cars business was closely tied to Honda, but they considered the possibility of acquiring just Land Rover or, if that was not possible, forging a contractual relationship with Honda but gradually building up Rover's independence. Within the 'Rover' portfolio, the BMW men could see the latent potential of what was, in their minds, the criminally under-exploited Mini brand name, and while MG might have had some attraction, it was

BMW's second-in-charge to Chairman Bernd Pischetsrieder at the time of the purchase of Rover Group was Professor Dr.-Ing. Wolfgang Reitzle, a perfectionist whose unnerving eye for detail made him many admirers and not a few enemies too. In later years, he cited the Rover purchase as a tactical error by BMW. (Jaguar)

ROUTE OF DESTINY

Serbian-born designer Marek Djordjević was a young designer at the Designworks studio in California in 1994 when he drew this concept sketch for a possible new MG sports car, predating the launch of the MGF. BMW was Designworks's main client – and Reitzle masterminded the outright acquisition of the studio in 1995. (Marek Djordjević)

comparatively incidental in their minds, although Pischetsrieder had seen potential in the RV8.

Many people both inside and outside the company believed that Reitzle had seemed destined to take over the reins from BMW Chairman Eberhard von Kuenheim. Two years earlier, in 1991, the two men had been on a visit to Japan when they began discussing possible ways that BMW might expand its business portfolio without diluting BMW's core brand and the 'Ultimate Driving Machine' mantra. According to David Kiley in his book *Driven – Inside BMW, the Most Admired Car Company in the World* (John Wiley and Sons, 2004), the ideas that Reitzle put forward to his then boss were to buy Porsche, buy Rolls-Royce (and Bentley), buy Land Rover or buy Mini.

Of these, the idea of acquiring Rolls-Royce subsequently moved towards the crux of a deal, until von Kuenheim scuppered the idea. Reitzle was forced to eat humble pie with Rolls-Royce's owners, Vickers, but he called on George Simpson and talked about buying either Land Rover, Mini or maybe both. Reitzle did not want Rover – or, presumably MG, although that marque seems hardly to have registered on the radar: Reitzle told Kiley, 'the numbers on Rover were terrible ... we only wanted Land Rover and Mini, and I was not interested in any deal that included Rover'. However, Simpson was not likely to be persuaded to sell just the choicest bits, and so the options for BMW seemed less attractive.

By the end of 1993, a job offer from Ferdinand Piëch to Reitzle had effectively blocked the latter's chance of succeeding von Kuenheim as BMW Chairman, and so the job went to Bernd Pischetsrieder instead. So by the time of the 1993 Frankfurt show, the two senior BMW men were wary allies, both of whom had wanted the top BMW job. Pischetsrieder rekindled the Rover project, and as the new chairman was able to make the plan his own; he was less concerned than Reitzle at the prospect of taking on Rover along with the 'premium' brands, and so went back to negotiate with Simpson.

So it was that in January 1994 BMW stunned the world by making a cash offer to acquire the whole Rover Group business from BAe, taking the Rover Group Board as much by surprise as the rest of us. Supposedly hardly less shocked

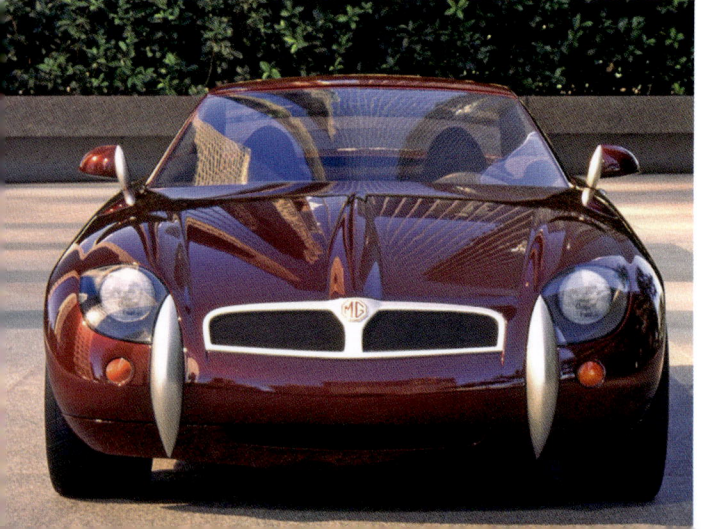

From the front, Djordjević's MG sports car proposal is an attractive blend of modern and traditional shapes. (Marek Djordjević)

From the side, the compact size and lack of front or rear overhangs gives Djordjević's MG proposal credence as an idea for a new MG Midget; this model predates the MG*F*. (Marek Djordjević)

were the Honda Board, although in fact BMW had tried to sound out the Japanese company. Honda Chairman Nobuhiko Kawamoto apparently did not respond to a letter from Pischetsrieder in which the Bavarian asked Honda to accommodate the deal.

After some further negotiation, Honda agreed to raise their stake in Rover Group from the existing 20 per cent to 47.5 per cent – in other words, still leaving BAe as the majority shareholder. However, BAe wanted out of car making, and so the BMW deal was agreed and swiftly ratified. All of this might have seemed academic with regard to the development of Rover Group's own PR3 sports car, which owed very little to Honda (in fact the only 'Rover' product outside the Land Rover family that owed less to the Japanese company was the Mini) had it not been for the little matter of BMW's own sports car plans.

What would become the BMW Z3 roadster, launched in 1996 with a cameo role in the latest James Bond film *Goldeneye*, had started as a typically thorough BMW design study that involved the creation of a brand new greenfield car factory at Spartanburg, South Carolina – in prime position for production in North America, the heartland of sports car consumption. Whatever one may think of it, the Bavarian car maker has always been thorough and seldom less than ambitious. Measured against this, the project to make an MG sports car out of Metro bits must have seemed very curious and inconsequential.

The British management, designers and engineers behind the new MG were right to be worried: the Germans were puzzled at the choice of a mid-engined layout (they thought that a traditional British MG would have a traditional transmission layout) and the lack of any US sales plans (even if that kept the way clear for the Z3), and some may have been disparaging of the low-cost and consequently low-volume solutions that the British team had adopted, even though many of these were clever choices forced by budget constraints rather than preference.

BMW definitely had concerns about the arrangement with Mayflower making bodies and sharing in the profits. Although they

Another view of Marek Djordjević's scale model. Nowadays, Djordjević is better known as the principal exterior designer of the mammoth Rolls-Royce Phantom of 2003. (Marek Djordjević)

might have been unhappy about the body-in-white compromises forced on the MG by this investment route, Greg Allport says that BMW senior management were sanguine about this: 'BMW understood why Rover Group's available funds were deployed on mainstream cars and therefore appreciated the MG*F* funding route'.

Allport does not feel that BMW had any major concerns about the body-in-white.

However, if one adds in the fact that BMW had the Z3 on the way and that BMW was already the established sports car marque in the extended family, it was clear that the MG would certainly have to give a good account of

The first time that BMW's senior management team laid eyes on an MG*F* prototype, it was a full-size GRP model finished in a pinkish red called 'Lipstick'. By all accounts, the Bavarians were somewhat nonplussed. (Rover Group)

ROUTE OF DESTINY

When the BMW team returned a few weeks later, the model had been refinished in a dark metallic British Racing Green: the BMW management pronounced themselves happy with the programme. (Rover Group)

itself. Accordingly, while Bernd Pischetsrieder, fresh from basking in the spotlight caused by the audacity of the Rover Group purchase, expounded thoughts on future directions for MG, his colleague Dr Reitzle asked for a high-level review of the MG, along with all the projects that were currently being worked on.

Things did not start very auspiciously. The fully detailed GRP-bodied model of the new MG had been painted in a rather bright pearlescent pinkish red rather like lipstick or nail varnish, as the team were hoping to have a special 'halo' colour exclusive to the top-of-the-range model (in the end, this would be 'Volcano', see Chapter Four). According to Brian Griffin, when Pischetsrieder and Reitzle arrived at Gaydon for the viewing, they were rather taken aback and Pischetsrieder asked for a review of the MG brand values: 'We arranged for a meeting with BMW's design director Chris Bangle so that he could review the car and feed back to Pischetsrieder'.

Behind the scenes, some of BMW's engineering team were also concerned about the British roadster project; a senior BMW engineer, Christian Eich (later to become head of BMW Mobile Tradition, and still later to be a victim, with his family, of the Concorde air crash of 2000), told *Classic & Sportscar* magazine's James Elliott, 'if we had run Rover at the time, the MG*F* would never have happened. It would have just been too much time and hassle for the return.' BMW's attitude to such joint ventures became clear when they cancelled Rover Group's proposed plan to build what became the Land Rover Freelander with Valmet of Finland, postulated under a similar framework to the Mayflower deal.

In the meantime, however, the project team collected together all the market research data they had been working on for a report to be presented by Nick Stephenson, and simultaneously arranged for the GRP car to be repainted metallic British Racing Green. The next time that Pischetsrieder came to see the MG, he saw it newly refinished in green and, according to Griffin, simply said 'I don't have a problem!' just from looking at the car. Chris Bangle recalls that this was broadly what happened, although he stresses that BMW Design had relatively little input to the MG*F* programme beyond that first appraisal.

ROUTE OF DESTINY

In truth, the MG project was so far down the road, and BMW was trying to tread a middle ground between interference and support, that PR3 survived by the skin of its metaphorical teeth. BMW largely left the Rover Group team to their own devices, and Nick Fell and his team concentrated on getting the car ready for the launch in Geneva. According to Greg Allport, then involved in Rover Group's brand management team, when the BMW and Rover people shared their sports car market research, they found that they were a very good match, which helped show the thoroughness of the work by each party.

'I developed a very good relationship with my counterpart at BMW', Allport says, to the extent that he would often be invited into BMW's engineering centre for *Weisswürste* (Bavarian white sausages) and beer during his regular end-of-week visits to Munich:

Their research for Z3 matched what we had done for MG, and their car had arguably a more overtly 'masculine aggressive' focus, while ours had a rather broader appeal across the spectrum, so in fact it was Pischetsrieder who said he could see there was room in the market for both MG*F* and Z3.

Even so, BMW could not resist playing with the concept of other MG products, including the lovely little roadster in the accompanying photos from Designworks designer Marek Djordjević (better known subsequently for the exterior design of the 2003 Rolls-Royce Phantom). According to Chris Bangle, 'Marek's beautiful little roadster came out of Designworks internal project budget, money I set aside for them to do whatever they wanted to. They made quite a number of nice scale models and later full size ones.'

The MG*F* model as shown to BMW management; the colour may look relatively innoffensive in this photo but a change to British Racing Green was deemed wise in order to ally BMW concerns! (Rover Group)

chapter four

Dreams Realized: The New MG*F*

MG*F*: THE GENEVA SHOW STAR

By the beginning of 1995 it was a fairly open secret that there was a new MG sports car on the way, one that many outsiders assumed would be the 'MGD'. (One personal number plate speculator was surprised when Rover Group's Denis Chick declined an offer to buy some 'MGD' numbers as a special deal.) In the run-up to the launch at the famous Geneva Salon de l'Auto, there was a great deal of hard work behind the scenes to ensure that the first all-new MG sports car in twenty-three years had a good send-off.

The famous Corgi Toys model company worked closely with Rover Group and was able to arrange a joint launch of a new 1:18 scale detailed model of the MG*F* on the MG stand at the show. As another strand to the launch activities, the MG Car Club decided to mount a trip to the show in a convoy of MG cars of various vintages that drove from Abingdon to Geneva in a couple of days, stopping at various French hostelries en route. The author, already booked for Press Day, agreed to join in the fun

Rover Group, like most contemporary car companies, rarely gave much prominence to its designers (other perhaps than the Design Director) and so when Gerry McGovern was allowed to assume the role of an 'ambassador' for MG, it was a refreshing change. McGovern would appear at many MG*F*-related events in coming years and still looks back on his MG days as amongst the happiest of his distinguished career. (Rover Group)

The MGF was shown to a small group of MG club officials and MG specialist writers, the author among them, at a preview session at Gaydon in February 1995.

along with his wife and his 1974 MGB GT V8. Our little convoy was trailed by a Rover Group-supplied Land Rover packed with spare parts in case of any mishaps on the Autoroutes, and we were also royally welcomed by the good people of the MG Car Club of Switzerland on our arrival.

Also shadowing us on our journey was a BBC Bristol film crew who were, we understood, making a special TV documentary about the wonderful things that BMW was doing to help the recovery of the Rover Group, the MGF launch being just one example. We supposed that film of a bunch of eccentric MG enthusiasts would make good viewing, but in the end all of the MG launch trip film ended up on the cutting room floor when the BBC showed the final documentary, 'When Rover Met BMW', in 1996.

The unveiling of the MGF on press day was a great affair, orchestrated by Greg Allport and his team with Nick Fell giving a preamble before the gold covers were pulled off the two cars on show. Journalists and rival designers were generally very complimentary, even if one or two of the latter said they thought that the design could have been a little bolder. Hindsight has generally shown, however, that the style of the MGF was – to most eyes – pitched just about right. Rover Group even took out a special licence to allow them to import Morland's Old Speckled Hen beer (then brewed in Abingdon) into Switzerland to help celebrate the MGF launch.

FINAL TESTING AND PRODUCTION

Clearly a great launch at Geneva (and the hearty acclamation of the world's motoring media) was one thing, but the work obviously did not stop at Palexpo, for the first cars were due to be delivered to their new owners before the end of the year, and so pre-production testing and line manufacturing had to be concluded before MGFs could issue forth in bulk from Longbridge.

We saw in Chapter Three how the 'Pizza Vans' and K-Series Toyota MR2 mules had been useful, and that some skilful GRP disguises had helped conceal the shape of the new car; but once the MGF was featuring on the pages of motoring magazines and newspaper car columns worldwide, some of the previous need for secrecy evaporated; the final stages of testing and pre-production build-up could begin with realistically representative cars.

DREAMS REALIZED: THE NEW MG*F*

The Origins of the MG*F* Name

The design and engineering of a new MG is just the start of a long journey; bringing it to production, spreading the message of its arrival and delivering the cars to customers requires an enormous amount of effort and sheer momentum, with a degree of effort that the general public may not appreciate. In the case of the PR3, one of the early steps was to resolve a name and model strategy for the new sports car. There had been various prototype models in the company's history with their own code names (some of them featured earlier in this book), but the name on a prototype did not necessarily have any particular bearing on the production side. Until the last MG TF Midget went out of production in 1955, most production MG cars had used series letters to define their model, with an additional suffix sometimes added to differentiate a new variant. Thus the 'TF' was the final incarnation of what had been known affectionately in MG circles as the 'T-Series Midget'.

When MG came to launch a brand new streamlined sports car in 1955, they were in something of a quandary, as it was clear that the model letters were coming towards the end of the alphabet. For a short time the new car was referred to internally at MG as the 'Series UA', as that was almost the only letter left (S, V and W had been used pre-war, Y was only just out production, and X was possibly confusing because of the XPAG engines and prototype connotations of that letter). An MG sports car called the MG U-Type, however, somehow didn't look very appealing, and so MG's John Thornley decided a new approach was needed.

The eventual idea was a clever one: to use 'MG' as part of the model name itself (thereby ensuring that every owner had to use the MG name when referring to their car, rather than talking about their 'T-Type' or 'Y-Type') and so combine it with a suffix starting afresh, right from the start of the alphabet. Thus was created the 'MGA' model name, and before long the 'MGB' name was being talked about at Abingdon for the new twin-cam derivative of the MGA (in the event, as we now know, the MGB name was held back for something newer).

The MGB was known at the factory as 'ADO23' but this codename had no bearing on the public profile of the car. When a larger-engine variant was designed with the intention of breeding joint MG and Austin Healey sports cars, the model name on the MG was decided as 'MGC', although this name too nearly ended up on another model, the Cowley-built MG 1100. The MG Midget of 1961 somehow escaped this new policy; probably it was decided that 'MG Midget' was a clear enough name without the confusing clutter of more letters.

When it came to another engine transplant in the MGB, there seems to have been no serious thought given to calling it the 'MGD'; as a result, like the MGA Twin Cam, the slightly clumsily named MG MGB GT V8 of 1973 was viewed as an engine variant rather than an entirely new model. As MG had suffered much criticism over the resemblance of the MGC to the MGB, perhaps this was not too surprising. However, even while the V8 was being developed, what was by now British Leyland was looking at what would eventually replace the MGB (for the story of ADO21, *see* Chapter One). This car, in whichever iteration might have been chosen, could well have become the MGD, but there never was a production MG with that model name, any more than there was an MGE.

However, the MG*F* name was seen as an attractive euphonious option that neatly linked to the exotic EX-E concept car, and also picked up on the work done on the F-16 project. So the new sports car was destined to be the MG*F* (preferably, in Rover Group eyes, with an italic '*F*'). Although the MG*F* name was being used from 1992, as some of the sketches prove, Greg Allport insists that the final decision to go with the 'MG*F*' name was not taken until 1994.

DREAMS REALIZED: THE NEW MGF

Once the use for 'Pizza Van' Metros and Toyota MR-2 engine mules had been exhausted, and testing moved beyond even the phase where heavy GRP disguises were acceptable, some testing – often at night – was undertaken with these vinyl masks. (Autocar)

In the wake of simulators, the next stage in development was the so-called 'DO1' prototypes, which were hand-built using a combination of hand-made parts and prototype components. This is never cheap, and so to make best use of each DO1 car they were each used for several tests. As explained on page 73, Brian Griffin recalled a single one of these cars being used for multiple testing. Brian remembered driving one of these cars in a partially wrecked state (with a crushed windscreen) around the Warwickshire

Inevitably the PR3 was caught out on test in the long telephoto lenses of onlookers: here in the long grass is one of the PR3 mules wearing its GRP disguise in NATO green. (Rover Group)

Immediately before and in the aftermath of the launch, some testing was done without any external disguise. Here an MG*F* test car races across the dusty Arizona roads in February 1995; during this trip some film was taken of an undisguised car, for use in a launch promotion video. (Leigh Richardson)

Prototype and Pre-Production Models

Code Description

- PR3 ADC   Running steel-bodied prototype built by ADC.
- SIM-1   Metro Van body mid-engined running prototype built by ADC.
- SIM-2 – SIM-4   Metro Van 'pick-up' body mid-engined running prototypes built by Rover Group.
- Toyota MR2   Four test 'mules' fitted with K-Series engines and used for emissions testing.
- SIM-7   Hybrid crash-test mule using a Metro front end and a hand-built PR3 rear. Tested 22 December 1992 to the North American specification 30mph rear end test (although the MG*F* was never sold in the USA).
- D01   First running prototypes (SIM-8, -9 and -10) with hand-made bodies, built at Rover Group's old Drews Lane plant. Some used for barrier impact tests.
- D02   Vehicle development phase after 'Day Zero' – Board Approval (November 1992). 'Soft-tool' bodies for engineering development.
- D1   First prototype off tools (July–August 1994). Two of these cars were shown to the MG clubs and specialist press in February 1995, two weeks before the Geneva launch.
- QP   'Quality Proving': first prototypes made almost entirely from tooling and on the production line (autumn 1994–spring 1995). The Geneva Show cars fell into this category.
- QC   'Quality Conformance': second stage of proving production processes.
- M   'Method Build': developing refinements to the on-line production processes prior to volume production (commenced 3 July 1995).
- AV   'Advanced Volume': just ahead of full production, addressing any problems identified during the previous stage. First production car (VIN No. 000251) completed on 24 July 1995; now forms part of the Heritage Collection at Gaydon.

DREAMS REALIZED: THE NEW MGF

Another MGF test car outside a desert motel in Nevada. These US trips took place during February, April and July 1995 in Nevada, Arizona and Death Valley, California. (Phil Gillam)

The 'QP' team stand proudly alongside one of the first MGFs to come through the early pre-production testing process. (Rover Group)

MGF Road Test Results

Magazine Model Date	Autocar MGF 1.8 20 September 1995	Autocar MGF VVC 8 April 1998	CAR MGF 1.8 October 1995
0–30mph	2.8	2.7	3.0
0–40mph	4.3	4.0	–
0–50mph	6.2	5.8	–
0–60mph	8.7	7.6	9.1
0–70mph	11.5	10.3	–
0–80mph	15.4	13.4	–
0–90mph	20.3	16.1	–
0–100mph	27.0	23.5	30.4
30–70mph through gears	8.7	7.6	–
30–50mph in fourth	7.8	6.5	7.8
50–70mph in top	12.1	11.0	–
Maximum speed	123	126	120
Fuel overall mpg	26.4	28.3	28.4

backroads, and being thankful that no one from the local constabulary happened to be around to stop and ask awkward questions.

Following the 'DO1' cars came the 'DO2' versions, which were built in larger numbers (twenty-six were assembled in the case of the MGF). These were closer to the real article and were needed for some aspects of the testing such as cooling and crash performance, where the earlier cars were not close enough to production specification. It was the DO2 cars that wore the GRP and vinyl tape disguises mentioned earlier. After the DO2 cars came thirty-four 'D1' cars, the closest yet to the showroom cars, using a greater proportion of 'off tools' components. Penultimately there were another sixty-four 'QP' or 'Quality Proving' cars, to test the production processes at Longbridge, and finally about a hundred 'M' cars, just before full production.

Various testing sessions were held in North America during February, April and July 1995, ranging from cold climate testing in Canada to much hotter sessions in Arizona and Nevada, with the inevitable trips to Death Valley, one of the harshest proving grounds available. (Incidentally, China now offers similar environmental extremes for MG's present-day owners.) Race driver Mark Blundell was invited to put the MGF through its paces at Gaydon in January, and some of his feedback was used in fine-tuning the production chassis specification. By September the first cars were ready to be delivered to their expectant owners, and for the magazines to report on the first all-new MG sports car since 1962.

DREAMS REALIZED: THE NEW MGF

MGF Models at Launch

Export sales to Japan had been an important factor for the MG RV8 and this proved to be important again for the MGF; here cars are lined up at Southampton on 22 October 1995. (Andrew Roberts)

From the launch in March 1995, and the start of series production the following September, the MGF came in two basic variants: the 1.8i and VVC. Both units were closely related but the latter had a more sophisticated high-tech valve operation system that dramatically increased power at higher revs (*see* Chapter Three). Both units had 1796cc capacity but the difference in model specifications was separated by more than simply the engines.

The 1.8i and VVC engines generated power outputs of 118bhp and 143bhp respectively. Standard equipment levels for all models included a remote central locking and dead lock system together with passive arming immobilizer and remote-activated perimetric and volumetric alarm, heated door mirrors (manually adjusted) and electric windows. The VVC added further to this standard spec to include electrically assisted power steering (initially an option on the 1.8i, but standard equipment from 1998), a boot-mounted additional brake lamp (again, standardized across the range in 1998), anti-lock braking and half-leather interior trim. From the launch, quite a good variety of options were available including more sophisticated in-car entertainment, fog lamps and passenger airbag (all models had a steering wheel-mounted airbag as standard), while there was even a factory hardtop with heated glass rear window.

Greg Allport says that the principle behind the car that supported its sales forecast was 'that it should be fun and easy to drive (Performance, EPAS), practical as possible (comfortable, big boot, easy hood operation) and have good residual values so

AN AFTERMARKET MG SUPERCAR: THE MGF CHEETAH

We saw earlier how the Rover Group engineers toyed with turbocharged versions of the K-Series engine and their possible application in what became the MGF. The engineers continued to explore the possibility of a turbocharged or even supercharged MGF, and would go on to show a concept for such a car at the Geneva Motor Show in 1998 (see below). In the meantime, however, it was a partnership between a go-ahead MG dealer and a well-known aftermarket forced-induction specialist that saw the first series production MGF with a supercharger.

Stephen Palmer Ltd, a Rover Group dealer

DREAMS REALIZED: THE NEW MGF

In the spring of 1997, three new colours were added to the MGF range, by which time the company had just celebrated the 20,000th MGF sold. Tahiti Blue and Nightfire Red pearlescents and Platinum Silver metallic increased the colour option on MGF to nine. These new colours complemented existing colours of Flame Red and White Diamond, British Racing Green (accounting for over 50 per cent of sales) and Charcoal metallics, Amaranth (Purple) and Volcano pearlescents. (Rover Group)

that owners could come in and out of the market, thus widening its appeal'. Allport recalls meeting Jaguar's Sir William Lyons, who told him 'if you have demand for 100 cars, then build 99, not 101'. Following this philosophy, advanced interest in the MGF – launched in March but not actually in showrooms until the autumn – was significant: Allport points out that 'MGF boasted an order bank equivalent to six months build – which in itself created a demand!'

Rover Group had been looking to find a unique 'halo' colour for the premium VVC model variant, but the 'Lipstick' colour that BMW management saw on the full-size GRP nearly scuppered the whole project. Conventional choices like red and metallic British Racing Green were obvious, but something special was sought in the knowledge that, while not everyone would specify it for their own car, it could be associated with cars through marketing and sales literature and other promotional activities. After much investigation, a bright pearlescent orange dubbed 'Volcano' became the halo colour, although, according to Brian Griffin, some at Rover Group called it 'Sarah' in honour of the hair colour of the Duchess of York.

Strangely enough, a Volcano-finished car was the very first MGF that the author saw on public roads, when a test car shot past him on the M40 one day. In production, however, few people actually specified it as a personal choice, and Volcano-finished VVCs (the colour was never offered on the 1.8i) are nowadays quite rare.

at Long Eaton in Nottinghamshire who had cleverly built up both new MGF sales and his own aftermarket business, SP Performance, had begun selling Milltek-developed exhaust tuning kits for the standard MGF from soon after its launch, aiming to offer drivers improved performance from their standard 1.8 models and a proper sporting exhaust note into the bargain. However Palmer was ambitious to offer his wealthier customers an alternative to swapping their allegiance to another marque, and so in a seven-month development period, starting in mid-1997, the supercharged 215bhp VVC-engined MGF Cheetah was the result.

Launched at the *Autosport* Show in January 1998, the Cheetah was certainly an eye-opener. Under the engine compartment cover, the engine retained the standard ECU but

DREAMS REALIZED: THE NEW MGF

Stephen Palmer tried hard to create a Porsche-beating MGF. (Stephen Palmer)

had been fitted with an exotic – and pricy – hybrid Danish-built unit known as the Rotrex Supercharger, supplied by Turbo Technics. This unit was driven from the crankshaft and formed a centrifugal compressor that provided instant response (eschewing the lag inherent in normal turbochargers) and, of equal importance, resulting in lower engine compartment temperatures.

All of this equipment was expensive (the complete engine upgrade, including the Rotrex system, alone cost around £5,000) but SP Performance decided to go one step further and dress up their car with a body kit designed by Krafthaus, larger (7.5J × 17in) wheels, uprated brake discs and Mintex pads, and, last but not least, a modified instrument display with illuminated 'cheetah eyes'. The end result was offered for a cool £29,500, firmly into Porsche Boxster money. *Autocar* tried one for their 4 March 1998 issue. The report, headed 'MG FF', admired Palmer's tenacity in seeing the project through (he was said to have sunk £100,000 of his own money into it), but their final verdict was 'admirable effort, but too many flaws to be considered completely successful'.

No one could argue with Stephen Palmer's determination to continue to be the premier MGF dealer in the UK, and to offer his customers something extra special, but behind the scenes all was not quite what it seemed. Rover Group, now part of the BMW combine, was fiercely protective of the image of its products and only a small number of third party 'customization' companies were ever approved by the factory.

Only substantial and well-respected businesses like Alpina have ever had support from BMW, and in that context it was always likely that what could unkindly be termed a cottage industry in the UK would not receive Rover Group sanction. It is one thing for a totally independent company to offer aftermarket bits for an MGF (and there have been many such businesses over the years), but quite another when that business is an officially licensed outlet of the manufacturer.

In 1998 relations between Rover Group and Stephen Palmer Ltd became more strained, and the breaking point came when Palmer refused to finance major changes to his showroom demanded by Rover Group. Palmer eventually lost the Rover Group franchise, and before long the Cheetah project was nothing more than a fading memory. A 0–60mph time of around 5.5 seconds and a top speed in excess of 150mph were remarkable figures, but in the end that heavy price tag meant that sales were pitiful.

DREAMS REALIZED: THE NEW MGF

Motor sports would feature high in the MGF retinue, just like all previous MG sports cars; here the first MGF racer is seen at the Autosport Show in January 1996, complete with a competition hardtop designed by consultant Peter Stevens. (Rover Group)

MG'S OWN SUPERCHARGED MGF: THE SUPER SPORTS

Even before Stephen Palmer had set out to create his own 'super MGF', Rover Group – in conjunction with Mayflower Systems – was also looking at ways of extending the performance envelope of the MGF. By this stage, some experience had been gained with a turbocharged K-Series in the EXF record car (see below), but there would be no turbo version of the K-Series until some years later. In some ways rather like Stephen Palmer's Cheetah project, however, the Rover Group engineers favoured a supercharger, perhaps as a stepping stone to yet further developments such as the all-new 'NG4' engine that BMW was developing and which might, it was envisaged,

The first real competition work with the MGF was for a race series in Japan; here Tony Pond does a demonstration lap for Japanese and British media at the Castle Combe circuit on 21 February 1996. (Rover Group)

DREAMS REALIZED: THE NEW MGF

A concept sketch by designer David Woodhouse for a 'weekday race car' based on the MGF: 'This sketch was made before the car; usually designers' sketches of that accuracy to a concept are drawn "after the fact", but not this one!' (David Woodhouse)

eventually supersede the K-Series.

For the design of what became the MG Super Sports, Gerry McGovern, by now immersed in design work on what would become the Land Rover Freelander, turned to one of his young designers, David Woodhouse, to lead on the concept car project. Starting with study of some of the classic MG racing cars and other makes of the 1950s, a theme that emerged was one that was redolent of James Dean's infamous last car, the Porsche 550 'Little Bastard' in which the actor died; indeed that name even

Work underway in the studio for what would become the MGF Super Sports: according to David Woodhouse, 'We used a little skunk works on the Gaydon site which used to be an Officers' Mess, and where the MG RV8 had also been developed'. (David Woodhouse)

DREAMS REALIZED: THE NEW MGF

Nearly there: the project known variously as 'The Rebel' and 'Little Bastard' (names inspired by James Dean's famous film role in *Rebel without a Cause*, as well as his ill-fated Porsche 550 Spyder) is lined up outside. The gold wheels would go, as would the legend on the tail. (David Woodhouse)

featured on some early studio shots of the car, but not in public. 'I was also working on Mini and Freelander at the time', Woodhouse recalls (he was the exterior designer for the Freelander, although he acknowledges that 'Gerry was head Chef!'). 'Influence from the James Dean Porsches was my doing ... I was tooling around in a little RSK Replica at the time, and had always been a huge Dean fan!'

McGovern described the Super Sports as 'an MGF that has been working out in the gym for three hours a day, every day – maybe having

Mayflower played an important role in creating the special wider bodywork for the MGF Super Sports. The distinctive rear bumper splitter is, according to the current owner (in 2008), actually made of MDF! (Mayflower Vehicle Systems)

DREAMS REALIZED: THE NEW MGF

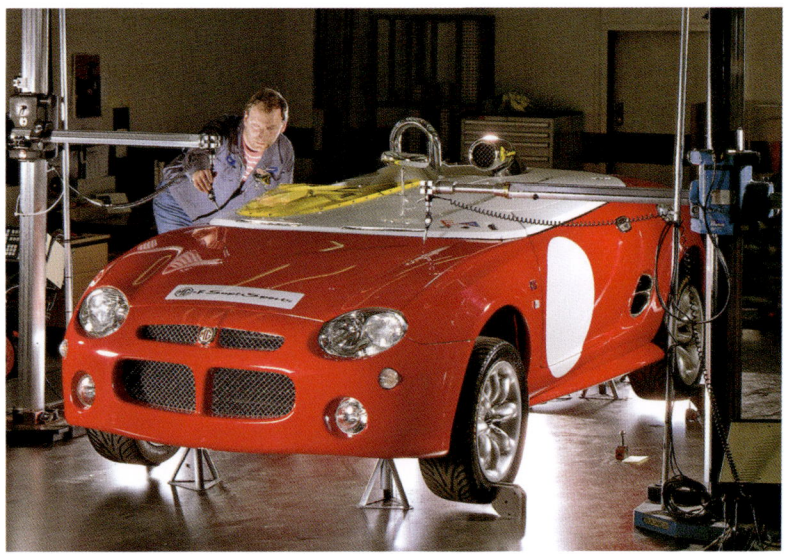

The MGF Super Sports poses for the camera at Mayflower's engineering workshop. (Mayflower Vehicle Systems)

popped a few steroids as well! It shows the extreme potential of "MG" in terms of how you can grow it, and for it to still work.' The reason that the Super Sports looked more muscular was pretty simple: the front and rear wings had been flared (they were wider by around 30mm and 40mm respectively, and had been formed in aluminium alloy) and there had been changes to every external panel, necessitating soft-tooling by Mayflower in order to reproduce the body shapes scanned from the clay.

As is so often the case in time-pressured projects that have a fixed deadline, in this case the Geneva Salon press day, not everything went smoothly and according to plan, as David Woodhouse explains:

My experience with the body was quite something. Having spent weeks finessing the highlighting on the exterior clay with

Young designer David Woodhouse, who already had the design of the special one-off futuristic 'Land Rover' vehicles from Sylvester Stallone's film *Judge Dredd*, was tasked with designing the MGF Super Sports. He is seen here sitting in the cockpit of his creation at the Geneva Motor Show in March 1998.

DREAMS REALIZED: THE NEW MGF

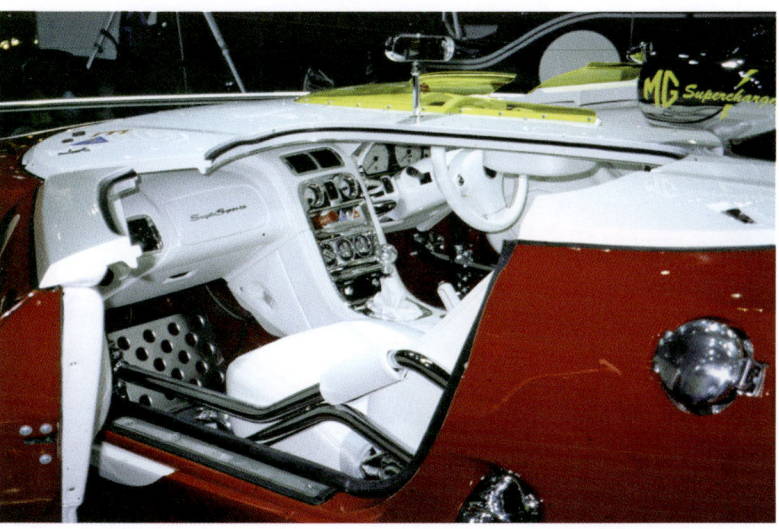

The interior of the MGF Super Sports was liberally covered with white Connolly Leather over just about every surface. Woodhouse says that 'the white was an acknowledgement of how flamboyant the pre-war race cars were in terms of their décor … and extended the old Abingdon racing colours nicely'.

Gerry, Mayflower had promised the earth with regards to accuracy of their aluminium panel process. However, at a very late stage, there was suddenly a realization that the panels were undersized and not matching the clay.

Time was rapidly running out:

We pulled the clay model in to the body shop responsible for the paint, where I had to literally direct the templating from clay to real car, and had to do modelling in bondo [filler] in cramped conditions: there were a few sleepless nights and a lot of work.

Woodhouse concludes that the actual car must weigh rather a lot more than it should have done as a consequence.

As shown at the 1998 Geneva Show, the MGF Super Sports featured a cut-down racing style screen in yellow Perspex and a definitely rather 'over the top' white leather interior, intended to

Various names have been suggested for the mysterious white-masked driver sitting in the cockpit of the MGF Super Sports during a photo shoot at Donington Park. In fact it was David Woodhouse behind the wheel, wearing his own retro race gear. Similarly attired in the K3 Magnette behind is owner Peter Gregory. (Rover Group)

DREAMS REALIZED: THE NEW MGF

BMW and MG: Curious Bedfellows

One of the few direct involvements that BMW had with the MGF was in the creation of the special one-off MINI ACV30 concept car, intended as a signpost towards the forthcoming 'real' new MINI and as a celebration of the thirtieth anniversary of the last major Mini Cooper rally victory. (BMW)

From the very beginning of BMW's ownership, decisions were made – or perhaps were not made – that would haunt the relationship until the very end. The appeal of Land Rover and the Mini brand name were easy enough to understand, but to an impartial outsider the attraction of Rover as a marque to a company like BMW from the perspective of 1994 was a little harder to see. Yes, Rover had made great strides and the Rover 600 was rightly viewed as one of the prettiest saloon cars on sale, but in crude terms it was in essence a more interesting Honda Accord in a pretty frock. In BMW's eyes, however, it seems that 'Rover' was viewed as the basis of a way to fight back against VW AG's Audi, but with an emphasis on understated luxury and comfort, keeping the BMW marque's role as the 'Ultimate Driving Machine'.

This was perhaps all very well, but it left a question mark over the role that MG should fill. Many of Rover Group's own product planners had hardly embraced MG with great enthusiasm from the word go; the battle to get the MGF on the programme is testament to that, so it is hardly surprising that Rover got the major focus. In hindsight, it seems that BMW made an error in failing to exert greater control over the Rover Group business from the outset, opting instead to give its new British subsidiary the independence and financial security it had long craved. In his book on BMW, David Kiley refers to a conversation between BMW's Bernd Pischetsrieder and Sir Nick Scheele, then running Jaguar for Ford. Pischetsrieder was expounding on the brand portfolio he had bought with Rover Group, but Kiley quotes Scheele: 'I told him that, honestly, outside of Land Rover and Mini and maybe MG, I wouldn't give him tuppence for the lot'.

There is no doubt that Rover Group had achieved miracles on a shoestring during the Honda-BAe years, but good businesses are seldom built on miracles alone. We have already seen that BMW had reservations about the MGF; there would be several studies aimed at rebodying it, and improving the component make-up and build quality, but none of these exercises received the focus they needed while the mainstream Rover portfolio was demanding the main attention. As early as 1994, even before the MGF was launched, various third parties were playing with ideas of what a new MG could look like. These, however, such as Marek Djordjević's sketches and models developed at California-based Designworks studios, were more thought-provoking exercises than hard-wired programmes.

When it came to the matter of powertrains, the picture was quite simple: Ian Pogson says that the K-series engine and PG1 box were viewed as 'legacy' units: 'along with all our powertrains they were scheduled for cessation and replacement by BMW units (NG, New Generation engines) or proprietary gearboxes from Getrag and ZF'. Pogson became involved in the BMW project to create a brand new engine facility at Hams Hall where these new units would be built: 'I set all the targets for the factory and recruited many of the key personnel to staff it in the biggest recruitment drive in Manufacturing Engineering for 10 years. That was a hoot; something new and what I called "People Engineering".' The Hams Hall factory project was announced to the press in November 1996.

In the midst of the review process, the UK designers began to explore options for the future with the greater scope that BMW patronage could offer, as Dave Saddington recalls:

DREAMS REALIZED: THE NEW MG*F*

I got a philosophical debate going about MG's post MG*F* future – including a choice between North South front engine Rear wheel drive, and doing another transverse mid-engine. We made a couple of 40 per cent clay models. I think Julian Quincey looked after the mid-engine and I did the front engined version.

As a consequence of this, Saddington remembers a trip to Munich: 'it became clear that we weren't to join in on the next platform (Z4) as collaborators – we could have the Z3 platform when it was superseded'. Even so, according to Saddington, this makes a certain kind of sense: 'BMW had the markets defined by having premium and mainstream vehicles in each sector – BMW/Rover; BMW/Land Rover; BMW/MG'.

As soon as it became obvious, however, that Mini was going to be given attention, BMW ramped up the attention from Munich: with the creation of the 'Mini/MG' engineering and design teams, it began to become a little clearer how BMW could envisage MG's position in the family. Insiders from the time began to talk of MG and Mini (or 'MINI' as BMW styled the name) sharing platforms or at least major components, suggesting something like an 'MG Midget' or, as the BMW Z3 replacement moved upmarket (the Z4 would be an exclusively 6-cylinder engine car) slotting into the family.

The period from 1996 onwards saw increasing tensions and upheaval at both Rover Group and BMW; John Towers announced his resignation in April 1996 (recorded on the BBC TV documentary mentioned above), then Wolfgang Reitzle held the post in 1996 and 1997. Reitzle's German successor, the Anglophile Walter Hasselkus, who came to Rover from BMW's motorcycle division, eventually fell on his sword in December 1998 as costs at Rover Group spiralled upwards even though a deal had been brokered with the unions. When both Pischetsrieder and Reitzle left BMW on the same day in February 1999 (Pischetsrieder's place was taken by Professor Joachim Milberg when German unions and, it is said, the key BMW shareholders, the Quandt family, refused to accept Reitzle as his successor), many wondered if things could get any worse.

Behind the scenes, though, some fascinating studies continued. Tony Hunter was involved in various exercises looking at possible evolutions of the MG*F*. There was even an exercise to create a new MG, which he dubbed the 'MG TH' ('designers and their egos, eh?' he jokes – *see* page 120) and was intended to be a front-engine alloy space frame chassis sports car 'to take MG back to its roots, being more masculine, muscular and raw, with looks inspired by the MG TC Midget'.

On the 'higher plane' of BMW AG, the approach with the British marques available as a result of the purchase of Rover Group was cautious, according to Chris Bangle, who was then BMW's design supremo but since 2009 has run his own design business:

> Despite many exciting proposals from design there wasn't too much activity to start a Riley or revamped Austin Healey product line. We felt they were more suited to boutique solutions, spun off the Z8 [a low-volume BMW sports car], for instance, plus I think that there was always this reluctance to over-invest in brand build-up given the uncertainties regarding the main family lines of Rover and Land Rover. But of course design always produced proposals, even to keep ourselves fresh and excited.

Meanwhile in 1997, in order to mark thirty years since the last factory Monte Carlo rally event by the BMC Mini Coopers, BMW decided to create a special one-off mid-engined concept car that was also intended

continued overleaf

BMW at one stage had serious designs on recreating the dormant Austin Healey marque – dependent, of course, upon the willing collaboration of the Healey family. Julian Quincey produced this achingly lovely evocation of the classic Austin Healey 100 of 1953. (Julian Quincey)

BMW and MG: Curious Bedfellows *continued*

The idea of a new 'Big Healey' was further explored through scale models. This one, built to the same proportions as BMW's 'Z07' concept car (later to evolve into the BMW Z8), was by Julian Quincey. A similar one was developed at Designworks by Anders Warming. (Julian Quincey)

This quarter scale model of an idea for an MG Midget based on BMW MINI components – dating from 1999 to 2000 – survives at Longbridge.

to give some clues to the ideas being developed for the all-new Mini planned for the coming decade. This car, the 'ACV30' (for 'Anniversary Concept Vehicle'), was based on the mechanical innards of an MG*F*, but even so it was clear that relevance to the MG family was minimal at best; Chris Bangle says that the ACV30 was the only MG*F*-based prototype that BMW (as opposed to Rover Group) ever created. BMW subsequently kept ACV30 and even brought it out in 2009 as part of the press launch of the new MINI Speedster concept, although perhaps unsurprisingly there was no mention in the press material of the Rover Group drivetrain.

At another stage, there was a session where sales and marketing people came to the UK from all over the world for a workshop entitled 'Beyond BMW with Great British Brands', at which 'brand identities' were mapped out for the future. Tony Hunter became involved:

> If I recall correctly – and there were some rather late nights and copious drinking was involved – the favoured direction ended up being to bring back Triumph and let MG slowly pass away. I think it was felt MG had a lot of baggage whereas Triumph still had a good name and any negative connotations were a long way in the past, and probably extinguished by links with the Triumph motorcycle brand. We looked at all aspects of pushing the brands forward, and even unique Brand Centres which built on the respective brand values.

In the end, Triumph could have been as much a rival for BMW as the 'sporty' brand; perhaps for that reason, among others, the idea never moved forward. 'Brand Centres' were seen at Land Rover and MINI, and some themed 'MG Garages' in Australia were an echo of this idea.

A key BMW insider from the time recently confirmed that MG was on the radar but the Rover issues continually overshadowed other projects:

> The plans had been to use the MINI platform to build an MG*F* successor. The idea was to use the concept that was later shown as the MINI speedster as the MG*F* successor and to use the 4-seater as the MINI convertible. Positioning was to be against the Miata. If that worked we wanted to expand by offering more models using BMW Group (Rover or BMW) platforms.

So in effect what is only now going on sale in 2010 as a two-seater MINI could possibly have seen the light of day, with some subtle remodelling, as an MG. Perhaps we might also have seen a larger rear-wheel drive MG sports car to go up against the Honda S2000?

All that is spilt milk now, of course: obviously a lot has happened between 2000 and 2010, and the MINI itself is now on its second generation. Even so, the same BMW insider says of Tony Hunter's concept, 'the similarities to the MINI Speedster are obvious'.

DREAMS REALIZED: THE NEW MGF

The first 'LE' version of the MGF started out in overseas markets as just the 'MGF Limited Edition' but was soon rebranded, for the UK at least, as the 'MGF Abingdon', a suggestion of Stephen Cox. (Rover Group)

contrast with the red bodywork in a manner that echoed the old BMC rallying colour schemes of the 1960s. Coupled with liberal use of chrome and a raised air intake for the supercharger, which looked rather like a silver hairdryer, the effect was certainly striking, although it has to be said that not all of the rival professionals who visited Rover Group's stand at the prestige auto show were as complimentary about the Super Sports as they had been concerning the original MGF at the same venue, just three years before.

Photos of the MGF Super Sports were taken in an outdoors setting at Donington Park with Peter Gregory's vintage MG K3 Magnette in the background. Considering his role, it was appropriate that David Woodhouse, who had made his debut in historic racing that same year at the Goodwood Revival, should be seen in the driving seat:

> It is me in the car wearing my own personal racing kit. You will see that I matched the kit exactly as the sketch ... I took the old white leather driving helmet and vintage kit along for Peter to wear that day, and later we also took proper driving footage of the car at Cobham ... again with me behind the wheel in the full racing kit.

From the spring of 1997, special optional leather trim could be specified, such as this distinctive green finish to the seats and steering wheel. Note the embossed MG badges in the head restraints. Four tailored, leather trim combinations were offered; Light Stone Beige, Red, Black and Green, all with contrasting piping. (Rover Group)

DREAMS REALIZED: THE NEW MGF

Recapturing the Record-Breaking Tradition: MGF at Bonneville

MG racing cars had arguably been at their zenith in the pre-war years, when Abingdon-built MG Midgets and Magnettes had performed well and occasionally dominated the race circuits and road racing events throughout much of Europe. After 1935, however, MG sports cars were seldom in the rarefied upper echelons of the racing theatre. This was just as well, perhaps, as they probably would not have retained their accessible everyman status and might have become the province of the rich playboy. However one rather unusual area of motorsport in which MG maintained an active interest was that of record breaking, an arena championed by British motor racing legends and record-breakers in their own right like 'Goldie' Gardner and George Eyston. These *Boy's Own* heroes had been behind the wheel of some exotic, but often home-brewed and expensively built record-breaking monsters, and yet the MG marque allowed them to chase record-breaking activities in a wide range of categories where they had a reasonable chance of success while the new boys – people like Sir Malcolm Campbell – could nudge the upper limits of ultimate land-speed record-breaking. MG put these record-breaking exploits to good use – as of course did their sponsors (Eyston, for example, was a director of Castrol Oil) and right through to the last such outing

Just to prove that the sketch was part of the inspiration behind the EXF, here is David Woodhouse crouched alongside the car at Bonneville. (David Woodhouse)

in 1959, special streamlined MG record-breakers chased new speed figures on the famous Utah salt flats.

Once or twice in the following decade there were tentative thoughts about returning to this publicity-generating but quite expensive activity, but the BMC of Sir George Harriman was a different animal to the old Nuffield Organisation. Even in the Leonard Lord years, MG's John Thornley found himself sailing close to the wind with some of the racing and record-breaking exploits that Abingdon undertook. The fact that the MGB was in essence the last Abingdon sports car and needed all the small team's attention to remain on sale meant that there was little time or corporate inclination to mess about with such supposedly peripheral activities as record breaking.

With the reinvention of MG through the all-new MGF, however, there came a renewed appetite for fresh attacks on the salt flats, not so much for out-and-out record breaking but because of the publicity that could be gained through that greatest record-breaking philosophy of doing it 'because it is there'. The first MG exploit in this vein was the 'EXF' record-breaker of 1997 (later renamed the MG EX253, latching on to the famous Abingdon MG EX Register numbering system). One option briefly considered was to shoehorn a Hart Grand Prix racing engine into an MGF shell, and aim to shatter Phil Hill's 1959 MG record, but this idea

David Woodhouse says that he always likes to weave in a little humour into his work, hence the small snapshot of famous British actor John Le Mesurier (perhaps best known as Sergeant Wilson in BBC TV's 'Dad's Army') looking up at the MG record-breaker. (David Woodhouse)

DREAMS REALIZED: THE NEW MGF

was swiftly discarded as being the wrong way to go – even though the basic idea still appealed.. Since Speedweek was essentially an event for amateurs, some thought that a heavy-hitting approach by Rover might backfire. 'To break the Stirling Moss and Phil Hill records, we would have been looking at a potential 300mph', project engineer Wynne Mitchell confirms. Not many engines in the Rover Group portfolio fit the bill for the 800–1000bhp needed. Eventually, Mitchell says,

> Common sense prevailed, and because of the short space of time, we decided that we would go with something which looked as much as possible like an MGF and using a K-Series engine. Once we had settled on that, we set ourselves a target of 200mph, the objective being to be able to show that we had created the fastest MGF.

Using Dave Woodhouse as design lead (it was Woodhouse who styled the MGF Super Sports) and Geoff Howell as aerodynamicist, eventually a body shape emerged that looked like the illegitimate offspring of an MGF and EX181. Rover persuaded Terry Kilbourne, a technician at a Land Rover dealer in California's Simi Valley, near Los Angeles, to drive the car since he had previous experience at Bonneville and so knew the ropes. Once at the salt lake, and having overcome various last-minute hurdles, Mitchell says that all the effort paid off: 'We did something like 215mph between the fourth and fifth mile mark, with a terminal velocity of 217.4mph'.

A year later, the team were ready with a new car named EX255 (EXF had been renamed EX253, while EX254 was the code name given to the MGF Super Sports). This time they had 'gone large', building a longer car with a very powerful engine based on the Rover V8. To drive the car, Rover Group had secured Andy Green, RAF pilot and World Land Speed Record holder, and there was bold talk of smashing the Phil Hill figure and even going for 300mph. Although the team reached Bonneville,

continued overleaf

RIGHT: *The EXF was beautifully constructed, as this photo showing the innards clearly demonstrates. Woodhouse explains that 'I chose battleship grey as a cool contrast to the Brooklands Green exterior'. (David Woodhouse)*

The EXF team fuss over their charge at Bonneville in the heat of the desert sun in August 1997. (David Woodhouse)

DREAMS REALIZED: THE NEW MGF

Recapturing the Record-Breaking Tradition: MGF at Bonneville *continued*

Californian Land Rover technician Terry Kilbourne, who happened to possess the necessary SCTA licence, drove the EXF (later known as EX253) to more than 349km/h (217mph) on 20 August 1997. (Rover Group)

ABOVE AND LEFT: Following on from EXF, plans were laid for an even bolder MG record-breaker that might have been expected to shatter the Phil Hill record still held by EX181. 'These are the two initial sketch pages I produced for the successor to EXF', Woodhouse explains, 'much less reminiscent of MGF, an extreme, pure streamliner, but with soft form, shapely. Note the tail ending in a point, with flaps, fins and full underbody ground effects, tiny minimized canopy, and Union Jack parachute! A bit like having Union Jack underpants!' (David Woodhouse)

DREAMS REALIZED: THE NEW MGF

The MG EX255 prototype saw extensive wind-tunnel testing at MIRA as part of the process of developing the aerodynamics. (Rover Group)

Although record-breaker Andy Green was ready and willing, sadly EX255 refused to cooperate and the idea of breaking new MG speed records had to remain a dream for another decade. (Rover Group)

sadly EX255 never ran there in anger. Despite upbeat words about a return the next year, the plans came to nought and EX255 ended up as a museum curio. The same fate did not befall EX253, however, for in 1999 it was brought out and suitable modifications were made so that it could be driven by a blind policeman, Ken Moss, on an attempt on the blind speed record in aid of the St Dunstan's charity. During the afternoon of Saturday 16 October 1999 Moss took the car up to 131mph, his run being filmed by BBC Television for its popular *Tomorrow's World* programme. In later years, EX253 languished until it was sold off to Jonathan Suckling and Daniel Nash, who took it back to Bonneville in 2007 and 2008 together with a record-breaking MG ZT-T (X15, *see* Chapter Five).

The second record-breaking adventure was with the dramatically altered EX255, which went to Bonneville in 1998. (Rover Group)

For a while, it appears there were thoughts of entertaining a return to the salt in later MG Rover days (note the MG TF side intakes and XPower Grey paint finish), but financial realism killed this off. (MG Rover Group)

DREAMS REALIZED: THE NEW MGF

ECHOES OF MG'S PAST: THE MGF ABINGDON

Although MG sports cars are now linked strongly with Longbridge, the connection was not always as firm. For long-time MG fans, the 'real' home of MG will always be Abingdon-on-Thames in Oxfordshire (even if MG cars have also hailed from nearby Cowley). For the first MGF 'limited edition' special, therefore, MG turned up the nostalgia dial and created the MGF Abingdon LE in the spring of 1998. A unique paint colour was specified ('Brooklands Green', a non-metallic deep green more like the British Racing Greens of old) and walnut beige leather interior trim was specified. In fact the idea of a 'Limited Edition' matching this specification had begun with an announcement at Frankfurt in September 1997, to mark two years since the MGF had entered production, but by the time the first cars were being built for most markets the following spring, the 'Abingdon' name, suggested by Steve Cox of MG Cars, had been approved.

Chrome-plated accessories were fitted in and outside the car: the first production MGF variant, for example, was seen with chrome door handles, polished stainless steel grilles and new six-spoke 16-inch alloy wheels, fitted with Goodyear F1 214/40 R16 tyres. For the first time too, a non-black hood colour was specified. At the 1998 MGF 'birthday party' hosted by MG Cars at the Heritage Motor Museum, Gerry McGovern turned up in his personal MGF Abingdon, and he told the author that he had lowered the suspension slightly on his own example to give the car, in his view, an even better stance.

ANNIVERSARY CELEBRATIONS: THE MGF 75TH ANNIVERSARY

For many years MG's various owners had held to the view that 1924 was effectively the start of the MG story. Even if some might argue, for example, that the octagon came earlier (1923 at least) or that 'real' MG cars as opposed to tarted-up Morrises did not come until later, the

1999 marked seventy-five years since the first 'true' MG sports cars turned a wheel, and so MG Cars, as part of Rover Group, decided to do another Limited Edition special version of the MGF. (Rover Group)

110

DREAMS REALIZED: THE NEW MGF

Although UK market MGF 75 LE models only came in Black or Mulberry, overseas markets also saw Silver being offered. All variants, however, had the same Grenadine leather interior trim. (Rover Group)

date of 1924 was arguably as convenient as any to form the basis of an anniversary.

In March 1999, therefore, Rover Group announced their second official Limited Edition of the MGF, restricted to just 2,000 examples – although, as had been the case with the 'Abingdon', both 1.8i and 1.8i VVC versions were offered. The car was premiered at the Geneva Motor Show. For the home market, limited to 500 cars, it came in a choice of Mulberry Red or Black. Contrasting hood colours were black with the red car or Grenadine Red with the black. The 16-inch eight-spoke 'Minilite' style wheels were fitted with 215 × 55 Goodyear Eagle F1 tyres. For other export markets, the MGF 75 LE was also offered in silver with Grenadine trim.

The interior on all MGF 75 LE variants was trimmed in Grenadine Red leather, while a wood interior trim package was applied to the centre console and air vent surrounds along with a chrome ashtray. The chrome theme was also extended outside the car to the door handles, grille and bodyside air intakes. To mark the 'exclusivity' of the model, there were special badges inside and out, with a numbered identification plate mounted on the rear panel between the seats.

Just as the MGF 75 LE went on sale, another low-number limited edition was introduced exclusively for the Australian market, in the form of the MGF Targa Trophy, available in Solar Red, British Racing Green and Tahiti Blue. MG Cars Australia had been allocated just 100 examples of the MGF 75 LE, to which they added fifty MGF Targa Trophy models, announced on 5 February 1999 and marketed to coincide with the annual 2,500km Targa Tasmania race scheduled for April. MG Cars Australia would later go on to market other special variants, even listing an 'MGF Coupé' as a third model line (in fact it was simply an MGF offered with the hardtop included in the price).

THE 2000 MODEL YEAR

Gerry McGovern, the MGF designer, explained at the 1998 Geneva Motor Show that he and his

Sitting at the famous Goodwood race circuit for the press launch in July 1999, this is a 2000 Model Year MG*F*. Some of the changes in the facelift can be seen: new wheels, body-coloured windscreen pillars (instead of black), clear smoked indicator lenses and new paint and trim options. (Rover Group)

Out on the road, a silver 2000 Model Year MG*F*. (Rover Group)

DREAMS REALIZED: THE NEW MGF

The interior of the 2000 Model Year MGF was basically the same as the original car, but both the quality and the trim options had been improved. For the Swiss market, Rover Group offered the limited edition 'MGF Silverstone', 100 examples of which were offered in a choice of Platinum Silver, Anthracite or British Racing Green, but were otherwise more or less identical to other 2000 Model Year cars. (Rover Group)

Arguably the most significant innovation for 2000 was the new Steptronic CVT gearbox option, which married a 120PS engine with a new clutchless transmission, with a choice of traditional centre 'gear selector' or push buttons on the steering wheel. (Rover Group)

The steering wheel buttons on the MGF Steptronic were not the same as F1-car style 'flappy paddles' but they could be fun. Take-up of the Steptronic (later to be rebranded as 'Stepspeed' post-BMW) was never especially high. (Rover Group)

A Solar Red 2000 Model Year MG*F* at speed; note the body-colour windscreen pillars and 'clear smoked' indicator lenses. (Rover Group)

Two classic MG sports cars flank the second road-going version of the MG*F* Super Sports at Goodwood in the summer of 1999.

DREAMS REALIZED: THE NEW MGF

The same wider stance seen on the earlier 'weekend racer' concept was also seen on the roadgoing Super Sports. (Rover Group)

The second iteration of the MGF Super Sports; this time the official photo shoot was at Brooklands on the old banking, and in attendance were Julian Quincey (seen here behind the wheel) and David Saddington, but there was no sign this time of a white helmet and gloves. (Rover Group)

Unusually, Rover Group repainted and retrimmed the second MGF Super Sports and showed it again at the September 1999 Frankfurt Motor Show. It is seen here at a photo-shoot organized for the author's benefit two months later at Gaydon: the author is pretending to drive a car with no engine management system fitted at the time. (Michael Whitestone)

DREAMS REALIZED: THE NEW MGF

To accompany the respray in 'Chromaflair' Green, the Recaro seats and other interior trim were recovered to match. (Michael Whitestone)

team were already working on what he called the '1999½' model year facelift. Very little of the Super Sports would translate into a road-going car, but the exercise had clearly been part of the process of refining the MGF line for the next decade.

What actually transpired was a modest facelift, covering such things as interior trim improvements, a more adjustable steering column, new trim (plus two new paint colours), some new alloy wheel choices, electrically adjustable door mirrors, smoked lenses on the indicators (and repeaters) and body colour paint for the windscreen pillars (in lieu of the previous black) – all of which were welcome fillips but hardly earth-shattering. In engineering terms, the most significant arrival was the optional 'Steptronic' transmission, which allowed drivers more used to automatic transmissions the chance to drive an MGF with the added novelty of gear-shift buttons mounted on the steering wheel. Other less obvious but worthwhile changes included a double-skinned petrol tank and an improved electronic power-steering specification.

For anyone expecting more radical changes, especially given the promise of the Super Sports concept, the 2000 Model Year MGF was arguably a bit of disappointment; this is not to say it was a bad car, but just a little underwhelming to those who had been tantalized by the radical concept of the previous year. However some excitement came from the appearance, first at Geneva in 1999 and later at Frankfurt, of a road-going version of the Super Sports, still showing broadly the same exterior features below the scuttle, but with a conventional windscreen and interior. This time round, the creation of the show car had been led by Julian Quincey, one of the team of designers who had been intimately involved with the sketching process for the 1995 MGF, although, as Quincey explained to the author, there was less scope to influence the outcome as Mayflower had already produced the body panels.

In the engine bay, the Super Sports also showed performance potential, for as 'Mini & MG' Engineering Director Chris Lee told the author at Geneva that year,

> We've driven it in anger ourselves, and it uses the 1.8 litre K-Series 'base' engine supercharged to give a stated 200 PS – although in reality we got a bit more than that.

DREAMS REALIZED: THE NEW MG*F*

This sketch by David Woodhouse dates from 1997 and shows that he was thinking in terms of a roadgoing MG*F* 'Speedster' even before the MG*F* Super Sports was built: 'A wide body, housing bigger boots, and chopped speedster windscreen all contributing to a really powerful statement that could have transformed MG*F* from timid hairdresser's runabout to purposeful potent sports muscle car!' (David Woodhouse)

The gearbox is basically the PG-1 unit out of the standard car, but suitably upgraded to cope with the higher output.

It all sounded very promising.

The 1999 Geneva show saw this car finished in black with a red interior, and in fact it was on display in this guise during the MG*F* 2000 Model Year press launch at Goodwood a few months later, in July 1999; for the September Frankfurt show, however, the road-going Super Sports was refinished in Chromaflair Green and re-trimmed with a matching green leather interior. No one at Rover Group would be drawn to give much detail as to what future, if any, the Super Sports had in production terms, and the author became hardly any wiser at a photo-session he organized with the car at Gaydon in November 1999. According to Julian Quincey,

> I think that there was every intention of producing the Super Sports when it was being developed, but I know there were issues that came up that made it difficult due to the fact the parts developed for the standard MG*F* could not take excessive loads – not least the wheel bearings with the increased track. I don't think that BMW took the MG*F* seriously, especially when they had engineered their Z3 without the restrictions that the MG*F* team had.

Of course, what none of us knew at that time was that BMW, which had also just facelifted its Z3 sports car, was already looking to a future without Rover Group.

chapter five

Another New Start

ALCHEMY, PHOENIX AND MG ROVER GROUP

The first really public sign of a fractured relationship between Rover Group and its German parent came at the launch of the Rover 75, the company's first all-new product in four years of BMW ownership and which was undoubtedly intended as a vanguard of great things to come. The press material for the new car made no mention of the rear-wheel drive BMW 3-Series – as though the similarly sized executive saloon did not exist – but highlighted the admittedly front-wheel drive Audi A4 as a rival.

Also unveiled at the October 1998 British Motor Show was Jaguar's new S-Type. Although no one outside a very small circle in Rover Group knew at the time, BMW Chairman Bernd Pischetsrieder had brought forward the Rover's launch, which had originally been set for the March 1999 Geneva show, to steal some of Jaguar's limelight. Nevertheless, the launch of the Rover 75 went exceptionally well, with Nick Stephenson walking around the cars on stage and proudly showing off their features. Having seen this promising debut, many of us wandered off to the far side of the show to attend the traditional BMW press conference – where our jaws collectively dropped at what the chairman had to say.

It was fairly well known that BMW was unhappy that the recently elected British Government of Tony Blair had not embraced the euro, and was sticking resolutely to the independent pound sterling. This meant that it was often difficult to control trading costs across the two currency sectors. Since many investors liked the status of sterling – as the euro wobbled – it meant that building cars in Britain was seen by the Germans as expensive. Added to this was the fact that apparently the British public did not love Rover sufficiently, at least to the extent of buying its products in high enough numbers, and so the BMW Chairman listed a catalogue of problems, hinting darkly at the possibility of BMW rethinking its investment plans. This was hardly the message one normally expected to hear at a new car launch.

Later, from the convenient perspective of a new job (he resigned on 5 February 1999), Pischetsrieder would admit that he had deliberately used shock tactics as BMW was at a critical stage of negotiations with the British unions over productivity, as he told the *Financial Times* in December 2000, 'there was no chance to get the unions to do that without a crisis, so we manufactured a crisis'. This certainly reflects what the Rover and even the BMW public relations people who were there subsequently told the author: Pischetsrieder deliberately veered away from the prepared script in order to drop a bombshell that none of them knew was coming.

Meanwhile, in the autumn of 1999, unbeknown to all but a tiny number of people, a British venture capital company, Alchemy Partners, had made tentative approaches to BMW with the bold idea of buying out the Rover Group

ANOTHER NEW START

Tony Hunter occasionally got to look at facelift ideas for the MG*F*; this is a proposal of his from March 2000. (Tony Hunter)

operation by the clever process of encouraging BMW to sell off Land Rover and offloading the rest to Alchemy. It was a bold and audacious plan, but one that for obvious reasons was initially conducted in the greatest secrecy, to the extent that many BMW senior officers had no inkling of the discussions.

At the January 2000 Detroit Motor Show, the BMW Senior Executive responsible for worldwide sales, Dr Henrich Heitmann, suggested that his company had no current plans to bring MG back to the USA. In February, a year on from the sudden departure of Pischetsrieder and Reitzle, the German magazine *Der Spiegel* compounded the alarm among MG and Rover watchers when it reported that BMW was looking at ways to abandon its British subsidiary. 'This is not going to happen. Closing Longbridge is out of the question', a BMW spokesman tersely retorted to press enquiries from the Reuters news agency. Following Heitmann's speech at Detroit, the author contacted him to seek some assurance that MG actually still had a purpose and a future in the BMW hierarchy.

In a reply from BMW's Head of Research & Development Wolfgang Ziebart on 13 February, it was suggested that the main obstacle to US sales was really the K-Series engine, in particular its non-compliance with contemporary US emissions legislation:

> To make it comply would mean a whole redesign of the current K-Series engine ... this does not mean, however, that in the next generation, where new engines will be introduced, the return to the US market could [not] be considered again.

On 3 March 2000 I also had a response from Wolfgang Vollath, 'brand manager for Mini/MG', who added that:

ANOTHER NEW START

The Last Days with BMW...

Towards the end of BMW's ownership of Rover Group, there was some activity on concept work for possible future MG sports cars – if and when priorities, time and budgets permitted. Tony Hunter was a key member of the small 'Mini & MG' design team led by David Saddington: this is one of Hunter's sketches. (Tony Hunter)

Tony Hunter labelled this sketch the 'MG TH'. (Tony Hunter)

We have seen how the news that BMW had decided to finally divest itself of Rover Group, apart from Mini, came as a shock throughout the entire organization. The team at Mini & MG were no exception to this bolt from the blue, according to Tony Hunter, who had worked at Rover Group on the original MG*F*, gone away in 1992 to work for Renault in France and then come back during the BMW ownership of Rover Group:

> We were a very small team in Mini & MG. I had been responsible for the interior design of Mini and also did all the accessories and merchandise, while Frank Stephenson was responsible for the exterior and David Saddington was overall chief designer for the Mini and MG brands. Very little was being done on MG at the time though; I'd had a play with some concept ideas but there was no real push – so when Gerry McGovern left to take over Lincoln design, David took on the role that Gerry had vacated as Chief for Land Rover 'temporarily', whilst still retaining MG and Mini responsibilities.

This all changed almost immediately when the news came that BMW was planning to sell the business.

'The plan we were told initially was that personnel would be split according to the brand they were assigned to, Rover guys to Rover, Land Rover guys to go with Land Rover and so forth.' Clearly people with feet in both camps had more choice, and so David Saddington went with Land Rover. 'This left Frank and me as the only people at Mini MG – and since Frank was BMW, by default I ended up (luckily for me, I thought) looking after the MG brand.'

This was still, however, a rather unsettled period. 'It was a pretty unhappy and messy time whilst we

The Tony Hunter 'MG TH' concept got as far as a two-fifths (0.4) scale model. Inspiration came from the classic MG TC of 1947 and the idea was to use the new MINI mechanical components but in a Lotus Elise-style chassis. (Tony Hunter)

ANOTHER NEW START

This is a proposal for a radical redesign of the MGF by Tony Hunter dating from the beginning of 2000, drawing upon his earlier all-new MG sports car concept. (Tony Hunter)

A race-car inspired MG sports car cockpit concept, from the closing days of the BMW era, again by Tony Hunter. (Tony Hunter)

Note the use of classic MG news clippings from the 1930s in this concept sketch for a new MGF by Tony Hunter. (Tony Hunter)

all waited to find out what would actually happen to the company', Hunter says, but suggests that it did at least, as he puts it,

> kick MG back into action as we started looking at facelifts and possible future products; I remember having a meeting with the guys from Alchemy and they did seem to be very enthusiastic about turning the company into a sports car producer again, and their plan for lower volume but more premium certainly made a lot of sense. Of course, by making their proposal to BMW all they did was open a can of worms, and of course it didn't work out in their favour.

At this stage, Hunter revisited his MG TH proposal:

> I wheeled out my grey MG concept and we started looking at developing that design direction and the facelift of the MGF to look that way. Exciting for me for the time that it lasted.

When the split happened, Hunter says, for most people the direction they would take was pretty clear cut, but for him things then got quite confused:

> BMW didn't seem interested in retaining any of the design team that had been on Mini, save Frank of course, as the car was only a few months from production and they basically had what they wanted ... so I was left as the only design person on the MG brand and when things settled down, that would have meant me going off to Longbridge with Phoenix. Since I was in a fairly unique position in the design team, I was given a choice where I could go. I seriously considered staying with MG as it might have let me achieve the goal of properly being chief designer there, but I was advised by a number of people not to take this route, and to stay with Land Rover. So when the companies parted, I stayed with Land Rover and my MG time was finished.

although currently there are no concrete plans to have the MG brand return to the US in the near future, this does not mean that there are no projects analyzing the possibility of an MG return.

This was perhaps as reassuring a message as I was likely to get at that stage. Vollath went on to stress that:

at Mini/MG brand management, as well as in many other places within the BMW Group, there are enthusiasts who are working on keeping the Mini and MG dreams alive. You can rest assured that the British sports car heritage and tradition is well taken care of within BMW Group.

Within days of that last message from Vollath, Rover Group showed a concept for a more sporting version of the Rover 75 at the Geneva show, an idea that seemed almost heretical when BMW had decreed there should be no crossover between the BMW and Rover sales pitches. It was later learnt that this car, with lowered, sportier suspension and a jazzier trim palette, was the basis of what some inside Rover Group would secretly have liked to have become a new 'MG Magnette'.

The staff at Rover Group, in particular those in the West Midlands, were told that Longbridge had a great future ahead of it, even if much of the investment remained 'in the future'. Ian Pogson recalls the briefing sessions:

We were shown a model of how Longbridge would look under BMW management for the new R50 MINI production. Buses were commissioned to pick up employees from Gaydon, Warwick, Solihull and so on. Just weeks later the order was given to return to Munich. Trucks were assembled at Longbridge to remove the store which had just been built at the end of CAB 1 and take it away!

BMW had often proclaimed that they pumped £3 billion of investment into Rover, but Ian Pogson poses the question that some asked:

I could walk you around the site and ask you to show me 'Where is it?' A large part of the investment was £0.5 billion in Hams Hall and whatever into Cowley and Swindon, for BMW's own ends on MINI. A lot of the rest was monies to support the BMW employees and families whilst living here, many of whom we liked and respected and were sad to see go.

Before long, however, this would all be academic, for the story suddenly broke that BMW was planning to do a deal with Alchemy (with MG sweetening the deal), selling Land Rover to Ford and holding on to Mini. Suddenly all the fine words about MG in BMW's tender care seemed meaningless, although there is no reason to doubt the sincerity of the two Wolfgangs; indeed, one of them later confessed to the author that losing control of MG had been his single greatest regret over the debacle. Henrich Heitmann and Wolfgang Ziebart were among the immediate casualties in senior BMW management; both left as the Rover deal was announced on 16 April 2000.

Speaking in 2010, by which time he was the CEO of an exciting new German sports car maker, Artega, Dr Ziebart confirmed that, while there had been positive noises about MG under BMW, this concealed a lack of serious action:

Not very much happened during that time regarding MG. The MG*F* was on the market not for too long and so no urgent need for action was seen. In general, within the wide portfolio of different brands bought by BMW through the Rover acquisition, MG was considered as a brand to cover the lower segments of the sports cars, especially roadsters. So the MG*F* for instance should have a similar image like the Z3, but in a lower segment. However, not very much happened in executing that strategy.

In that context, therefore, it was clear that,

whether they liked the idea or not, the sale of MG to a third party might not really upset BMW plans too greatly.

For a while, it seemed likely that the deal with Alchemy would go through, and Managing Partner Jon Moulton enthused about grand plans to develop new low-volume MG sports cars with Lotus, return to the North American market and stage a return to the Le Mans 24-hour race. In the company's business plan of 18 April 2000, it was recorded that 'The MG Car Co has approached Lotus Engineering, a division of Lotus Cars, with a view to develop a new MG sports car, which will be finished by end 2002, using aluminium/composite technology and at the leading edge of technology'. Volume Rover production would be run down over time, and the focus would very much be on MG sports cars. For many MG fans at the time, it was music to our ears, even if there were some very worried people in the West Midlands concerned at potential job losses.

Within days of the announcement, however, news broke of a rival bid, overseen by former Rover Group Chairman John Towers and soon working under the umbrella title of the Phoenix Consortium, ironically embracing a name previously associated, as we have seen, with the creation of the MGF. For a time the new bid, lacking finance, appeared doomed to failure, but the proposals, which included the retention of volume production and widening the stretch of the MG brand, won Towers and his colleagues many more friends in Birmingham than Moulton, who was being demonized in some quarters as the great destroyer of Longbridge.

There then followed a political and financial battle of wills, which eventually led to BMW breaking off its exclusive negotiations with Alchemy and becoming more receptive to the overtures from Phoenix. Through persistence and by building up their bid using an intimate knowledge of the business, which to some degree had to compensate for the lack of time to do proper due diligence, eventually the Phoenix Consortium managed to persuade BMW of the sound basis of their bid and were allowed access to the financial information they needed.

Within a matter of days BMW broke off negotiations with Alchemy, and instead agreed a deal with John Towers and his colleagues that, in return for a symbolic ten pound note, brought them ownership of the Longbridge factory, some other property, a number of brand names (most importantly MG and Rover, but also Austin, Morris and Wolseley among others) and, last but not least, a so-called dowry from BMW that would suffice to keep the business afloat while it sought new external partners. For the time being, BMW held on to the powertrain business that produced many of the engines and gearboxes that MG and Rover relied upon, but eventually (May 2001) that operation was sold to Phoenix on similarly generous terms.

FROM ROVER GROUP TO MG ROVER GROUP

With the reversion from BMW ownership to independent British ownership, the future of Rover Group looked both exciting and daunting; under the wealthy rule of BMW there had often been a thought that, if all else failed, Munich's money could be thrown at problems – but the Bavarians' patience had finally snapped, and Rover Group had been cast adrift, albeit with a significant sum of money to keep the business afloat for some time. In fairness, too, the BMW management had scored a number of own goals too, as Ian Pogson points out: 'Remember they ceased the volume-selling Metro with no replacement, ceased 600 (good car) and 800 (not so good, but better in R17/18 guise) and only kicked off one new car, the Rover 75'.

Several key things had become apparent during the divorce proceedings – not least the value of the MG name, which had been one of the key issues that shaped some aspects of negotiations. We shall see later how the sports car badge would also become one of

ANOTHER NEW START

From left to right in this photo are Nick Stephenson, John Towers, Peter Stevens, Rob Oldaker and Chris Lee. (MG Rover Group)

the last things that the new owners would let go; but that part of the story lies five years in the future.

Better use of the MG name had been core to the respective strategies of both the Alchemy and the Phoenix camps. Where the two had differed was that Alchemy had been prepared to let Rover eventually go the way of all flesh, whereas Phoenix saw a healthy future for both their core marques. John Towers and his team set about planning how to lift the MG presence, in part by developing MG cars closely based on Rover models.

Just a few years earlier, the concept of badge engineering had become discredited, and indeed as recently as his January 2000 speech at Detroit, BMW's Henrich Heitmann had made it clear that BMW did not and would not adopt a policy of mere badge differentiation for any of their models using different brands. Now that BMW control and even Dr Heitmann's influence within BMW had passed, however, the new British owners were able to think differently if they so desired.

To avoid any charges of heresy, however, the new team would need to ensure that any new Rover-based MG cars, developed as they would have to be without the benefit of a bottomless bank account, were credible and desirable. To do this, they also needed to secure the help of the right top people, and in the summer of 2000 they recruited a new chief designer, Peter Stevens, and persuaded former Rover engineer Rob Oldaker to return after four years at Rolls-Royce/Bentley as director of product development.

In the autumn came a change of name as well, as Rover Group became MG Rover Group, with the two marque badges given equal prominence and reinforcing the message that MG would be in for a considerable share of the fresh investment.

MGF WEDGWOOD

Despite the whirlwind of change that swept in with the departure of BMW, the regular

One of the first bits of product action with the MG*F* was another limited edition, the MG*F* SE finished in Wedgwood, a distinctive metallic light silver-blue. (MG Rover Group)

clockwork-like appearance of an MG*F* limited edition was not allowed to be deferred for too long. July 2000 therefore saw the unveiling of the MG*F* Wedgwood Limited Edition, offering a bundle of standard equipment upgrades to the in-car entertainment and trim, along with a unique paint colour, a light metallic silver-blue called 'Wedgwood'. On the rear deck, the limited edition came with a neat spoiler, the first from the manufacturer and hinting at a similar one that would subsequently form part of the package making up the next limited edition in the following New Year.

MG*F* TROPHY AND MG*F* 1.6

For those who were looking forward to the outcome of Nick Stephenson's promise to deliver harder-edged MG sports cars, the wait arguably came to an end on 3 January 2001, when MG Rover Group announced a two-pronged extension to the MG*F* family. At the bottom of the range, a new 'lower spec' variant had been added in the form of the MG*F* 1.6i, which was basically a 'de-contented' MG*F* 1.8i fitted with the sweet shorter-stroke K-Series (the 1.6 engine had bore and stroke of 80mm and 79mm respectively, versus the 80/89.3mm of the 1.8i). However the real news was at the top of the range, where a new 158bhp (160PS) version of the MG*F* VVC had been introduced in the form of the MG*F* Trophy 160SE.

As well as an engine output that had been hoisted to 160PS, the MG*F* Trophy boasted a phalanx of changes intended to differentiate the car both visually and dynamically. Starting with the looks, the most distinctive features were arguably the bold new colours of Trophy Yellow and Trophy Blue, married to distinctive 16-inch alloy wheels (through the front ones of which, distinctive bright red 'MG/AP Racing' brake callipers could be seen), new front and rear spoilers, black finish to the headlamps and body-coloured trim panels inside the cockpit.

As well as the in-house studios, both Rover Group and later MG Rover Group also looked to outside companies for inspiration. This is a concept board for a whole MG range, proposed by Richard Hamblin's OMNI Design Consultancy, with everything from a facelifted MG*F* at the left, an MG sports tourer at the rear and, in the foreground, a V6-engined MG coupe intended to sit above the MG*F*. (OMNI Design)

LEFT: Inside the cockpit, the MG*F* Trophy had body-coloured trim sections and on the rear deck was a spoiler honed in the wind tunnel. (MG Rover Group)

BELOW: Even before BMW parted company with Rover Group, a number of senior managers in the British company wanted to see 'harder-edged' MG sports cars. Their dream was realized in 2001 with the MG*F* Trophy LE, with stiffer, lower suspension, vivid new colour schemes and a number of motor sports-inspired changes that BMW, in all probability, have never sanctioned on a road car. (MG Rover Group)

ANOTHER NEW START

A rare photo of quite a rare car – the 'bargain basement' MGF 1.6i with black painted side air intake (which actually cost MG Rover more money!). However, at least – unlike the cheapest Mazda MX-5 – the MGF 1.6i still came with alloy wheels as standard.

Throughout most of the MG*F* and MG *TF* story, motor sports in various guises (the Mayflower Cup and Trophy Series) have remained essential parts of the MG sports car ethos and pedigree. (MG Rover Group)

Whereas others have suggested that the boot spoiler on the MG*F* Trophy was the same as that on the previous year's LE model, Graham Fairhead, the company's Project Director, Sports Cars Product Development, explained in an interview with the author at the time that the Trophy spoiler was in fact different, with a shape arrived at through wind-tunnel work at MIRA:

> We've been very fortunate to have had Peter Stevens's involvement in this project, as he is very sensitive to aerodynamic effects, and in combination with the chin spoiler at the front, the Trophy has clearly benefited considerably in aerodynamic terms.

The suspension had been subjected to a raft of improvements too, with the overall ride height lowered by 20mm and uprated Hydragas units fitted, giving a much firmer but more sporting ride/handling balance. Anti-lock brakes were not offered, a surprising omission in some people's eyes, but perhaps a reflection in part of the approximation of a track-specification for the Trophy.

Some journalists were invited to a track session at the Knockhill race circuit near Dunfermline, where the Trophy's talents were perhaps best appreciated. Even so, Greg Allport of MG Rover Group External Affairs recalls that the ride of the Trophy was rather harsh, even allowing for the circumstances.

A further minor change around this time was the name of the CVT transmission: it was the same ZF unit but, as BMW retained the rights to use the 'Steptronic' name, the MG Rover Group settled on 'Stepspeed' as the new word to identify the optional unit.

In early March 2001 the sight of an MG*F* surprised visitors to the stand of Chapman-Arup Consultants at the SAE Show in the Cobo Center in Detroit, Michigan. MG Rover Group said that this was 'an opportunity to update the company's knowledge of current US perceptions and awareness of the MG brand', acknowledging that MG had not been marketed in North America for twenty years. A Platinum Silver 2001 model year MG*F* was displayed on Chapman-Arup's stand and visitors were invited to fill in market research questionnaires.

According to Chapman-Arup's Barrie Wills, staff on his stand were asking 'what the brand name MG brings to mind when

ANOTHER NEW START

Chapman-Arup took an MG*F* to the SAE Show in the Cobo Center in Detroit, Michigan, USA, in March 2001 and gauged reaction. In hindsight it was a slightly odd place to undertake market research, but it got some publicity and feedback. (Barrie Wills)

they hear it, what price they believe the MGF should sell for, what current products on the American market they consider would compete with it and other key questions about the car's attributes'. However, as we have already seen, the MG*F* itself was never engineered with US sales in mind, and as MG Rover Group rather pointedly explained in their own press statement, 'the MG Rover Group five-year business plan assumes no planned sales in the US market'. Rob Oldaker says that the costs of around £8 million at the time could not be justified: 'we tried a number of times to get [MG*F*] in the programme, but we couldn't get the numbers to stack up'. However the way that MG Rover Group was beginning to review this approach for the medium term would become apparent within the following few months, since unknown to outsiders, the company had been out on a buying spree.

MG XPOWER

Both Alchemy and Phoenix had proclaimed that a return to Le Mans would form part of their game plans for rebuilding MG's sporting credentials; following the success of the Phoenix Consortium's bid and the creation of MG Rover Group, work began behind the scenes on creating a suitable vehicle for this return to the Circuit de la Sarthe, and the first outward sign came with the release of a sketch by Peter Stevens on 12 December 2000.

Just over four months later, on 26 April 2001 (and by complete coincidence, the very same day that BMW Mini production began at Cowley), MG Rover Group's director of product development Rob Oldaker stood on the stage in front of a packed conference theatre at Longbridge and announced the creation of a special subsidiary of Phoenix Venture Holdings (parent of MG Rover Group) called MG Sport &

ANOTHER NEW START

The first indication of plans for even more exciting MG sports cars came with this artist's impression of what was called the 'MG*F* Extreme' in 2001. (MG Rover Group)

Racing Limited, together with an associated sub-brand known as MG XPower.

Oldaker, who assumed responsibility as managing director of this new subsidiary alongside his existing duties, explained that the idea was to support various motor sport programmes, including engineering work on the vehicles themselves, and to assist with the associated performance parts and merchandizing operations. It soon became apparent that MG Sport & Racing would also be responsible for the creation of some of the more extreme road-going creations to wear the MG badge.

Oldaker explained that the function of the MG XPower sub-brand was

> to bind together and symbolize all MG Sport & Racing's activities. The letter 'X' stems from historic MG associations, such as the 'EX' engineering project numbers and the 'XP' engine number prefix. We already use 'X'

This concept sketch shows effectively the 'MG*F* Extreme' concept, but in fact is taken from the major facelift programme for the 2002 MGF, which eventually became the MG *TF*. (David Arbuckle)

ANOTHER NEW START

Part of MG Rover Group's ambitious plans to rebuild the MG brand was a return to the Le Mans 24-hour race with this MG Lola EX257. Although we didn't know it at the time, the tiny grille at the front, with its horizontal centre vane, was a hint of a new design face in the pipeline for future MG road cars. (MG Rover Group)

codes for today's MG prototype model codes, and our new motorsports cars have 'EX' code-numbers.

Oldaker said that the thinking was

> to sum up the brand essence of MG in the phrase 'outrageous fun for all'; to our way of thinking, outrageous fun is a serious business, so we have set up a serious business to generate that fun.

The motor sports programme took in a return to Le Mans (using a specially developed derivative of a Lola race car and an AER-developed engine) as well as campaigns involving the ZR and ZS saloons and hatchbacks. However the first sign of developments in the more mainstream MG sports car area was the unveiling on 10 May 2001 of an artist's impression of a proposed 'super MGF' – perhaps the spiritual successor of the aborted MGF Super Sports (*see* Chapter Four) – in the form of what was called the MGF Extreme.

MG Rover Group explained that the idea was an extension of its philosophy of three 'core' model specifications for each of the MG cars then on sale (MGF, MG ZR, MG ZS and MG ZT), comprising, in their words, 'Entry, Core and Ultimate' models. The idea of an 'Extreme' variant was to push the boundary between the road cars and the competition variants, as the company proclaimed, 'The MG Extremes are one-off vehicles, which are being specially built for demonstration and promotional purposes and they are truly outrageous'.

The MGF Extreme was said at the time to be powered by a '450 horsepower MG XP20 XPower Le Mans engine', based on the unit in the EX257 Le Mans cars. Under the

ANOTHER NEW START

The MG*F* XPower 500 was designed to run the same AER 500hp 4-cylinder two-litre engine as the EX257 race car out on the Le Mans circuit (although the only example built had a Ford Cosworth engine). This was the first sight of what would become the future MG *TF* headlamps. (MG Rover Group)

specially formed bodywork, we were told rather euphemistically that 'suspension components have been modified to embrace this triple expanse in power output from the standard car'. What we did not know until later was that these changes presaged the abandonment of Hydragas. Alongside the MG*F* Extreme, the MG ZT Extreme was spoken about with 500hp expected from its Ford-derived V8 engine.

The first time that the MG*F* Extreme appeared in the solid was at the Le Mans 24-hour race, where MG Sport & Racing displayed it inside a marquee where the company did good business selling MG XPower regalia. The name had changed: it was no longer the MG*F* Extreme but, in line with the XPower branding, the one-off prototype (formally announced on 15 June 2001, the eve of the Le Mans race) was now to be known as the MG*F* XPower 500, the '500' intended to represent the 500PS output now claimed for the engine. The transmission was said to be a six-speed sequential X-Trac competition gearbox, while the front and rear track had been increased by 100mm and 150mm respectively. Tyres were 225/35 R17 at the front and 265/35 R17 at the rear.

Of greater significance, and something that would not become apparent until later, was the restyling at the front of the MG*F* XPower 500, which previewed the new headlamp units that would be seen in September on the X80 and the following January in the MG *TF*. Interestingly enough, the simple 'twin nostril' nose of the XPower 500 also has even stronger echoes in the MG *TF* LE500 of 2008 and *TF* 135 of 2009.

What was not apparent in the summer of 2001 was that the MG*F* XPower 500 (later 'rebranded' as the *TF* XPower) had been built by David Paveley of DPRS. Although we were all told the new AER-Lola Le Mans racing engine had been fitted in place of the normal K-Series, thereby linking the project to the MG-Lola single-seaters, according to Peter Stevens (and later confirmed by the author), the engine actually fitted was a Ford Cosworth unit, which doubtless explains why nobody from MG Rover Group was ever prepared to lift the engine compartment lid and show the contents to the press.

On 24 October 2001 another 'limited edition' appeared in the form of the MG*F* Freestyle SE, available in 1.8i, 1.8i Stepspeed and 1.8i VVC versions, which added new front and rear spoilers (similar to those of the Trophy SE), new 16-inch wheels and special 'Freestyle' badges. Colour options for the MG*F* Freestyle SE were Solar Red, Tahiti Blue, Platinum Silver, British Racing Green and Anthracite. At the end of that month, an optional body-

ANOTHER NEW START

Project X80: The MG Supercar

On 19 June 2001 MG Rover Group surprised the automotive world by announcing a new project for an MG sports car based closely on the chassis and running gear of the Qvale Mangusta. Qvale Automotive Group, based in San Francisco, had been building a specially designed Ford Mustang engine sports car at a dedicated factory in Modena, in the heart of Italian sports car country, but had been finding the business hard. The project had begun as a joint venture whereby the American company, whose business had once relied strongly on importing MG and other British sports cars to the USA, effectively bankrolled the creation of a new De Tomaso with the eponymous Argentinian-born sports car maker.

When the Qvale and De Tomaso families fell out over the degree of influence Alejandro De Tomaso could wield over the project, Kjell Qvale decided that his name was sufficient on its own for the new car's badge. Sadly, not enough customers shared the great man's optimism, and so MG's new owners, still flushed with the success of their deal with BMW, were soon persuaded that a deal to acquire the Italian assets of Qvale Automotive Group could form the basis of a swift route towards a new MG for North America.

MG Rover Group's Chief Executive Kevin Howe suggested that:

> the MG X80 will be an excellent fit at the top of our family of MG cars; it also provides an opportunity to look at markets where we are not currently represented – in particular, the USA market, the world's largest sports car market, where we can now seriously evaluate the full potential for the MG brand.

At the time, it was claimed that X80 would be seen in both coupé and roadster form, with both manual and automatic transmissions.

At the Frankfurt Motor Show, on 11 September 2001 (a date that would tragically become associated with terrible events in New York), MG Rover Group chose to unveil the TWR-built concept model for the proposed MG X80 coupé, which had been developed from the initial studies shown in Peter Stevens's sketch first released in June. There was a bit of drama at Frankfurt when the hot spotlights on the stand damaged the model. Neil Simpson, then at TWR, takes up the story:

Quite often, translating a designer's ideas to the round when there are all manner of packaging and production constraints can be a nightmare: remember the Austin Allegro? The Qvale Mangusta wasn't the easiest starting point, but this elegant sketch from Peter Stevens shows that the right intentions were there. (Peter Stevens)

ANOTHER NEW START

The final proposal for MG X80 was shown to the press on that ill-fated day in September 2001 when the attention of the world was on terrible events in New York. Meanwhile, the MG XPower girls gamely posed to conceal a split in the full-size foam model. (MG Rover Group)

We built the Frankfurt show car; it was actually milled from dense foam blocks which were glued together, and that was the problem when two started to delaminate under the hot show lights. I was the first to notice the crack after first thinking it was a trick of the light. I can say that my blood ran cold: we'd never had anything like that happen before but it was a new technique which we never used again! Peter Stevens was very cool about it but we straight away phoned our painter in the UK who prepared some Di-Noc [plastic film] and flew over with it that evening so we could 'fix' the problem after the show closed that evening.

In the meantime, a couple of 'MG XPower Girls' were asked to pose alongside the car in a way that concealed the damage.

In its press statement at Frankfurt, MG Rover Group said that the X80 was 'set to challenge the established world sports car market, with a dynamic technical specification, and high performance characteristics'. Perhaps if the indicative UK prices had indeed started from under £50,000, as projected, there might have been a good chance of this; however the story of the X80 project, which eventually evolved into the much more pricey and exotic MG XPower SV, would prove to be a far more protracted journey than a simple translation from prototype to production. (For a full account see David Knowles, *MG XPower SV*, The Crowood Press, 2005.)

Ironically, one of the prominent styling features of the X80 concept – the almond-shaped headlamp units shared with the MG*F* XPower 500 – would not make it to production on the MG XPower SV but would be seen instead on the major MG*F* facelift at the beginning of 2002.

ANOTHER NEW START

coloured hardtop was also announced, with a special introductory offer of £795 (a saving of £500) that ran through to the end of the year. With a heated glass rear window and neat headlining, the optional hardtop truly turned the open MGF into an attractive coupé.

A MAJOR CHANGE OF GEAR: THE MG *TF*

The MGF Trophy had shown how much 'harder' the MGF could be made in line with Nick Stephenson's aim to stretch the MG sports car, but it also showed some of the limitations. The Hydragas suspension was now unique to the MGF (other cars that had used it had been the Austin Allegro, Leyland Princess and more recently the Metro) and as such further production development had stagnated with the death of those other cars. Furthermore, some of the equipment and tooling involved needed periodic renewal and, with only one customer and one model, the costs involved were becoming uneconomic.

However there were other factors at work; although the suspension could provide an excellent ride and handling compromise, tuning the balance for the optimum in a manner that would remain true throughout the life of the vehicle was hard to achieve. If the MGF platform was to have an extended life ahead of it, it seemed logical to look at a switch to more conventional steel springs. As a consequence, work began to design and develop brand new suspension set-ups front and rear, adapting to minimize the need for significant body-in-white changes but nevertheless resulting in new demountable coil-spring suspension units to replace the old Hydragas units, and thereby finally breaking the link with the old Metro.

Building on the lessons learned from the MGF Trophy 160SE, MG Rover Group looked at simple substitution of the Hydragas units with high-rate compact coil springs, but it was swiftly appreciated that this alone would not be

Although the design is almost there, the label on this image tells a story; the facelift was still seen as the '2002 MG*F*' at this stage. (David Arbuckle)

ANOTHER NEW START

It was pretty obvious that in order to make much of an impression, the facelift of the MG*F* would have to show some visible changes to the nose and tail. Changes to panels had to be minimized and so, while a new headlamp could be considered, it had to fit in more or less the same 'hole'. This yellow concept sketch shows the whole of the 'grille' shifted below the bumper. (David Arbuckle)

At the rear of the same concept, the back bumper is squarer and the tail-lamps subtly different. (David Arbuckle)

sufficient to deliver an accomplished all-round package. Computer-aided design processes had advanced in recent years, and through the use of new software and 'virtual engineering' modelling techniques, experiments were undertaken on the computer to optimize the suspension geometry and elasto-kinematic characteristics. A simulator test vehicle was then built, which of course at first looked like any normal MG*F* from the outside. Rob Oldaker explains how the development progressed:

> My chassis guys had a bee in their bonnets about this. They said that the MGF was not stiff enough at the rear, which gave rise to a low polar moment of inertia and a propensity to spin. We did some Adams software modelling to see if we could make a difference using

Similar to the yellow car, but more of a halfway house, retaining the familiar grille 'nostrils', this grey car has new driving lamps and again rather squarer bumpers front and rear. (David Arbuckle)

Again, like the yellow sketch above, this proposal differs little from the original MG*F*.

Underneath the facelifted car, there were significant engineering changes proposed, but most of them would remain invisible to casual inspection from the kerbside; this concept showed a neat 'technical' look for the rear bumper to hint at the changes under the car. (David Arbuckle)

steel springs and dampers – and of course these would be much less susceptible to temperature than Hydragas.

Oldaker took the simulator to the Dunlop test route at MIRA:

It was conclusive as far as I was concerned that this was the right way to go; my initial impression was that it was better by leaps and bounds, although funnily enough in production form the gap didn't seem quite so large.

A subsequent thorough Main Board test drive session led to a green light for Oldaker to move the new suspension project forward to full production.

The new suspension drew much interest from the media, many of whom were amazed at such extensive changes as part of a facelift: many other manufacturers would have only considered such alterations as part of a wholesale model change, and also would often have expended far more than the £25 million or so that MG Rover Group spent. Within the rear suspension, the trailing-arm pivots from a forward extension of the subframe, forking at the rear to attach, via firm bushes, above and below the hub carrier. This provided longitudinal wheel location and reacts to torque purely in the vertical plane. A maximum-length link runs from the rear base of the hub carrier to a pivot on the centre rear of the subframe, thus completing what is effectively a very wide-based lower wishbone with a large swing radius.

The other links comprise the upper suspension arm and a lower steer-control link mounted forward of the hub carrier. A new

Yet another sketch – this time with a centre exhaust and twin rounded tail-lamps. New tail-lamps were on the designers' wish-list but were an easy budget casualty. (David Arbuckle)

ANOTHER NEW START

Starting with the premise of minimal changes to any of the panel work, this is the 'do minimum' facelift, with a new bumper and a narrow slot for an upper air intake. (David Arbuckle)

A squared-up rear bumper (with vertical 'overriders') and only minor changes to the detailing of the side air intake; this concept did not even feature the one-piece sills, but did show an idea for a new style of tail-lamp. (David Arbuckle)

rear anti-roll bar, with modifications to suit the new configuration, was introduced, operating via a short swinging link connected to the hub end of each trailing arm. This new suspension combined better camber control with much greater resistance to unwanted steer effects. This proved to be key to the more responsive and throttle-adjustable handling of the new car, along with an improved steering 'centre feel'. In addition to the standard set-up, MG Rover Group also offered an optional 'Sports Pack 1' with the suspension lowered by a further 10mm (i.e. 20mm lower than MG*F*).

Both front and rear subframes were modified, with raised and angled turrets for the top mountings of the coil over damper units. By moving the lower operating pivots for the spring units further outboard on the

This clay modelling on an MG*F* nose shows work in progress towards the finished article. (David Arbuckle)

Again we see the squarer rear bumper, but this time there is the new sill and air intake profile (needing panelwork changes). The budget trade-off is retention of the MG*F* tail-lamps. (David Arbuckle)

Further work has brought the style even closer to the finished article. (David Arbuckle)

Almost there, including the new grille 'vanes'.

upper suspension arms, more conventional leverage ratios and spring rates could be employed compared with the previous system. The change also meant that the damper forces were contained within the stiff subframes instead of being fed into the bodyshell. The subframes themselves were now solidly mounted to the bodyshell, as on the previous MG*F* Trophy model, contributing to enhanced structural stiffness and precision of control. Another advantage cited for the new suspension was that it allowed a 10mm lower ride height to operate, to the benefit of appearance, stability and handling. The lower centre of gravity also helped reduce pitch under acceleration and braking.

At the front, the wishbone suspension configuration otherwise remained similar to that of the MG*F*, but with reduced camber and parallel tracking in place of toe-out, plus revised pivot bushes and a stiffer anti-roll bar, up from 19mm to 20mm diameter, to complement the improved steering system. Tyre life was said to have been improved with this revised geometry. It was in the rear suspension (especially important on a mid-engined car), however, that the most fundamental changes were made. A completely new multi-link axle was engineered to provide precise control of rear wheel geometry in all conditions.

The MG*F* had featured electric power-assisted steering from the start, and a CVT transmission option from the 2000 Model Year. These features were retained for the MG *TF*, although the steering was retuned, accompanied by a 10 per cent faster geared rack. The 1.6-litre engine had accounted for one in eight MG*F* sales, and so was an obvious option to retain in the new model. The engine outputs were used to define the model and so the 1.6 became the MG *TF* 115, and the automatic model (with a 118bhp 1.8-litre engine) the *TF* 120. At the top of the range, the *TF* 160 adopted a regular-production 158bhp

With the new projector-type headlamp units and paint detailing, this is almost the final MG *TF* style. (David Arbuckle)

ANOTHER NEW START

Separate one-piece side sills contributed to a 20 per cent increase in torsional stiffness, not to mention improved crash roadworthiness. (David Arbuckle)

development of the MGF Trophy 160 SE unit (the previous MGF with VVC engine managed 143bhp), while the core model was the TF 135, using a combination of TF 160-style induction and exhaust systems and high-lift cams to raise power output from the 118bhp of the old MGF 1.8i to a new output of 134bhp.

Alongside the powertrain and fundamental suspension changes, there was just enough money left in the kitty to allow a modest facelift and a change to the body structure that allowed the use of a single sill section running front to rear, thereby increasing the overall stiffness of the bodyshell by some 20 per cent, reducing

The tail of the new car featured a longer boot-lid with integral rear spoiler; this is almost there but not quite the finished item. (David Arbuckle)

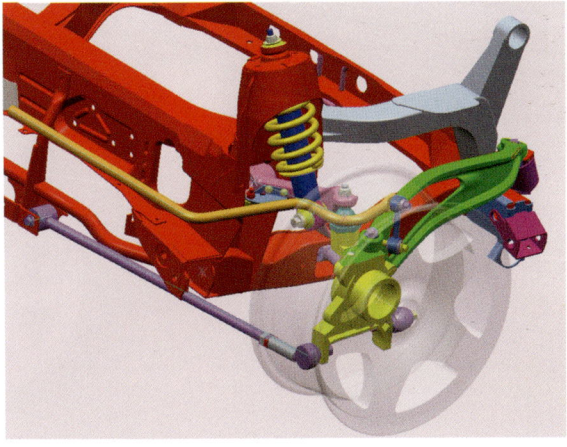

For the new MG TF, steel coil springs finally usurped the Hydragas units. (MG Rover Group)

139

ANOTHER NEW START

MG Rover Group was justifiably proud of the crash test performance of the new MG *TF*, which was tested by Euro-NCAP and received an excellent four-star 'occupant safety protection' and a class-leading three-star rating for 'pedestrian safety protection' (the contemporary Audi TT scored one star in the latter category) in January 2003. (MG Rover Group)

As well as front- and rear-impact testing, modern cars have to meet strict side-impact criteria: here an MG *TF* has survived a side swipe at MIRA. (MG Rover Group)

ANOTHER NEW START

The pedestrian safety rating is a measure of how likely a pedestrian would be to survive if struck by a car and thrown on the bonnet. Clearly this is a function of various issues such as shape, height and the existence of hard objects under the bonnet, and a mid-engined sports car has many advantages in such circumstances. Even so, the three-star Euro-NCAP rating was well deserved. (Adrian Guyll)

scuttle shake and undoubtedly contributing to the excellent NCAP impact test results that the new car subsequently achieved.

Subtle changes to the front included a slightly longer nose, with reshaped headlamp units, now with integral indicators and neat projector lamps built in, and a new corporate grille with a body-coloured central horizontal vane, similar to that first seen on the Le Mans cars. Completing a look that Peter Stevens had honed in the MIRA wind tunnel, the tail featured a slightly longer boot-lid, while the new one-piece sills included a sharper 'dart-like' shape to the engine bay air intakes.

Sadly the budget could not stretch to a major interior facelift, although in fairness many of the rough edges of the 1995 MG*F* original had been honed with the 2000 Model Year facelift.

A pre-production MG *TF* is lined up at Longbridge alongside a contemporary MG*F* and shows the differences between the two cars. (David Arbuckle)

ANOTHER NEW START

Note the longer boot 'deck' of the MG *TF* at right, as well as the new one-piece sill pressing.

According to David Arbuckle, a senior member of the MG Rover Design team who had been with the company since 1983, the original plan had been in effect an 'MG*F* Mark II' in design terms, but:

> we managed to get a lot for MG *TF* – in fact a lot of what we ended up with was not in the original plan. At first, there were going to be some modest changes to the bumpers and some trim changes – but it soon became apparent that we needed to do more; the car didn't look that much different to the original despite all the changes underneath.

Arbuckle and his colleagues were convinced they could – and should – do better:

> so we managed to do a lot more – to sharpen up the styling – and then we modelled in a new headlamp. Mayflower found a way to help us by changing the press tooling cheaply – and

Peter Stevens stands alongside a British Racing Green MG *TF*, with the MG XPower MG*F/TF* concept behind, during the *TF* press launch.

ANOTHER NEW START

Posing in the early morning Portuguese sunshine, this Solar Red MG *TF* with small Italian licence plates could almost be a bambino Ferrari. Bellissimo!

none of this was in the original brief, but it all came through design pressing for more changes.

Along with the new interior that the designers had wanted, they had to make do without new tail-lamps that they lobbied for: the budget could only stretch so far.

New paint colours and trim specifications were introduced, allowing a greater degree of personalization. XPower Grey appeared first on the MG *TF*, and Trophy Yellow and Trophy Blue were also available as mainstream colours, having first been offered on the MG*F* Trophy. 'We also tried an experiment with special soft paint finishes for some of the interior plastics,

As well as passing for a small Ferrari in red, a simple change of colour to metallic grey or silver, as here, means that the MG *TF* takes on the style of a mini Aston Martin. (MG Rover Group)

ANOTHER NEW START

In March 2003 the MG *TF* won an award as the 'World's Most Beautiful Cabriolet' at the awards ceremony held by L'Automobile più Bella del Mondo, in Milan. A panel of thirteen international judges, made up from design experts outside the automotive industry, gave the award 'for blending great originality and typical elements of MG tradition, with a strong casual and dynamic character'. (MG Rover Group)

but they proved too expensive', according to Rob Oldaker.

Colour-keyed hoods were also offered for the first time, although for the time being the same plastic rear window as the old MG*F* was retained. 'Ash grey' continued as one of the interior colours, although 'walnut' was replaced by 'tan', while deep red 'grenadine' and a light grey called 'smokestone' were offered. New fabric options included the use of Alcantara mock-suede surfaces and an upmarket 'Oxford' leather trim, all aimed at giving the MG *TF* a more contemporary and luxurious feel to compensate for the fact that the basic interior architecture was really little different from the MG*F*. That meant, for example, that the cockpit ergonomics remained less than ideal, and some of the equipment, gauges and switchgear were beginning to show their age when compared with some of the younger opposition.

Following a press release with a single image on 8 January 2002, there was a public debut at the Brussels Motor Show on 15 January, while the full-blown press launch of the new MG

Unsurprisingly, the MG*F* XPower 500 was trotted out again for the MG *TF* launch, although it was 'rebranded' as the MG *TF* 500. It still had the same prototype grille style, however, rather than the 'vaned' grille of the production *TF*.

144

ANOTHER NEW START

It is somewhat ironic that despite 'rebranding' as the 'MG *TF* 500' the original grille shape was retained: however, it would later prove to be inspiration for the 2008 MG *TF* facelift! (*see* photo on page 187)

The MG *TF* came as the culmination of a long line of MG sports cars, as the evocative old posters show on this photo staged for the launch press material. One wonders what the Portuguese building owner made of all this. (MG Rover Group)

TF took place at the tail end of that month in the Algarve, Portugal. The launch had been scheduled for the summer of 2002, but MG Rover Group managed to bring it forward by six months with the hope of benefiting from spring and summer sales.

Meanwhile, on the roads of the Algarve, journalists (the author among them) were favourably disposed towards the car. MG Rover Group had already wrought miracles in turning the stodgy Rover 25 and 45 into the outstanding MG ZR and ZS models; since essentially the same chassis team had been set loose on the new *TF*, it was hardly a surprise that the end result was so professionally executed. However, quite a few drivers mourned the luxurious soft nature of the old MG*F* suspension; it was hardly surprising that the new steel spring set-up was much better on the track, but some of the on-road comfort had been traded off – especially on the sharper-handling *TF*s fitted with the optional sports packs. This latter

The attractive hardtop that had been offered on the MG*F* continued as an option for the MG *TF*. (MG Rover Group)

ABOVE LEFT: There were three basic colour options for the MG *TF* interior at the time of launch: this was 'Grenadine', a deep red as seen on the MG*F* 75th LE. (MG Rover Group)

ABOVE RIGHT: 'Smokestone' offered a range of light grey and charcoal. (MG Rover Group)

LEFT: 'Tan' was a light, expensive-looking beige, often teamed with a walnut trim kit. (MG Rover Group)

Why the 'MG *TF*'?

We saw earlier how 'PR3' had become the MG*F*, even though some pundits had guessed incorrectly that it would be the MGD. A similar dilemma was faced by MG Rover Group when it came to the major facelift they had planned for their mid-engined sports car for 2002. On the one hand, the new car was clearly evolved from the MG*F*, but on the other it was a sufficiently thorough upgrade that the changes perhaps warranted a change of name to mark the new direction.

Designer David Arbuckle is of the view that the changes, which had been hard fought by both the engineers and the designers, had clearly helped make the case: 'as a consequence of our efforts, marketing saw that they could justify a new name'. MGG had long ago been ruled out of contention; it looks odd, sounds terrible in most languages and of course there was always the old equine joke about 'gee gees'. Some of the concept sketches in the BMW period showed 'MGH' badges and there was even, as we saw earlier, Tony Hunter's 'MG TH' concept (really a tongue-in-cheek reference, he admits, to his own initials), but these were never the subject of any serious marketing analysis.

British pop singer Sophie Ellis-Bextor was recruited by MG Rover to help launch the MG TF to the public at the Brussels Motor Show on 15 January 2002. (MG Rover Group)

A clue came with the naming used for the MG saloons that had been introduced in 2001; these had cleverly echoed the last true Abingdon MG saloons, the MG ZA and ZB Magnette, and there had been some thought about using the Magnette name on a variant of the Rover 75 in the latter stages of the BMW era. By using the 'Z' prefix for the ZR, ZS and ZT, MG Rover Group cleverly came up with modern and stylish branding that at the same time cleverly echoed the older models and so provided a rather neat heritage link.

So when it came to selecting a name for the facelifted MG*F*, a precedent had been set. When the MG ZA Magnette was introduced at the 1953 Motor Show, it shared the MG stand with the new MG TF Midget sports car. The step from there to adopting the name for the new car was a fairly short one, and Greg Allport credits MG Brand Manager Richard Hudson with the idea.

Kevin Jones, like Allport a key member of the public relations team at the time, recalls the genesis of the new name:

> From a marketing point of view, it was largely that we neither had the time or money to re-market the car, so it had to evolve. What better than to cross paths, so to speak, with our past? We appreciated the sensitivity towards the re-use of the classic 'TF' name, but at the same time felt it was hardly a unique occurrence; after all, we'd returned to using '75' as a model name for one of our Rovers.

Lots of people had been hoping for an all-new car, but the changes to take the MG*F* to the MG *TF* were nevertheless a pretty thorough package. Greg Allport says that the new car was explained as having been 're-engineered' rather than facelifted: 'the journalists welcomed that honesty, in my view – and in the event, quite a few of them still wrote about the "new car". The use of "*TF*" also had a neat link back to the "MG*F*" name, so it worked very well.' The practice of italicizing the '*TF*' is also an obvious link to the MG*F*.

ANOTHER NEW START

would be addressed some three years later.

JUBILEE – 1.5 MILLION MGS

We have already seen how the people behind MG have seldom been reluctant to celebrate significant dates of one kind or another (the existence of '75th', '80th' and most recently '85th' MG anniversary specials is testament to that), but in 2002 Public Relations Manager Kevin Jones saw an opportunity for something of a double celebration, in the form of the '1.5 Millionth MG Jubilee Special'. Jones had calculated – with a little help from Steve Cox, British Motor Heritage and author Jonathan Wood – that a total of one-and-a-half million MG-badged cars had been built in the seventy-eight years since the first MG 14/28 of 1924. The split was roughly a million roadsters and half a million saloons.

However, 2002 also happened to be the Golden Jubilee of Her Majesty, Queen Elizabeth II. Since a precedent had been set by creating a

The MG *TF* fell neatly into line to celebrate a couple of key milestones: the Golden Jubilee of Her Majesty Queen Elizabeth II and also the 1.5 millionth production MG built. (MG Rover Group)

BELOW: Seventy-seven years separate the 1925 MG 'Old Number One' and the 2002 MG *TF* Jubilee, seen at Longbridge on 16 April 2002. (MG Rover Group)

ANOTHER NEW START

MG Rover Group's Chief Executive, Kevin Howe, was on hand to help celebrate the production of the 1.5 millionth MG. (MG Rover Group)

BELOW: Adrian Guyll, who was 'vehicle safety protection manager' at MG Rover Group, also races an MG TF when he gets the chance. Adrian joined SAIC following the collapse of MG Rover. (Adrian Guyll)

one-off MGB GT 'Silver Jubilee' special back in 1977, the decision was taken to repeat the exercise with a specially finished one-off MG TF160, finished in a new 'Monogram supertallic' paint finish, coincidentally and ideally dubbed 'Jubilee Gold'.

Unveiled to the press on 16 April 2002 at a special ceremony at Longbridge, the MG TF 'Jubilee' (bearing VIN Number SARRDLBPC2D604127) featured specially embroidered seat backs (with the Golden Jubilee crown logo), a variety of special badges on the exterior (even the wheel centres) and the registration 'MG02 OTF'. A special Queen's

ANOTHER NEW START

MG Rover's MG *TF* Limited Editions

In a climate where sales were becoming critical, and as the opposition snapped at MG's heels, it was hardly a surprise that there would occasionally be limited edition variants that set out to offer extra value by bundling in special features not always on sale otherwise in quite the same combination. The key *TF* limited editions were:

- MG *TF* Sprint SE (July 2002). Available in both 135 and 160 engine tunes. Colours offered for the 600 cars built were Le Mans Green, Solar Red, Starlight Silver, Trophy Blue and XPower Grey. Seats were trimmed with Gunsmoke Alcantara and black leather. Sports Pack 2 suspension fitted as standard, colour-coordinated hood and chrome trim, 16-inch wheels as per the *TF* 160.
- MG *TF* Elegance SE (December 2002). Available for the Dutch market in 135 engine tune, finished in Royal Blue metallic or British Racing Green and with a matching Dark Blue or Green hood. Wheels were 16-inch square spokes, and a 'wood' pack was fitted, covering the centre console, door panels and steering wheel, along with a chrome pack and front fog lamps. Interior trim was Alpaca & Tan Leather.
- MG *TF* Cool Blue SE (March 2003). Available as 115 and 135 engine tunes. Colours offered were Anthracite, Starlight Silver and Trophy Blue; in all cases, fitted with a blue hood and blue Alcantara seats. Six-spoke 'Minilite' style alloy wheels.
- MG *TF* SunStorm LE (October 2003). Limited to 500 and available in 115, 135 and 160 engine tunes. Three colours: Nightfire Red, Raven Black or Starlight Silver. Body-coloured hardtop supplied as standard, and a Smokestone interior with seats trimmed in black leather and Gunsmoke Alcantara. Sports Pack 2 suspension and 16-inch eleven-spoke wheels.
- MG *TF* 80th Anniversary LE (January 2004). *See* main text.
- MG *TF* Coupé LE (May 2004). Just thirty built for the Australian market. Available as 120 (Stepspeed) or 160 engine tunes and with a body-colour hardtop fitted as standard. Colour choice was either Starlight Silver or a choice of two colours from the Monogram bespoke colour programme – Monogram Nightshade Blue and Monogram Black Olive. Air-conditioning was included, as was a wood and leather steering wheel and Monogram beige leather interior.
- MG *TF* Spark SE (July 2004). Limited to 1,000 for the UK market. Available as 115, 135 and 160 variants. Suspension as per SunStorm. Colours offered were Firefrost Red, Sonic Blue, Starlight Silver and XPower Grey. Chrome trim pack and interior in Ash grey with black Alcantara seats.
- MG *TF* Vintage Racing LE (October 2004). For French market only and premiered that month at the Paris Salon. Distinctive Dover White colour

The MG TF *Sunstorm LE. (MG Rover Group)*

ANOTHER NEW START

The MG TF 80 LE. (MG Rover Group)

The distinctive interior of the MG TF 80 LE. (MG Rover Group)

scheme with bold blue stripes and standard hardtop. Just thirty were built and this is arguably the most collectable *TF* limited edition variant.
- MG *TF* Oxford LE (February 2005). For the Dutch market only. Available in *TF* 135 guise only. Colours were British Racing Green or Pearl Black and the interior trim was in Oxford leather, fitted with a 'wood pack', a wooden finish for the centre console and door panels, chrome pack and Sports Pack 2 suspension and wheels.

Something of a rare and sought-after limited edition is the MG TF 160 Vintage Racing, which was made available for the French market. It featured a special white livery with bold blue stripes and debuted at the 2004 Paris Salon. Just thirty were built and they are understandably quite sought after in left-hand-drive markets. (Erik Baekelant)

Another low-volume special was the MG TF Swiss Blue. (MG Rover Group)

ANOTHER NEW START

Jubilee parade along The Mall on 4 June saw the one-off *TF* taking part. The colour was available as an extra-cost option as part of MG Rover Group's 'Monogram' paint programme, although the Jubilee car remained a one-off.

Spring 2004 saw yet another anniversary and the introduction of the MG *TF* 80th anniversary limited edition with 500 reserved for UK sales (as had been the case with the MG*F* 75th LE of 1999). The Retail Trust's Hollywood Ball at the Grosvenor House, Park Lane, featured a charity auction conducted by fashion celebrity Jeff Banks and the bid for one of the *TF* 80 LE models reached a remarkable £275,000.

Three 80th Anniversary *TF* LE versions were available with colour coordinated hood and trim combinations, and features that included unique identity detailing, with a choice of 135, 120 Stepspeed (CVT transmission) or 160 power units, making the choice rather wider within the small number built. Black and Goodwood Green MG *TF* 80 LE models have commanded a small premium on the second-hand market due as much to their rarity as to their attractiveness as good-looking and reasonably well-equipped models, although the Starlight Silver variants arguably looked less distinctive.

Photographed in the studios of Dove Company in Norfolk, this is Peter Stevens's special one-off 'MG GT Coupé'.

MG *TF*: EVOLUTION AND GT

As will become apparent later, MG Rover Group was looking optimistically at major improvements to its sports car portfolio; the plan to drastically overhaul the *TF* was still being investigated in earnest during 2003 and 2004, but sadly would eventually come to nought. However, some of the work in tandem with these more advanced studies did spill over

MG *TF* production on 'System Two' at Longbridge in the days of MG Rover Group. (MG Rover Group)

ANOTHER NEW START

The rear window in the prototype is fixed, but from the outset it was obvious that a more flexible solution would have been needed for a production version. Under that engine cover is not a KV6 but a 4-cylinder K-Series, despite what some people believe.

into production, perhaps the most laudable of which was the change from plastic to glass rear screen in the folding top. Mazda's MX-5 (Miata) had had such a feature for some time; indeed some cars with soft-tops had boasted glass screens for many years: the idea of a scratch-, discolouration- and generally damage-prone plastic window was an outmoded one for the new millennium.

Unfortunately, however, behind the scenes the MG Rover Group business was beginning to suffer from various major problems, not least the failure of the company to complete a partnership contract with a major company. Even though there was a down-payment of £28 million, the much-vaunted tie-up with China Brilliance collapsed (not helped by the company chairman fleeing arrest) and other deals with Proton of Malaysia and Daewoo in South Korea came to nothing despite much effort from Longbridge. According to Rob Oldaker, 'It was unfortunately a long drawn-out process – and it was time we could ill afford to lose'.

As soon as the Brilliance deal was off, however, a whole series of Chinese companies made contact and Rob Oldaker showed them round Longbridge. One day Oldaker took a call from a business acquaintance who had in turn been sounded out by a third party to see if MG Rover Group might be prepared to talk; that third party turned out to be SAIC: 'I went to see John Towers and Nick Stephenson, and it was agreed that we would meet SAIC at a forthcoming motor show, which was the start of our relationship with the company'.

Meanwhile, the large dowry that BMW had given to the Phoenix Consortium back in 2001 was being eaten into rapidly. MG Rover

The bold front spoiler helps to visually 'lengthen' the MG GT, although it might not have been completely practical as a production prospect. The wheels are 17-inch OZ alloy wheels finished in 'Gunsmoke'.

Inside the MG GT, not a lot was done other than to fit lowered Sparco seats (Peter Stevens says that the seat cushions were made thinner). The plastic side glass windows do not go up and down – but then surely that is what one should expect on a show car?

Group became engaged in a programme called 'Project Drive' aimed at slashing costs through cost-saving on various components and build processes. Many of the savings were clever (such as rationalizing door mirrors), but inevitably some of the cost reductions resulted in changes that ended up being visible – and in some cases not wholly attractive, such as changes to some of the switchgear in the *TF* cockpit.

The 2005 Model Year MG *TF* entered manufacture in February 2005 (and, as circumstances would prove, had only a short production run). The most important change was the new hood with glass rear screen (see above), but there were also new alloy wheel options, new colour and trim combinations, and some new badges. Of equal significance was a re-rating of the suspension as a response to criticisms that the *TF* ride had been too hard for some customers (a criticism that had been raised at the *TF* launch in 2002). Thicker anti-roll bars and revised suspension bushes all contributed to a smoother ride without a loss of the *TF*'s fine overall handling balance.

As negotiations with MG Rover Group's would-be partners went through twists and turns, Nick Stephenson decided that some special one-off prototype concept cars would help give a fillip to the negotiations and the public image of the company, both of which were coming under a battering in the press. Exploring both the Rover and MG themes, Peter Stevens was put in charge of the creation of two hand-built but running prototypes intended to give tantalizing clues as to what might lie in the company's future (there was a third car, but that was effectively a specially trimmed MG XPower SV).

Taking as his basis the Rover 75 and MG *TF*, Stevens created two-door coupé versions of both types. The 75 was transformed into a stunningly beautiful coupé with an elegant leather and wood interior, and could conceivably have become an MG ZT coupé with relatively little effort. The MG *TF* was built by the Dove Company in Norfolk, a small but highly professional outfit that had also developed the MG XPower SV body prototype and had worked with Peter Stevens on many projects before.

Peter Stevens directed the work by Colin Jones and his team and the result was an elegant coupé version of the *TF* with a number of aerodynamic tweaks, new larger wheels and lowered seats inside the cockpit. The *TF* coupé was built inside six weeks, according to Jones: 'the car came in as a standard *TF*, and Peter simply explained that we would be making it into a hardtop'. What Stevens did next was

ANOTHER NEW START

Electric Dreams: The MG *TF* 200 HPD

Officially announced on 23 October 2003 by Rob Oldaker and MIRA director John Wood at the Motorsport Industry Association's 'Clean Racing Conference', the *TF* 200 HPD (Hybrid Performance Development) was based on an MG *TF* 160. However, there the resemblance stopped, for the one-off prototype featured four-wheel drive, with electric power to the front wheels the key to extra motive force, and a claimed output of some 200PS without an adverse effect on emissions or fuel economy. City driving could be achieved with just the electric motor powering the front wheels. Body styling had been altered to suit and help ensure an evenly balanced 50:50 weight distribution.

There were plans for development between MG Rover Group, Powertrain and MIRA to continue 'with a view to a production model in the next couple of years – whether this will be on a *TF* or in a new saloon based vehicle is yet to be seen. The Government's Energy Saving Trust has funded the project so it is highly likely this project will run to fruition.' In fact, events at MG Rover Group eventually overtook these bold ambitions.

To supplement the conventional petrol engine at the rear, the MG TF 200 HPD also had a 40PS high-output electric motor driving the front wheels, through a separate automatic drivetrain. (MG Rover Group)

Technical Specification
- K Series 160PS, 1.8-litre VVC petrol engine driving rear wheels

The MG TF200 HPD was a joint project between MG Rover Group's Rob Oldaker and MIRA. Into the front of an otherwise largely standard MG TF was grafted an electric motor to power the front wheels, coupled with a mild restyle of the nose. (MG Rover Group)

- 40PS high-output electric motor driving front wheels, through CVT drivetrain
- Engine driven generator
- Hawker SBS8 battery pack delivers 72V at 400 amps
- BRUSA BRMD 506 motor controller
- Mathworks XPC vehicle management
- Aerodynamic Cd 0.32, zero front & rear lift
- 50:50 weight distribution
- Sprint power increased from 160PS to 200PS
- 0–60mph time improved from 6.9 to sub 6.0s
- All-wheel drive traction, maximum tractive effort and 'low mu' handling
- 'Hotshift' delivers continuous power through front wheels during gear changes
- 'City mode' feature enables relaxed urban motoring using electric front drivetrain.

ANOTHER NEW START

Phoenix MG Projects: The New Sports Cars that Never Came

The essential need for a new medium car as a replacement for the Rover 45/MG ZS (and, perhaps, the 25/ZR pair) did not blind the MG Rover Group management to the fact that the core appeal of the MG marque was crucially linked to the existence of a 'proper' MG sports car. Richard Hamblin hinted earlier at an ideal scenario, one where there was an 'MG Midget', an 'MGB' and, ideally, a slightly larger sports car – one that could offer some combination of greater luxury, more space and higher performance (past examples in MG history being the MGB GT, MGC and MGB GT V8) and capture more profitable 'high end' sales.

One obvious train of thought was to exploit the sports car the company already had (indeed one such exercise is soon to be discussed). However, it could be said that extending the MG *TF* much further upmarket, into a sector dominated by some pretty competent opposition, was not going to be easy. One route would be the 'X120' project described in this chapter, but even that relied heavily on the existing technology and mid-engined philosophy of the MG *TF*.

So there were thoughts about exploiting appropriate low-volume technology to create a class-leading MG sports car flagship, with a number of routes considered as ways to achieve this. The MG RV8, a 'limited edition anniversary special' though it was, showed the obvious evolutionary direction of a compact, reasonably lightweight sports car in the traditional front-engine rear-wheel drive MG mould. Had BMW retained ownership of MG, and begun to properly exploit the marque, it seems likely that this is roughly the direction that could have been followed; Alchemy too had postulated such a path.

In MG's case, the main exercise – from 2001 – was 'X70', with Rob Oldaker in the driving seat: 'There were lots of different priorities in those days – the MG *TF* was soon to be on its way and the MG saloons were my main priority.' However, Oldaker nevertheless initiated some work with outside consultancies to research the materials that would provide the stiffest platform:

> I'd just come from Bentley at Crewe, under VW ownership, and while I was there we had been directed by Dr Piëch to make the Arnage body structure stiffer; VW policy was to aim for a 50Hz body – which is a measure of stiffness – and while the Arnage was around 37Hz, VW quite rightly wanted it as stiff as possible.

Oldaker had therefore come to MG Rover Group with a keen interest in stiffer structures.

> We looked at three different approaches to a platform for a sports car, and the contract companies were keen and did the work at no cost to us. [The three companies were EPM Technology, ARUP and Corus.] We did a sort of beauty competition at the end – they were all front-engined rear-wheel drive sports cars of a given engineering layout – but we didn't do a great

Ben Hooper's sketch shows a possible sleek style for X71 – a junior relation to the larger X80 project. (Ben Hooper)

Neil Simpson was also part of the TWR team asked to look at the roadster and coupé pairing of X70/X71. (Neil Simpson)

ANOTHER NEW START

Julian Quincey was working at TWR by the time that MG Rover was looking at ideas for a new front-engine rear-wheel drive MG sports car. This sketch of his shows a modern aggressive stance not a million miles from that of the MG XPower SV. (Julian Quincey)

There is perhaps something of a latter-day Healey about the tail of this Julian Quincey sketch for X70.

deal of styling at the beginning – this could be left until the structure and layout was fixed by the engineering analysis. It was really looking at a platform to be clothed. It was mid-front engined – i.e. with the engine set back for good balance – and the idea was to be a spiritual follower of the MGA, with some classic 'hooks'.

At the end of this work, the studies came up with a structure:

It would probably have been in steel, funnily enough, although we'd looked at aluminium and a composite structure plus a largely carbon fibre body – and we'd also looked at Jim Randle's 'Lea Francis' prototype [in MG guise this was 'Project Viking' – *see* picture on page 170] which had very similar proportions.

Of course, none of these cars happened; priorities were elsewhere at that time and so these concepts were always 'for the future': 'the *TF* was being done, the saloons were done – and then there was room for maybe another MG *TF* facelift and of course the new medium car, which was the most important for us'.

continued overleaf

Another dramatic style for X70 from Julian Quincey. (Julian Quincey)

Rob Oldaker owns a 1959 MG MGA, and he has long had a bee in his bonnet about trying to recapture the appeal of this classic British sports car in a new MG. These sketches show some of a series of themes he asked his designers to explore; the ghosted view shows packaging for a 'front mid-engine' format with an in-line KV6 engine driving the rear wheels.

ANOTHER NEW START

Phoenix MG Projects: The New Sports Cars that Never Came *continued*

Interestingly enough, TWR, the engineering and design group that later collapsed, taking with it some of the design work on MG Rover Group's 'RDX60' mid-range car concept, also developed a number of open-topped and coupé concept sketches for both X70 and the related X71, as well as work on the rather different Qvale Mangusta-based X80, which eventually became the MG XPower SV. Graham Fairhead was the engineering liaison man at MG Rover: 'TWR did around thirty styles for us, which we shortlisted to around five, and I can remember having a look at them at TWR's very impressive 3D studio at Leafield'.

As well as the design work, there were some tentative experiments using a Caterham chassis to make a crude but effective mule, as Fairhead recalls:

> I remember being very interested in polar moments of inertia. Optimizing this enables you to make the slip/breakaway transition very progressive. We looked at weight distribution and wheelbase, and I remember comparison-testing a Boxster, an MX-5 and a couple of other cars.

Some of the modern and yet traditionally inspired ideas designers came up with for Rob Oldaker's idea of a 'new MGA'.

In the end, however, X70 and X71 faded away although, as we saw earlier, X80 had a second lease of life.

---

to take half a dozen thin splines of MDF and carefully stretch them over the roof area, before taping them down. He then retained the splines on one side, built a timber 'armature' just underneath the remaining splines, and carefully built up the clay on that armature to match the required shape: 'When Peter next came in, he was able to actually "pull" the clay into shape – so that he would get the shape to where he wanted it and allowing me just to tidy it to suit afterwards'. With the clay finished to Stevens's satisfaction, a mould was taken, a fibre-reinforced composite roof was laid up inside the mould and then the mould and the roof casting were both carefully mounted back onto the MG *TF* (to ensure correct fit and alignment) before the roof was fixed in place and the work of carefully detailing and finishing it could begin.

In the official press statement, Peter Stevens was quoted as follows:

> We would love to expand the MG *TF* range with a high-performance MG GT which has inspiring handling, practicality and great looks. The KV6 engine combines a superb soundtrack with a surge of power and a wider performance envelope to drive within – perfect for a sports car.

In fact the KV6 was never fitted, owing to difficulties in achieving this in the existing *TF* structure, and to this day Stevens remains a little piqued that he was misquoted in this way. The end result was certainly as striking as the Rover 75 Coupé; both cars made their public debut at the annual *Autocar* industry awards in November 2004.

ANOTHER NEW START

The prototype survives and is now owned by MG Motor. Despite what has been written elsewhere, it still has the same 4-cylinder VVC engine fitted. Stephen Cox was responsible for getting it going again after it had lain unused for three years:

> I had to break into it to move it off the stage in the conference centre as the battery was flat, meaning the electric door locks were disabled, and the keys were in the ignition! With the help of some genius blokes from the assembly team, we fiddled our way into it and I was able to get it going with a new battery. After at least three years of static display, it cranked into life immediately. The exhaust I would suggest is absolutely standard. Clearly, the display material suggests it has a KV6 but this is nonsense and it is also still a styling exercise rather than a developed car as the large wheels foul the inner wings ... but it is a super looking car and a pity it will never see production.

A KV6 engine has been fitted in an MG*F* by an enterprising enthusiast, but even he found that squeezing the much wider V6 unit into the compact MG engine bay necessitated changes to the bulkhead and a smaller fuel tank (arguably one of the last things needed for a thirstier engine). Ian Pogson confirms that the idea of putting the KV6 in a standard MG *TF* never got very far:

> There was only one V6 put in a subframe, but never installed, with a PG1 box. Steve Potter who was running the workshop at the time confirms that Phil Turner [chassis engineer] was asked on a number of occasions to do CAD checks to see if other engines would go in *TF*, but all they did was create a reduced boot area or hit the fuel tank.

Other engines could have been contemplated – especially if North America was to be in the frame – and might conceivably have included US-compliant Ford or Toyota units, but the preference was always to stick to in-house engines if at all possible.

Key Features of the 'MG GT' Coupé

(Note that the *TF* name was not used.)

- Composite roof and integral roll-bar on prototype;
- Aerodynamic drag coefficient cut from 0.35 to 0.31;
- 17-inch 'Gunsmoke' five-spoke OZ alloy wheels;
- Extended front aero splitter is balanced by a longer tail-spoiler integrated into the boot-lid design, thus generating reduced lift at speed;
- New door mirrors with integral side direction indicator lamps and switch for electronic door opening;
- Interior trimmed with Burgundy Red leather 'Sparco' seats with facia and door casings coloured to match.

The concept of the MG GT was an exciting one, but it seemed destined to remain little more than an interesting excursion in lateral thinking. For the time being, at least, that is exactly what it became – although there would be an interesting side-story two years later.

A NEW DIRECTION FOR THE *TF*: PROJECT X120

The changes that MG Rover made to the MG*F* to create the MG *TF* were, as we have seen, remarkably extensive, but even then they were nothing like as ambitious as many in the company really wanted to see, if funding could be found. The MG *TF* was very well received by the media, but even the most ardent MG supporters recognized that by 2002 the basic architecture of the car was already approaching its tenth birthday, and rivals in the marketplace were getting better all the time.

ANOTHER NEW START

Over at TWR, Julian Quincey was involved in concept sketch development for a major facelift of the MG TF, which could have fed into the X120 programme. (Julian Quincey)

Smooth, clean detailing – devoid of any unnecessary 'jewellery' – have long been MG hallmarks. (Julian Quincey)

The MG TF may have become Britain's best-selling roadster, but the Mazda MX-5 was snapping at its heels and Mazda was certainly giving no indication that it was about to give up the struggle. With the suspension issues largely sorted, and the outstanding NCAP impact performance, it was obvious that, in the TF, MG now had a good basis for further development.

In 2002, however, MG Rover Group was rather preoccupied with other things, foremost among them building a partnership deal to share the costs and effort of creating new mainstream MG- and Rover-badged products. With the exception of short-term work on the MG TF and the almost contracted-out low-volume MG X80 project, there were few resources and even fewer funds available to look at a new medium-volume sports car.

Needless to say, this was something of a dilemma for many people inside the company: the MG name was still very much rooted in its sports car legacy, and while the philosophy of MG-badged saloons and hatchbacks had been rehabilitated, the idea of an MG future without an MG sports car was no longer tenable. Accordingly, somewhat under the radar, an exercise was started to look at a way of taking

A key part of the X120 mission was to try to find a way to deliver a new MG Midget, derived from the MG TF platform. As is normal practice, this process started with concept sketches, such as this one. (MG Rover Group)

ANOTHER NEW START

Taking some cues developed from the concept sketch above, the designer has attempted to marry them to a slightly more realistic rendering, in which the MG *TF* origins remain fairly obvious. (MG Rover Group)

the work already done to make the MG *TF*, but extending it dramatically in order to give the basic platform an entirely new lease of life, with an opportunity to split what was effectively one model into three or more closely related but nevertheless more differentiated variants.

Project X120 was conceived in effect as a set of triplets, ranging from an 'MG Midget' (X121), effectively a cheekier junior version of the *TF*; a so-called 'New Large Roadster' (X122), in effect a replacement for the MG *TF* but with a longer wheelbase to allow the fitment of the KV6 engine; and, at the top of the range, a stylish 'MG Coupé' (X123), which would have competed with the Audi TT and was even intended to knock at the door of the Porsche Boxster market sector (hinted at in 2004 with the MG GT Coupé discussed above).

Dave Lindley was responsible for looking at the X120 study, which, given its 'below the radar' status, was not a fully sanctioned programme but, in the best tradition of such ideas, a 'skunk works' project that was nevertheless carried out with the tacit support of such key people in the company as Nick Stephenson and Rob Oldaker.

Lindley saw the X120 mission as, in his words, 'extending the MG sports car family

Another slightly bolder, more 'edgy' looking Midget sketch – drawn, like others in the series, as one of a trio of related images intended to represent X121, X122 and X123. (MG Rover Group)

ANOTHER NEW START

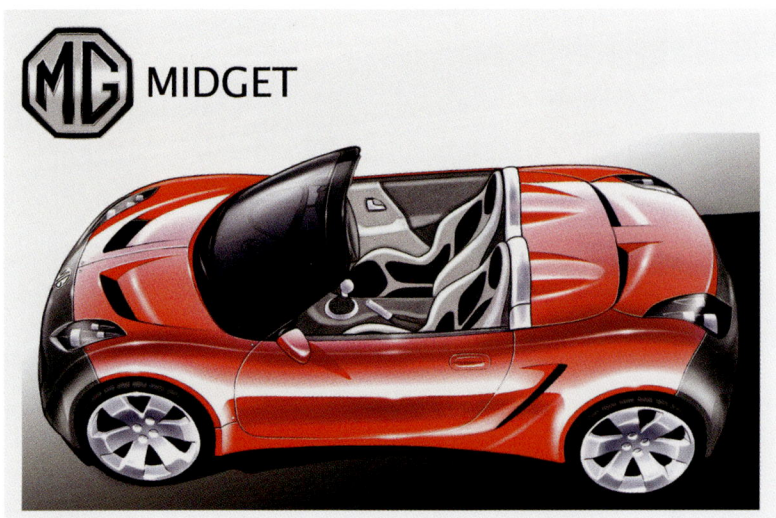

Of all the 'X121' Midget sketches the author has seen, this one seems somehow to best capture the youthful, fun image that one associates with the concept of an MG Midget. (MG Rover Group)

and getting the marque back to where it could be'. There were very tentative thoughts about opportunities for other brands, the most obvious example being Austin Healey, but there was also perhaps a chance to satiate the appetites of MG Rover Group's partner organizations, particularly SAIC, which was hungry for the opportunity to create a new Chinese brand of its own to add to its core business of building VWs and Buicks under licence.

Dave Lindley had been at Lotus, where he had been heavily involved in the exciting but ultimately abortive M250 project, shown in prototype form at the 2000 Motor Show but never taken forward to production. At Lotus there was obvious expertise in the use of plastic materials for automotive bodyshells, but also a great deal of cunning in the concept of a common basic architecture from which could be spawned a number of different products for marketing under different brands: the Opel Roadster/Vauxhall VX220 and, more

Eventually, the concept sketches and ideas for the 'X121' Midget were whittled down to a prime contender and more detailed, realistic renderings were produced. (MG Rover Group)

The final 'virtual' stage of visualization of a concept is often a 3D rendering produced using Alias software: this is an Alias view of the X121 proposal. (MG Rover Group)

recently, the Tesla Roadster, for example, were all heavily dependent upon the Lotus Elise, but the end results were very different products.

Bringing this expertise to MG Rover Group would be an interesting challenge, but there would be potential savings in tooling costs and greater flexibility, not only through creating different variants but also in managing the process of facelifts, thereby granting a potentially longer lifespan for the platform.

As we saw earlier, the MG*F* (and indeed the MG *TF*) had relied strongly on a partnership between what had been Rover Group and Mayflower Vehicle Systems. The Mayflower relationship (latterly Stadco, in the wake of Mayflower Vehicle Systems going into administration on 1 April 2004) had been an invaluable and very clever route into sports car production, but as with many such arrangements, cost-based decisions made in the early stages had consequences that

Compare this view of the four-tenths scale clay model of the proposed X121 Midget with the Alias software virtual model view. (MG Rover Group)

ANOTHER NEW START

From above, this hardtop version of the X121 Midget looks quite far removed from the MG *TF* platform from which it had been developed – a considerable and successful achievement. (MG Rover Group)

frustrated the design and production engineers alike.

The tooling and jigs used by Mayflower were not getting any younger, and some of the body design compromises that had been acceptable back in the early 1990s frustrated later efforts to improve quality, consistency and an ability to react to impact legislation that was already on the horizon at the turn of the millennium. The new body sides of the MG *TF* had dealt with one of the MG*F* body-in-white issues, but there was still a lot more that could be done as part of a further, even more substantial, facelift.

There was no doubt, however, that the basic central structure of the MG*F*/*TF*, the so-called 'tub', was a very sound design, even if some of the cockpit packaging was no longer quite up to the standard of the latest opposition. By taking this 'tub', shorn of the entire front and rear-end sections, and dealing with some of the basic packaging problems, Lindley and his team believed that they could build the basis of a class-leading platform, which could provide the basis of a new range of products with the 'flexible architecture' needed to accommodate their tripartite X120 aspirations.

The concept therefore involved completely new front-end and rear-end structures, incorporating the necessary crushable sections needed for impact test compliance (including the potential to meet the tougher US rear-end tests), but with the exterior panels designed as bolt-on units, which could be plastic, steel or a combination of the two. Furthermore, building on some of the opportunities for sourcing that the new relationship with SAIC offered, there were some thoughts about using normally exotic and price-excluding materials like magnesium for seat frames and structural cross-beams. (China is the world's biggest source of magnesium, making the use of this exotic and extremely lightweight metal a more realistic prospect in the present day than it might otherwise have been.)

Lee Mitchell was one of the designers who worked on the X120 project and this is one his renderings for the X121 Midget. (Lee Mitchell)

ANOTHER NEW START

Another view of the clay scale model of X121. Sadly, the MG Midget project was an early casualty of budget constraints late in 2004. (MG Rover Group)

come opportunities for small but welcome improvements to visual stance, road-holding and side-impact performance, allowing for better cockpit room as well as the latest safety paraphernalia, such as side airbags.

The front and rear track of the MG *TF* were 1,404mm and 1,410mm respectively; this would have increased by 46mm at the front (to 1,450mm) and by 90mm at the rear (to 1,500mm) for all models, Midget included. Where the really significant changes came, however, was with the wheelbase and overhangs: the latter, of course, was possible to achieve flexibly through the use of the all-new front and rear sections, as already mentioned. The basic MG *TF* has a wheelbase – effectively the distance between the centrelines of the front and rear wheel centres – of 2,375mm; for the X121 Midget, this would have increased by just 12mm to 2,387mm, and for the closely related X122/123 Roadster/Coupé the increase was greater, by a full 100mm to 2,475mm.

In addition to new exterior bodywork all round, X120 offered opportunities to improve on the variety of powertrains, trim and equipment, including the possibility of an all-new Z-fold roof for X121; this could have been co-engineered with the German company Edscha, which rather rashly issued a press release back in January 2001 to tell the world that they 'have landed the order for the development and series delivery of the convertible roof system for the Roadster successor of the MG*F*'.

All three variants – X121, 122 and 123 – were to have a wider track than that of the *TF*, which by now was not only an unusually petite car, judged by the standards of its newer competitors, but was also tight in terms of packaging. With slightly greater width would

For both X121 and X122/X123, the increases were intended to accommodate powertrain options that had not been on offer back in the days when the original PR3/MG*F* had been planned and yet were still denied the *TF*; the modest-seeming 12mm extra for the 'Midget' would have been enough to 'package protect' for a possible turbocharged K-Series 4-cylinder variant (perhaps even a high-revving 1.4 turbo, as envisaged a dozen years earlier with the ADC PR3 running prototype?), while the more substantial increases proposed for the larger cars would have allowed fitment at last of the

Sitting just above the Midget in the three-model 'X120' family would have been the MG *TF* replacement, X122. This concept sketch shows what looks like a more expensive car with crisp styling. (MG Rover Group)

ANOTHER NEW START

The 'California' licence plate gives a clue to MG Rover's hopes and ambitions for their sports car range: sadly it was not to be. (MG Rover Group)

The tail-lamps in this rear view of an X122 concept sketch by Lee Mitchell have an echo of the MGB.

KV6 engine, considerably extending the reach of the MG sports car into rival territory.

Perhaps even more intriguing was the matter of the overall lengths, since in order to achieve a more compact size, the front and rear overhangs of the X121 were to be reduced from those of the *TF* by 150mm at both ends, resulting in a car fully 300mm (or almost an imperial foot) shorter than the *TF*. Coupled with the slightly longer wheelbase and greater track, this meant that the Midget would have had quite different proportions from those of the *TF*, more in line with target competitors, seen at the time as including the Smart Roadster and Ford StreetKa. As far as positioning of X121 was concerned, the product concept called for it to be 'the spirit of the MG Midget, reborn', offering the proposition of 'the most affordable sports car on the market' and a role as the '*TF*'s younger brother'.

Eventually the MG Rover team opted for this design for further development as the basis for 'X122'. (MG Rover Group)

ANOTHER NEW START

LEFT: As with X121, a four-tenths scale clay model was made to represent the X122 'medium roadster' concept. A longer wheelbase and changes to the rear platform would have allowed the engine range to have expanded to include a KV6-engined version if needed, although a turbocharged 4-cylinder K-Series was also feasible. (MG Rover Group)

The proposed X122 MG roadster would have had a longer wheelbase that X121 and, in turn, the MG TF from which both were to have been derived. (MG Rover)

The shorter rear overhang for the Midget would have necessitated various packaging compromises, including the obvious one of luggage capacity, but in order to address this Lindley and his team envisaged a different kind of roof structure using lift-out panels instead of the traditional but space-hungry folding roof mechanism of the *TF*. Some sketches for X121 even showed flowing rear roof buttresses similar to those on the Lotus Elise, which also has a lift-out roof panel. Meanwhile, the X122 and X123 would have kept broadly the same front and rear overhangs as the *TF*, meaning that overall length of these two variants would have gone up by the same 100mm as the wheelbase.

Target rivals for X122 and X123 were seen as the Mazda MX-5 and Toyota MR2 in the case

LEFT: Sitting above X122 would have been a coupé derivative, 'X123', intended to go up against the Audi TT and Porsche Boxster. V6 power was an obvious attraction, although the KV6 would always have struggled to match the kind of power outputs available to the German rivals. (MG Rover Group)

The X123 coupé could have been a really striking rival to the established Audi TT and Porsche Boxster, as these concept sketches by Lee Mitchell show; sadly the KV6-powered coupe was the first casualty of cost-cutting within the X120 project.

ANOTHER NEW START

The 'chassis buck' of X120 survives at Longbridge, even if it does not look likely to turn a wheel again in the near future.

of the roadster, and the Audi TT, Mazda RX-8 and Nissan 350Z in the case of the coupé; the product plan described the goal of X122 to be an 'affordable Porsche Boxster', while that of the X123 coupé was to be 'an affordable Porsche 911', both obviously building on the mid-engined selling point.

The MG TF interior packaging certainly offered scope for improvement. Even the latest MG TF variants of 2010, while hardly poor in this regard, have received some minor criticisms from the press when compared with newer-generation rivals. Among the obvious sources of criticism about the MG TF, and equally valid in relation to the MGF, had been the fact that a driver tended to sit 'on' rather than 'in' an MG TF, a consequence in part of the Metro architecture that had been used.

Whereas a driver of, say, an MGB tends to sit much lower and laid-back longitudinally, with the steering wheel and gear lever falling nicely to hand, the driver of an MGF or MG TF has a driving experience rather more akin to that of a small conventional car. Another criticism of the MGF/TF is the alignment of the steering column, which is not dead-centre with the driver's seat; while not a problem for everyone, this is less than ideal and can prove slightly uncomfortable over long distances for certain sizes of driver.

As a result, a great deal of work was undertaken to develop the cockpit packaging for X120, using a special seating buck that used modified facia and interior parts taken from the MG TF, Rover 75 and other potential sources. Lindley and his team used the services of a local university where students undertook ergonomic 'clinics' to evaluate the effectiveness of the proposed changes, which included a lower cowl height, more adjustable and better aligned steering wheel, and repositioned

Experiments took place to upgrade the facia for the proposed X120 family: the idea was that clever use of trim components and optional instrument cowlings would help to distinguish the various Midget, roadster and upmarket coupé versions.

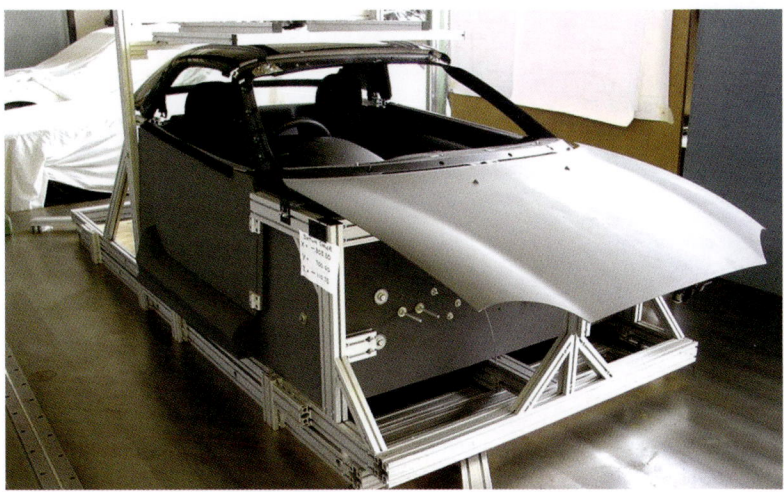

This is the initial X120 interior buck, which shows how various parts had been moved from the original MG *TF* layouts in an effort to improve the ergonomics. (MG Rover Group)

gear lever and handbrake, all designed to improve overall comfort, meet the latest design standards and market requirements, and of course, above all, to render a sportier driving experience.

The outcome of the ergonomic trial proved very rewarding: some 90 per cent of the testers reported that they were in favour of the proposed changes. In order to differentiate the variants further in the eyes of customers, there were proposals to use a common facia armature but to dress it differently according to model: different surface finishes and textures, a variety of fixtures and fittings, a range of instrument cluster binnacles and centre console arrangements would have allowed a pecking order with the X123 coupé at the luxury end. Similarly, different interior door casings were schemed out, with a more 'basic' specification for the Midget.

As well as improvements to the packaging in the central 'tub', the X120 programme also envisaged, as touched on earlier, all-new front and rear sections, varied as necessary to suit the Midget and Large Roadster/Coupé variants. At the front, all non-crushable components just forward of the front bulkhead were to be packaged behind a common line to allow proper crash performance in the modular nose; this allowed opportunities to make significant improvements over the *TF* in terms of the packaging of such components as the optional air-conditioning condenser, which, in the case of the *TF*, intrudes into the left-hand footwell.

Building on his experiences at Lotus, Dave Lindley also envisaged a top-exiting radiator, which would have both cooling and aerodynamic benefits. In order to meet changes in EU and US vehicle safety legislation, in

Some of the altered positions of controls inside the X120 buck – such as instruments, steering wheel and gearlever position – can be made out in this photo.

X Marks the Spot: The MG Rover Group Prototype Codes

MG	Rover	Project
X10	RD10	Rover 75 and MG ZT
X11	RD11	Rover 75 Tourer and MG ZT-T
X12	RD12	Rover 75 V8 and MG ZT-260 (V8)
X13	N/A	MG ZT-T 260 (V8)
X14	RD14	RDX14 was the 2004 Model Year facelift of RD10 and X10 with EU4 engine and mild facelift
X15	RD15	RDX15 was the 2004 Model Year facelift of RD11 and X11, as per RDX14. X15 was also the given name for the Bonneville MG ZT-T, but this was less official.
N/A	RD16	Rover 75 long-wheelbase
N/A	RD16C	Proposed facelift (improved interior and exterior) of 75 platform for SAIC; 'style reviewed' at the same time as RDX130 and 140 in March 2004, with the hierarchy of SAIC in attendance
X20	RD20	Rover 45 and MG ZS
RDX21		2004 Model Year facelift of the Rover 45 and MG ZS
X30	RD30	Rover 25 and MG ZR
RDX31		2004 Model Year facelift of the Rover 25 and MG ZR
X40	N/A	Project code for the MG *F* as inherited from Rover Group
X50	N/A	Improved MG *TF* platform

One of the projects that never saw the light of day: this is a sketch by Jonathan Gould for RDX130. (ARUP)

One of the MG projects that did not get an 'X' number was 'Project Viking', which was an exercise based on an all-aluminium Lea Francis concept masterminded by Professor Jim Randle. No production MG came from this idea but it did help inform the thinking behind the Morgan Aero. (Jim Randle)

MG	Rover	Project
RDX60		Project for a new medium car to replace the MG ZS and Rover 45
RDX65		Proposed tourer version of RDX60
X70	N/A	Proposed MG sports car with front engine, rear-wheel drive
X71	N/A	Coupé version of X70
X72	N/A	Proposal for a doorless open sports car based on X70 platform (but with same wheelbase as X90, see below)
X80	N/A	Proposed MG 'supercar' based on Qvale Mangusta
X81	N/A	Proposed MG 'supercar' roadster derived from X80
X90	N/A	Shorter-wheelbase version of X70 as a kind of front engine, rear-wheel drive MG Midget
RDX100		Proposed small Rover as a possible Rover 25/MG ZR replacement (packaging and styling only and a review of platform suitability)
N/A	RD110	Rover 'CityRover', joint venture with Tata
X120	N/A	Proposed family of mid-engined sports cars derived from MG *TF* basis
X121	N/A	MG Midget derived from MG *TF* platform
X122	N/A	New MG Roadster derived from MG *TF* platform
X123	N/A	New MG Coupé derived from MG *TF* platform
RDX130		Evolution of RDX60 in five-door hatchback form (see RD16C above)
RDX140		Evolution of RDX60 as a four-door saloon

Other projects from this period included the 'TCV' and 'HPD200' concepts, and 'Project Viking'.

particular that related to passive pedestrian safety, such new features as break-away wiper spindles, crushable or break-away light units and other passive safety measures were explored, although not developed in great detail as part of the initial studies.

The four-star European NCAP test score for the *TF* had been highly commendable, but Lindley and his team had no desire to rest on their laurels, and so part of the X120 mission was to increase the new sports cars to the five-star standard. In order to achieve this, the benefits of the latest software were used when designing the new front and rear structures, and finite element analysis showed that X120 was well on the way to meeting both European and North American NCAP test compliance.

Although the suspension changes for the *TF* had brought many benefits, there were still some compromises. As part of the comprehensive fresh set of improvements, X120 would have had a front axle with new double wishbones, modified rear axle, electro-hydraulic power-assisted steering with a subframe mounted rack (giving improved steering feel and tuneable side force steer characteristics) and a significantly greater range of wheel travel, allowing better ride and handling compromises. A chassis simulator was built and at the time of writing still survives (see photo on page 168).

The case for the Midget was an emotionally compelling one and everyone involved, both on the programme itself and around the periphery, would have loved to see a British MG Midget on sale. The key obstacle, inevitably, was cost – in particular balancing a realistic price point with a need to recoup the investment needed – and barring special factors like Chinese sourcing and an improved business position for the company as a whole, it was always going to be hard to extend the case for X120 in the direction of X121.

Without the core product, X122, none of the programme would be viable, and so efforts focused in the summer of 2004 on the Large Roadster, with or without the coupé option, and with options of steel or composite bodywork. By September 2004, when there was a presentation on X120, costs were in the range of £60 to £80 million, a small sum to a company like Ford, BMW or Honda, but still big money to a company like MG Rover Group, which was embarking on its cost-cutting exercise, known as 'Project Drive', aimed at reducing the production costs of existing product. Set against that background, the work on X120 was reluctantly put on hold to await better times. Sadly, however, the optimism of 2000 was shortly to be badly undermined.

Whereas the MG GT Coupé survives as a demonstration of how the MG *TF* might have evolved under MG Rover ownership, all that survives of the X120 project, apart from the many sketches, is the test mule seen in the accompanying photographs. Beyond the lack of funds, there was also a nagging feeling that spending so much money on re-engineering the *TF* platform might not have been as logical as starting afresh, as Rob Oldaker summed up: 'In the end, we would have been spending an awful lot of money on what amounted to a very clever repackage'. Under present-day management, the current financial constraints versus those faced by the Phoenix Venture Holdings management are not really comparable ...

END OF THE LINE FOR THE PHOENIX CONSORTIUM

Seen from the perspective of early 2000, the prospects of the Phoenix Consortium making a long-term success of the Longbridge operation were not given much credence by many in the media; indeed the apparent hostility of some of the news press appeared to be aimed at being able to say 'we told you so' if everything went wrong. Arguably the media had given Jon Moulton more tacit support, on the back of his undoubted corporate successes in many business arenas, whereas John Towers and his colleagues were inevitably portrayed as yesterday's men, even if they had a track record in the car manufacturing business. However you would have been hard pressed to find a pessimist outside Longbridge's 'Q' Gate in those early days.

At first MG Rover Group seemed to be doing so many things right – the MG saloons and the MG *TF* model were good examples – but all the time that these successes were being achieved, the company was continuing to eat in to the BMW dowry. Key to a long-term future, as we have seen, was supposed to be a strong partnership with another company,

Near the end of MG *TF* production in 2005 came a much anticipated improvement: the substitution of a proper glass rear window for the plastic one offered hitherto. (MG Rover Group)

ANOTHER NEW START

MG Rover Group offered a very extensive palette of optional paint colours under the 'Monogram' programme: this MG *TF* is shown in 'Chromescent Shot Silk', a paint finish whose colour 'flips' dependent on the light and the position of the observer. (MG Rover Group)

By the beginning of 2005, when the financial problems of MG Rover Group's parent company were coming to a head, arguably the best evolution of the MG *TF* up to that point appeared, with a new hood, wheels, brakes and suspension settings. (MG Rover Group)

ANOTHER NEW START

but for various reasons none of the on–off engagements was ever fully consummated.

By the beginning of 2005 matters were becoming increasingly desperate as Phoenix began selling chunks of the estate, business and intellectual property in order to keep the business afloat. At the time, negotiations were continuing with a consortium of Chinese businesses led by SAIC (since 2004) and Nanjing Automotive (NAC), the latter as a 'junior partner'. As talks moved on, however, so the financial situation at Phoenix Ventures deteriorated, to the extent that it seemed highly likely that the company would become insolvent before any deal could be concluded.

The precise sequence of events, as well as their background, need not concern us here for reasons of space, but suffice to say that on 8 April 2005 the crisis came to tipping point and MG Rover Group and some of its associated businesses entered administration, with the appointment of PricewaterhouseCoopers (PwC) to take over the companies from their directors and begin the process of disposing of the company assets in the interest of the creditors.

SAIC, having stepped back from concluding a deal, doubtless felt in the strongest position, having bought intellectual design rights from Phoenix in the previous months, but it seems not to have reckoned with the tenacity of its erstwhile business partner, NAC, which soon entered the fray as a rival bidder for the remaining assets, including the production equipment and tooling at Longbridge. By just over a month after MG Rover Group went into administration, PwC said that there were at least twelve 'credible' bids, but it was not long before the number of realistic ones were reduced to a handful of 'contenders'.

SAIC formed an alliance with some key motor industry figures, including Martin Leach, former head of Ford's European operation, together with others under the umbrella of 'Magma Holdings', and for the time being appeared likely to be the leading contender of a trio of bidders that swiftly emerged as the three favourites. Second bidder in this top three was Nanjing Automotive, whose plans seemed similar to those of SAIC/Magma but involving less commitment to UK production. The third bidder was led by David James, a corporate troubleshooter best known for having been called in by the British government to revive the ill-fated Millennium Dome. James had been working with SAIC, but in mid-July he smartly switched to a solo bid as SAIC teamed up with Martin Leach. With a nod to MG history, James called his bid vehicle 'Project Kimber'.

The bidding process and analysis was over before the end of July. The winner was announced as NAC, which had bid a little over £50 million. NAC seemed almost taken aback by the success of the bid, a spokesman telling the *Oriental Morning Post* that they were 'surprised' by their success. Perhaps no less surprised was SAIC, who had reportedly underbid their rival and would now face the strange situation of owning the rights to a number of cars and powertrains (Rover 25, 75, K-Series and L-Series engines, bought from Phoenix in 2004 for £67 million) but not the equipment to build them, nor the prized 'MG' name.

The outcome of this bidding was arguably a muddle, although as both Nanjing and SAIC are ultimately owned by Chinese political bodies it was felt likely that a deal between the two would be brokered before long. Common sense would eventually prevail, but not before there had been the curious spectacle of the 'MG' and 'Rover' halves of the former business going their separate ways and following parallel evolutionary paths.

ANOTHER NEW START

Project Kimber

As the Phoenix Consortium crumbled, and with it the future of MG once more lurched into peril, a number of keen groups and alliances formed with a view to purchasing the remaining assets from the administrator. Some of these groups appeared more firmly anchored in the real world than others, although none of them lacked ambition. Some offered great ideas but no finance, others offered off-the-wall ideas and positive-sounding noises about finance that may or may not have been there in the background.

One of the more convincing bids had come from a group headed up by David James (Baron James of Blackheath from 2006), a high-profile figure and corporate troubleshooter whose eminence doubtless gave the bid an air of believability, realism and respectability. One of the lead figures behind the figurehead was Barrie Wills, whom we saw earlier as one of the principals involved in the Chapman-Arup team that took the MG*F* to Detroit shortly after MG Rover had been formed. Wills has a lifetime in the industry, and one of his more colourful episodes was the time he spent at De Lorean (some of which is told in the author's *Triumph TR7 – The Untold Story*, Crowood, 2008).

Once Nanjing had been successful in purchasing the manufacturing assets and MG name, James's team continued (under the banner of 'Project Kimber') with an impressive team of marketing people, engineers and designers. Project Kimber set out to buy the MG name from Nanjing, and at the same time to acquire the recently discontinued Smart Roadster tooling from Daimler-Chrysler, planning to set up shop at Coventry instead of Longbridge (later changed to South Wales) and possibly build both a mildly facelifted Smart Roadster and MG *TF* as part of a new MG range.

In the event, the process came to naught; Nanjing was not prepared to sell or licence the MG name at the level of finance and agreement on offer from Kimber, and so a deal was never done. For a while Project Kimber's attention turned towards licensing or acquiring the 'AC' name, and the facelifted 'MG Midget' based on a Smart Roadster was shown with 'AC Ace' badging. By 2008 the project appeared to have been abandoned altogether.

Although their main focus appears to have been an attempt to acquire the rights to Daimler-Chrysler's Smart Roadster and turn it into an 'MG Midget', the Project Kimber team also proposed to facelift the MG TF. (Barrie Wills)

chapter six

Eastern Promise

NANJING: THE BIRTH OF THE MODERN GENTLEMAN

With their bid accepted, the men from Nanjing did not take long to take stock of their new acquisition. Within weeks, fleets of lorries were coming in and out of the Longbridge site as machine tools and equipment were swiftly dismantled, crated up and shipped out to China in 4,000 standard shipping containers. Meanwhile, work got under way to build a brand new factory at Pukou, just across the Yangtze River from the city of Nanjing. Rob Oldaker remembers visiting the site of the factory just days before the opening ceremony, and thinking it looked as though it would never be ready – and yet in a matter of a weekend the site was completely transformed as if by magic.

Simultaneously, work continued to allow modestly facelifted versions of the last MG saloons, in particular the MG ZT (reincarnated as the MG 7), to be launched in China. The MG *TF* was proudly displayed at various Chinese events as China's first sports car, in a generally conservative nascent car market quite unused either to two-door or soft-top cars of any kind. Some work was done with Arup and its senior automotive designer, Jonathan Gould, to look at facelifts of both the MG *TF* and the MG ZT; Rob Oldaker remembers a session with Wang

Testing of the MG *TF* resumed. Here a prototype for the new Chinese market model is seen in Tulufan, China, during endurance testing in 2007. (NAC-MG)

Hong Baio of NAC-MG. However the MG *TF* proposals never moved forward. A similar joint venture proposed with the 'Great British Sports Car Company' also foundered, despite talk of grand ideas.

Nanjing Automobile Corporation (NAC) was proud of its status as China's oldest automotive business, dating from 1947 (before the Chinese Communist Revolution), and so 2007 was always destined to be a key date that the company would want to celebrate – and the Chinese have always been especially good at celebrations. The new owners of the celebrated British MG brand were also undoubtedly very proud of their acquisition of a slice of British 'automotive royalty', and proceeded to stage bold theatre at various events in mainland China. There has long been a fascination in Eastern markets (as elsewhere, of course) with what is perceived as 'Britishness', sometimes expressed with a vigour and appetite that can seem peculiar even to the British themselves,

As well as testing in extremes of temperature and humidity in China, the new MG *TF* was also subjected to essential testing in other countries, such as here at the Millbrook test circuit. (NAC-MG)

There was an excited media frenzy at the unveiling of the first Chinese-built MG cars. (NAC-MG)

The end of May 2007 saw a big party staged by NAC-MG at the Longbridge factory to celebrate the relaunch of the MG *TF* in the form of the limited-production MG *TF* LE500 – although it would be more than a year before any customers got their hands on one. (NAC-MG)

A few months later, MG *TF* production did restart, albeit in a modest way. These are pre-production cars with the older style nose cones. (NAC-MG)

EASTERN PROMISE

The MG *TF* assembly line at Longbridge in the autumn of 2007, now under Chinese ownership and using some components, such as the bodyshell, shipped in from China.

The MG *TF* production line under NAC management included the careful hand spraying and polishing of the paintwork to a very high standard. From 2008, however, bodyshells were shipped in fully painted.

EASTERN PROMISE

Professional services giant ARUP undertook some early consultancy work for NAC-MG, looking at possible future evolutionary paths for the MG *TF* in 2005–6. (ARUP)

At the time of ARUP's involvement, their senior automotive designer was Jonathan Gould: this is his interpretation of an MG Midget – perhaps a redux of X121 or, as suggested in some contemporary reports, an idea based on the MG ZR platform? (ARUP)

An exotic-looking concept for an MG coupé that has overtures of the classic Dino Ferrari. This sketch actually dates from MG Rover days. (ARUP)

EASTERN PROMISE

ARUP continued to contribute ideas to NAC-MG and the Great British Sports Car Company: this is another concept for an MG *TF* facelift. (ARUP)

and in the early days of Nanjing's ownership this enthusiasm certainly seemed to spill over into the eccentric. March 2007 saw the sixtieth anniversary of NAC and the company celebrated by unveiling the brand new factory at Pukuo.

Someone decided, without any advice from the small British enclave still at Longbridge, that MG now stood for 'Modern Gentleman' rather than the time-honoured 'Morris Garages', and several of the public outings for MG products at high-profile Chinese motor shows involved a galaxy of synthetic British themes, including the inevitable 'guardsmen' and the use of British landmarks as backdrops. The message that NAC treasured the British heritage of

One of the more modest proposals for a facelift of the MG *TF* from ARUP dating from the NAC period of MG ownership. (ARUP)

Note the Chinese-style licence plates on the front of this ARUP concept sketch for a possible future MG *TF*. SAIC is now in charge and has its own in-house design team, and so these ideas from the early days of NAC ownership are unlikely to reach fruition. (ARUP)

One of the changes to the MG *TF* LE500 is the new instrument display unit, with integral digital warning displays. The change was one that had been in the pipeline towards the end of MG Rover's existence.

The smooth nose profile of the MG *TF* LE500 (and the subsequent variants for 2008 onwards) features clear twin 'nostrils', a bold MG badge and a subtly revised front spoiler profile.

the MG marque was undoubtedly welcome, even if the impression in the UK was that their vision was slightly skewed. MG's new chief at Longbridge was Wang Hong Biao, and his neat appearance and good looks earned him the nickname of Humphrey Bogart.

NAC decided that their plans to rekindle manufacturing at Longbridge with a facelifted MG *TF* should benefit from a big launch. The MG clubs and international media all converged on Longbridge on 29 May 2007. Following a press conference led by Yu Jianwei, the assembled guests were invited to see the first orange MG *TF* LE500 driven out of the factory by Wang Hong Biao accompanied by the Leader of Birmingham City Council, Councillor Mike Whitby. There was no doubt about the excitement of the occasion, but despite the spectacle it would be some time before anyone would be able to get their hands on their own MG *TF* LE500 (see below).

The LE500 engineering work was driven through by a small team, listed by Ian Pogson as having a:

> day-to-day life of only a few UK engineers; about eight folk on the whole vehicle, a handful of Integration people, a few engine-testers and builders and very little else. There were only nineteen people building the cars throughout 2007 to 2009. A skeleton crew and they deserve credit.

For a while, Stadco remained part of the picture (and was involved in the discussions for a US venture) but eventually the projected volumes for the *TF* were reduced, and NAC decided instead to bring in bodies ready-built from China. All that remains at the time of writing in Longbridge's CAB2 building are a few gantries, part of the simple track and a handful of bodyshells.

SAIC: A NEW ERA BEGINS

We saw earlier how two rival Chinese companies variously cooperated and competed over first a deal with MG Rover Group and then ownership of the assets that were being liquidated. As both companies were ultimately owned by political institutions (SAIC is owned by the city of Shanghai, while NAC is owned by the government of Nanjing state), it was surely inevitable that eventually some form of rapprochement would be concluded; rivals building separate cars using similar but not totally interchangeable components was hardly a recipe for efficiency. The process of forging a union, however, would be delicate because of the intense regional rivalries involved.

At the end of July 2007, however, it was announced that SAIC and Yuejin, NAC's parent company, would begin work on closer cooperation and integration – code-words for a face-saving merger of the NAC and SAIC automotive businesses, with SAIC in the driving seat. Despite Nanjing's greater age, the younger SAIC was already a much larger player with two major cooperative ventures and ambitions to make more than a million vehicles per annum, and so the deal made sense. As SAIC was already firmly established in the UK with a team based at Ricardo's premises at Leamington Spa, the news was undoubtedly good from the perspective of a continuing MG design and engineering presence in the UK.

On 26 December 2007 a deal was announced that effectively saw SAIC take control of NAC. The Chairmen of SAIC and Yuejin – Hu Maoyuan and Wang Haoliang, respectively – signed the cooperation agreement in the People's Congress Hall in Beijing under the watchful eyes of the Chinese Vice Prime Minister and various civic dignitaries from Shanghai, Jiangsu Province and Nanjing's municipal government.

While the main priorities of the newly merged but as yet unintegrated SAIC and NAC understandably remained China-focused, progress with the MG TF at Longbridge was made as there was a lot of activity behind the scenes, working with suppliers, marketing, dealers, endurance testing of pre-production prototypes and fitting out the factory itself. Arguably the event in May 2007 had been somewhat premature, but by the summer of the following year the first customer cars were ready to come off the production lines. The official start of production was 1 August 2008, with the first cars delivered to showrooms a few weeks later.

In the meantime, SAIC began the process of consolidating its design and engineering facilities with those of NAC UK, starting with the relocation of the main SAIC UK Technical Centre (under David Lindley) from Leamington Spa to the former Longbridge Sales & Marketing block, accompanied by major IT investment to link Longbridge with the Chinese and South Korean technical centres and the subsequent move to a brand new studio for the SAIC UK design team, managed by Tony Williams, who had been a key member of the original MG Rover MG TF design team back in 2001–2.

For a while in 2007–8 there were tentative thoughts of a fairly thorough facelift of the MG TF, doubtless drawing upon the talents of the new team, although for understandable reasons the details of this work are not ready for disclosure at the time of writing. However, the world financial position did not prove conducive to such investment and so the visual changes were abandoned for the time being. Development on the suspension by the skilled chassis team, many of whom had been involved with the car since the early MGF days, was followed through, and the benefits seen on the MG TF 85th LE, described on pages 190–1.

By the end of 2009, therefore, the MG TF family comprised three distinct models: the MG TF135, the MG TF500 LE and the MG TF 85th LE.

2009 Colours (2010 continues MG TF135 colours)

MG TF500 LE
Six colours: Vibrant Orange (pearl); Intense Blue (metallic); Crystal White (pearl); Graphite Grey (Micatallic); Raven Black; Scorched Red.
MG TF135
Seven colours: Racing Green (metallic); Platinum Silver (metallic); Oceana Blue (Micatallic); Frost White; Radiant Red (pearl); Raven Black; Storm Grey (metallic).
MG TF 85th LE
Three colours: Intense Cassis (metallic); Ice White (metallic); Enigmatic Silver (metallic). Special stripes and decals, new Clarion stereo head unit, special gear knob, 'Twist of Pepper' alloy wheels finished in a colour called 'Liquid Boron'.

EASTERN PROMISE

Oklahoma! An American Diversion

An early action of NAC was to put in place a new management team to oversee the British part of their acquisition. Affairs in China were very definitely to be managed by a Chinese team. NAC was keen to exploit the Britishness of the MG name, but for the Western world they decided to appoint a team based at Longbridge to run 'MG Cars of Europe and North America'. At the head of this enterprise they recruited a larger-than-life American with a larger-than-life name, Duke Hale, late of Mitsubishi and Lotus Cars of North America.

Hale saw the MG job as a great challenge, and he also saw the US market as an obvious draw. Grand plans to re-enter the US market were conceived, but of course grand sales plans also need suitable product, and the MG *TF* was arguably not the easiest basis for this, even if it was the only one on offer. Undaunted, Hale and his team began to flesh out a plan to not only sell MG cars in the USA but to build them there too, using kits of parts flown in from China and the UK. A potential factory site was found

A friendly handshake at a ceremony in Oklahoma in July 2006 between NAC Chairman Yu Jianwei and MG Motors Chairman Duke Hale. A week later, some of those who had been present at this ceremony would be confused by mixed messages at a subsequent press conference in London. (Oklahoma Chamber of Commerce)

MG Motors of North America Inc issued this composite of sketches showing the proposed MG TF Coupé, which the new Ardmore factory was intended to build. Stadco, who had acquired the assets of the defunct Mayflower body manufacturing business, was the intended partner in this venture. (Stadco)

for 'MG Motors Corporation' in the unlikely seeming location of Ardmore Air Park in Ardmore, Oklahoma, where there could be significant tax grants and the possibility of a deal to site the factory on land owned by the Chickasaw Indian Nation. A design and research facility was proposed at Norman, Oklahoma.

The car they chose to build was surprisingly not the existing MG *TF* roadster but a production version of the MG GT, which had been further developed with the assistance of Stadco. At a ceremony hosted by various civic dignitaries and investors in Oklahoma on 12 July 2006, Yu Jianwei was quoted as stating:

> Nanjing Motors is fully committed to the restoration of the MG brand to markets around the world. This will be the key component of Nanjing's effort to join leading automakers in the manufacture and sale of high quality, high character automobiles. As we finalize the installation of MG assembly lines in our new Nanjing plant, we are pleased to confirm plans to build the *TF* roadster once again in Longbridge, UK, and the new *TF* Coupé at a completely new facility in Ardmore, Oklahoma, USA. We will have even more to say about our plans during our press conference next Monday, July 17, at the London Motor Show.

In the accompanying press release, it was claimed that approximately 550 jobs would be created in Oklahoma, including headquarters operations, assembly operations, parts and distribution operations, and research and development. The statement concluded, 'The company expects to start construction of the Ardmore assembly facility early in 2007 with production to start by the third quarter of 2008'. There was also some expansive talk from Hale about the coming range of MG 'sedans', which he suggested could be brought in whole from China to support an MG dealer network.

Five days later, the British media turned out in some force to hear Yu Jianwei expound the next part of this grand plan. Present in the audience were a number of newspaper heavyweights whose interest in MG affairs was noteworthy: not many of them would have been seen at a similar press conference for most other car makers, but then the ongoing MG Rover saga still helped sell newspapers. To everyone's surprise, the Oklahoma project was

Alias software had been used to produce this 3D rendering of the proposed MG TF *Coupé, which had clearly evolved some way from the original Peter Stevens 'MG GT' we saw earlier. (Stadco)*

described as 'an idea' by Yu Jianwei. My own notes, transcribed from the simultaneous translation of the NAC Chairman's answers, record:

> We plan to have two bases – possibly three, depending upon the needs – but certainly Nanjing and Longbridge. On 12th July we held a press conference in Oklahoma to sign a letter of intent. So we might have three bases, but that is a thought; we have only signed a memorandum of understanding in Oklahoma.

This certainly seems to have come as a bit of a surprise to some of the people who had been present at the ceremony in Oklahoma a week earlier. In the event, the 'idea' never went much further. Little was heard until 28 March 2007, when R. Marc Nuttle of Oklahoma Global Motors, LLC refuted a press report that the deal was dead. Even so, before long it was: Wes Stucky, President of Ardmore Development Authority, confirmed as much to the author in late 2009: 'Close that chapter – Nanjing Auto was merged into Shanghai Auto. The project is dead.' Will MG cars ever be sold in North America again? We'll just have to wait and see, but perhaps the MG *6* of 2010 augurs well …

Key Events, 2005–10

Date	Event
2005	
22 July	NAC acquires the assets of the MG Rover Group and Powertrain Ltd
2006	
22 February	NAC signs a 33-year lease with St Modwen Properties, owners of the Longbridge site
10 March	NAC-MG Project approved by China's National Development and Reform Commission
27 March	NAC-MG Project's grand foundation stone laid in Nanjing Pukou New & High Technology Industry Development Zone
12 July	Ceremony in Oklahoma ostensibly to announce a deal to build MG in the USA
17 July	NAC press conference in London
13 October	NAC-MG Project sign a supply agreement with British car parts supplier Stadco
November	Roewe 750 shown at Beijing Auto Show with KV6 engine produced at SAIC's Baoshan engine plant
2007	
27 March	Sixtieth Anniversary of NAC; NAC unveils a new factory at Pukou in China, where MG7 (derived from MG ZT) is to be built. A British Racing Green MG *TF* assembled at Pukou is shown as being the first *TF* built in China
29 May	Longbridge inauguration event and 'official' relaunch of MG *TF*. In China, MG is said to stand for 'Modern Gentleman'
27 July	Cooperative deal announced between SAIC and Yuejin (parent company of NAC) to herald joint working and integration
28 September	Nanjing MG officially launches the MG *7* series in China. Versions feature engines derived from K4 and KV6
19 November	Guangzhou Motor Show. Launch of the MG3 SW (derived from Rover Streetwise) and MG *TF* CVT for China
26 December	SAIC takes control of NAC
2008	
20 April	MG and Roewe products both showcased by SAIC at the Beijing Auto Show; MG shows MG *TF*, MG *3* SW and MG *7*, while Roewe shows its new 550 alongside the 750
8 May	NAC MG UK Ltd announces the appointment of a new chairman, He Xiao Qing, in place of Wang Hong Biao, who had led the board of the Longbridge-based company since it was set up in 2005. It is also announced that MG *TF* LE500 production will begin in August; the new Chairman says, 'I am delighted to be in a position to talk about a launch date for the *TF* LE500 following a process of planning, reorganization, active quality improvements and parts optimization that we recognize resulted in frustration for our stakeholders. We are now fully focused on bringing our hard work to fruition.'

EASTERN PROMISE

Date	Event
1 August	MG *TF* LE500 production officially starts at Longbridge
2009	
8 January	NAC MG UK Ltd changes name to MG Motor UK Ltd
3 March	Completion of the move of the main SAIC Motor UK Technical Centre (SMTC UK) from Leamington Spa to Longbridge (design studio remains off-site until end of year) with an investment of £2.7 million
24 April	MG Motor UK Ltd is the primary sponsor of the Royal Windsor MG Heritage Festival event, at which the MG *TF* 85th LE is unveiled
15 May	Three versions of MG *TF* on sale: *TF* 135, *TF* LE500 and *TF* 85th LE
23 November	Production version of MG *6* (derived from the Roewe 550) launched at Guangzhou Auto Show in China, with a restyled MG badge and a reference to 'Morris Garages'
2010	
March	Production begins of 2010 Model Year MG *TF*; key difference is change to larger door mirrors to meet EEC legislation, and standard fit of 'twist of pepper' wheels formerly exclusive to LE 85th LE
April	MG 'Zero' concept car unveiled at Beijing Auto show. SAIC confidently talk of new MG range in coming years
21 May 2010	The last 2010 model year MG *TF* (finished in Ice White, and bearing chassis number SDPRDHBKCAD001156) comes off the assembly line at MG Birmingham (see photo on page 192)

The simpler 'nostrils' of the 2007–10 MG *TF* as seen on the MG *TF* LE500, *TF* LE 85th and here on the 2009 *TF* 135, harks back not only to the original MG*F* but also to the first efforts towards the first MG *TF* back in 2001, and as seen on the MG*F* XPower 500. The 2010 *TF* has larger door mirrors. (MG Motor)

EASTERN PROMISE

The cockpit of the 2009 MG *TF* is neat and compact, and especially with the optional leather trim is a pleasant place to be, even if the links to the 1995 MG*F* remain apparent. (MG Motor)

According to Ian Pogson, the MG magic remains part of the special appeal of the latest MG *TF* models:

> One of the things which distances the *TF* 85th from the Mazda is not the budget or engineering, but the fact that any customer can and does contact the Programme Manager directly, seeing me at shows and giving talks to clubs and other fans.

This level of personal service and enthusiasm was part of the spirit of MG as long ago as the 1930s, when customers were welcome at the factory at Abingdon:

> Through the 'Programme Manager's Factory Tours' both customer and MG Motor Manufacturing employee have had the chance to meet one another. Friendly banter has been exchanged across the assembly track, legs have been pulled by the Body Drop and both parties are left with a human face to customer and vehicle assembly worker.

Curiously, the Chinese market MG *TF*, which sold (in low numbers) at a premium price in a market where genuine sports cars are rare, retains the Peter Stevens-style nose with the horizontal grille 'vanes'. Production of the Chinese-market MG *TF* was suspended in 2009. (SAIC)

FUTURE TRAJECTORIES

Writing this conclusion in the summer of 2010, it is too soon to talk about life after the MG *TF*. It is somewhat remarkable – and a true testament to the work that has been done ever since the first PR3 running prototype turned a wheel nearly twenty years ago – that the same basic formula is still with us. It is pretty indisputable

EASTERN PROMISE

The first new MG since the MG XPower SV is the MG 6 (main picture), previewed in April 2009 and launched in production form the following November. Inset is the MG Zero concept, shown in April 2010, with its novel see-through Union Flag roof. Initially for China only, the MG6 is scheduled for production at Birmingham from the end of 2010, with a production version of the MG Zero likely to follow. (SAIC)

that the MG*F* and the MG *TF* that followed were both good-looking and brilliantly conceived true sports cars, of which their creators can rightly be proud. None of these cars was perfect, but all were cleverly conceived, developed with incredibly small budgets and launched despite so many obstacles along the way.

The fact that the MG *TF* – suitably evolved – should still be on sale in 2010 is a sign that, despite the presence of some very worthy younger rivals, developed with much larger budgets, the little MG sports car still has a lot going for it. It would be naïve, however, to imagine that this situation could remain static forever: changes in legislation, production requirements, customer expectations as well as new hardware and manufacturing techniques

If anyone doubted that MG had no future after the *TF*, the launch of the new MG 6 saloon at the end of 2009 showed that a new chapter is opening up for the marque, with a new black and chrome take on the classic octagonal badge.

EASTERN PROMISE

The New MG *TF* Limited Editions: *TF* LE500 and *TF* 85th LE

The decision to relaunch the MG *TF* in the form of a limited edition special was entirely understandable; as we have seen, 'limited editions' have long been a feature of both the MG*F* and the MG *TF*, and in fact had been used as marketing aids with MG cars since the 1960s. The new version of the MG *TF* is very similar in specification to the last of the MG Rover era cars, with the exception of a new instrument cluster (already under development before the 2005 collapse) and a new grille shape at the front that does away with the central grille vane and brings the appearance a little closer to that of the original MG*F*. Limited editions are often specially packaged with a number of features normally marketed separately as optional extras, and the first new NAC-MG MG *TF* for UK sale was no exception.

The MG *TF*500 LE – named for the fact that just 500 cars would be built – came as standard with a factory-fitted hardtop, air-conditioning, leather seat facings, a rear 'parking distance control' system and a high-specification sound system. Also setting the new car apart were some bold new exclusive colours, in particular the orange seen in many of the press photos, and some dark and moody graphite-colour eleven-spoke 16-inch alloy wheels (or 'shadow chrome' instead with some colours). At the price the *TF*500 was very well equipped, although some in the media questioned the wisdom

Seen outside the Longbridge Visitor Centre is one of the MG TF LE500 Press demonstrators in the distinctive 'Vibrant Orange' (Pearl) paint and contrasting black wheels that help set the LE500 apart from other TFs. Other colours available for the LE500 were 'Intense Blue' (Metallic); 'Crystal White' (Pearl); 'Graphite Grey' (Micatallic); 'Raven Black' or 'Scorched Red'.

of pricing the car close to that of a more basic but younger Mazda MX-5. The engine in the new car is a 135 horsepower version of the updated engine that is variously referred to as the N-Series, but to all intents and purposes is a reworked K-Series that now meets Euro-IV emissions targets and addresses some of the past service issues.

Following in the wake of the *TF*500 LE and the standard *TF*135, a further limited edition was launched in 2009 to celebrate the eighty-fifth anniversary of the marquee. This model benefited from a great deal of suspension work that should eventually transfer across to the rest of the *TF* range. Phil Turner, one of the key members of the MG*F* and MG *TF* chassis team right from the PR3 handover, explains some of the changes that were made for the *TF*85th LE:

> Ever since the MG Rover days I've been keen to follow the mid-engine philosophy of having different wheels front and rear. Before we had different tyre sizes but a common rim size, but now we've changed the wheels so there are 6.5 inch rims on the front and 7.5 inch on the back; that helps to make the tyres work better in a mid-engined application.

The MG TF LE 85th edition is available in a choice of three colour schemes: 'Intense Cassis', 'Ice White' and 'Enigmatic Silver'. (MG Motor)

EASTERN PROMISE

This kind of thing costs money, as two sets of tools (from supplier Rimstock) are involved for the wheels, but under SAIC the necessary funds were made available.

The style of these new wheels is known as 'Twist of Pepper' (and the colour 'Liquid Boron') and they were styled by Peter Andrews, a long-term MG designer, who also is responsible for those on the LE500. According to Ian Pogson,

> the wheels have only one known detractor in all the hundreds of people I have spoken to. So he was clearly wrong, or did not understand the question! Even the colour (Liquid Boron) is special; as with LE wheels, another fine creation from Rimstock of Birmingham. These wheels can also be seen on MG 6.

But there were other less visible improvements too:

> One of the other major changes is that we're putting Bilstein mono-tube dampers on the car in place of the standard twin-tube dampers; they are quite a bit more expensive, but they're what Lotus use exclusively on their cars, such as the Exige. The main thing is that you are able to have a much bigger piston, basically, which allows more oil to flow through and allows much more scope for valve setting. The damping force is the pressure times the area and if you've got a bigger area, then less pressure will develop. We think it greatly improves the ride-handling compromise.

Another big change is to the roll bars:

> The front roll bar is twice as stiff as the old one and we've increased the rate of the rear one as well. The anti-roll bar link – that is the link that connects the anti-roll bar to the lower arm – has changed from a rubber bushed item to a ball-jointed link; it cost us more, but Alan Phillips [senior chassis engineer for MG F and MG TF], the main man, is convinced he can tell the difference ... The overall roll stiffness of the car is up by 45 per cent, which is a huge jump really.

The anti-roll bar link came from TRW and the anti-roll bars themselves from Eibach, as China could not supply on time in this instance.

Ian Pogson sums up how the changes have transformed the latest TF on the track, which also rides a little lower than the standard car:

> The difference is – when you drive this car ... well,

Distinctive 'Twist of Pepper' alloy wheels feature on the MG TF 85th LE – similar wheels were also shown on the MG 6 premiered at the Guangzhou Motor Show in November 2009, and were offered in 2010 on the standard TF 135 models. (MG Motor)

> Alan's taken me around Bruntingthorpe in the dry, at the limit of handling with maximum grip, and at MIRA in the wet on the high speed bowl, with minimum 'mu' [friction co-efficient]. The difference is that if you are a clown in a TF and you go beyond your and the car's limit, enter into a roundabout and at that transition point where you set up your exit and then go – particularly if you're going straight on – a regular TF will smack you as if shouting 'please don't do that, Ian!' – it is a mid-engined car and physics takes over. But with this car it is more considerate – it sort of strokes you and says more gently 'don't do that, Ian'; it is much gentler and it is more of a 'sashay' through the exit than a snap. It is amazing and, as an observer, you can see the difference; even stood away from the car, you can see Al do his thing.

Externally, the unique colours and decals set the MG TF 85th apart, as Pogson explains:

> The 85th features decals which are the most complex set of such adornments on any production car. Sourced from GSM of Brecon, Wales, this is the same material and supplier used by BMW at Cowley. There are fifteen pieces in the decal set, tested to a Honda standard for adhesion and abrasion resistance. The style has spawned a host of lookalikes and imitators and may be repeated on future models. Tony Mortimer applied all of them to all cars and Kevin Fisher allegedly engineered them.

EASTERN PROMISE

will eventually mean that, in due course, a new MG sports car will be needed. The fact that SAIC successfully launched a very attractive new mid-range MG, the MG 6, at the Guangzhou Motor Show in November 2009, followed by the MG Zero small car concept at Beijing in April 2010, and has spoken confidently of production starting at Longbridge in 2010, is another very positive sign, as is the return to the old 'Morris Garages' name, almost bringing the MG story full circle to where we came in at the beginning of this book.

Some of the clever past ideas discussed here may well inform the decision-making processes that help to form that new sports car, or it may be something completely different: all we can be certain of at this stage is that there are many talented people involved in shaping MG's new destiny, and there is no shortage of new ideas: nor is the company as cash-constrained as it has often been. As already confirmed by SAIC itself, a new MG sports car is undoubtedly part of this new journey. Whatever form this next generation of MG sports cars may take, however, one thing remains certain: the MGF and the MG TF have rightly earned their prime positions at the pinnacle of more than eighty-six illustrious years of MG history.

After a break in production over the winter of 2009/10, the spring of 2010 saw production of a batch of 150 MG TF models for the new 'model year', distinguished mainly by the slightly larger door mirrors and the fitment (on 115 of the 150) of the 'Twist of Pepper' wheels first seen on the 85th Limited Edition. The main priority at 'MG Birmingham' (as Longbridge has become) is preparing for a new generation of MG cars, heralded by the MG 6.

Fifteen years span the gap between these two cars: the red MGF, affectionately known as 'Old Number One' (not to be confused with the car built by Cecil Kimber in 1925) bears chassis number 251 (a tradition derived from the old MG Abingdon telephone switchboard number); the white 2010 model year MG TF is SDPRDHBKCAD001156. Is the white car also the last MG TF? It is too early to tell, although significant changes – for example, day-time running lights and new supplies of key components – would be needed for a 2011 MG TF to become reality... (MG Motor)

chapter seven

MG Clubs and Specialists

THE MG FAMILY

From the early days of the MGF, Rover Group recognized that there was a large and loyal band of MG enthusiasts – either existing or yet to be recruited – who were worthy of support from the factory. In the planning of MG franchises, the brand management team spoke enthusiastically of dealers combining new and old MG sales, or even selling ranges of sports cars from multi-franchise sites. In practice, what happened in most cases was that an MG franchise was 'bolted on' to an existing but worthy Rover Group franchise.

MGF birthday parties have been held at the Heritage Motor Museum at Gaydon, Warwickshire, over a number of years; this is the first one in 1996. Each MGF owner at the event was given a miniature first birthday cake, suitably iced with MGF logos. (Rover Group)

MG CLUBS AND SPECIALISTS

Various celebrities have been associated with MG*F* and MG *TF* ownership. Anthea Turner, for example, had her MG*F* specially refinished in a classic MG green as part of a short-lived venture between MG Cars and British Motor Heritage. (Rover Group)

What was different, however, was the encouragement and support of the enthusiastic ownership experience, and for a few years the parent company even bankrolled some quite lavish 'birthday parties' for the MG*F* at the Heritage Motor Centre at Gaydon. Key guest at such events was usually Gerry McGovern, whose seminal role in the design of the MG*F* gave him star quality. In later years, particularly once MG was devoid of the deep pockets of an indulgent Bavarian parent, responsibility for the MG*F* (later to embrace the *TF* too) events was assumed by the MG*F* Register. Many firm friendships were forged through these events and a great 'MG family' feeling fostered that built upon the existing strong camaraderie inherent in the MG Car Club, the MG Owners' Club and the MG*F* Register amongst other groups

While a new MG *TF* will come with a factory warranty, it goes without saying that anyone who wants to own and run an older MG should consider approaching one of the excellent array of specialist MG groups that cater for the MG*F* and MG *TF* ranges. There are a number of acknowledged weaknesses in the older generations of cars – mostly either fixed or fixable nowadays – and it makes obvious good sense to tap into the wealth of knowledge that exists, some of it found the hard way through experience.

That is not to say that an older MG*F* or *TF* is especially likely to be a liability; these are generally excellent cars, which can be run on an everyday basis with reasonable care and attention, but as some of the older specimens lie at the lower end of the financial spectrum, it is inevitable that some will have been subjected to rather less care and nurturing than an MG sports car deserves. In general, sound advice would be to join one of the relevant clubs – the MG Car Club and the MG Owners' Club are the two largest organizations, and both have excellent reputations for advice, social contact and even the sale of spare parts – and if possible consider doing this before you even buy your car. Really useful MG forums can be found on the internet too.

It is always a good idea to meet people with experience of the MG*F* and MG *TF* first before you commit your own money to your first mid-engined MG, and you may even find that someone in the club will be prepared to sell you a suitable car. However, the social side of car club membership is admittedly not to everyone's taste, and so the second port of call should certainly be one of the specialists who serve these models: Brown &

MG CLUBS AND SPECIALISTS

Mick Hucknall of the rock band Simply Red was an early celebrity owner of an MG*F*, although he didn't go for the obvious red, choosing British Racing Green metallic instead. In the background is the special tour set from Simply Red's 'Life' tour (the album of that name was released in October 1995). (Rover Group)

Gammons, MOSS, the MG Owners' Club, the MG*F* Centre and indeed current MG dealers are just some of the better-known candidates. Many of these specialists offer on-line or mail-order catalogues as well as an invaluable fund of expertise from people who know the ins and outs of the MG*F* and *TF*.

There is not enough space in this book to do justice to the finer points of MG*F* and *TF* maintenance: for that, a factory workshop manual and handbook will be a good starting point, coupled with the information gleaned from the clubs, specialists and the various active internet forums. You will not find yourself moving far into this arena as a novice without coming across horror stories about head gasket failures and sagging suspension systems. The latter can be an issue as nowadays fewer professional garages keep the special equipment and fluids needed, but this is thankfully not a frequent service item and the various MG*F* specialists can help.

K-SERIES ENGINE – FRIEND OR FOE?

The K-Series engine, as we have seen throughout this book, was a remarkable and crucial element of the ambitious plans to rekindle the fortunes of Britain's last major indigenous car maker. The K-Series was not only a vital part of the process that allowed the MG*F* to be created but was even one of the factors behind Ford's brief dalliance with the idea of buying Austin Rover back in 1986. The engine design was truly revolutionary; even today, its low weight and modular construction are exemplary and there are few rivals as advanced: even the casting process was patented.

However, when designers push at the boundaries of the accepted technology of engine design, there are bound to be risks, and undoubtedly some of the parallel consequences of the K-Series engine's brilliance have proved unfortunate in the harsh and unforgiving real world. The engine was designed to be built up as a series of sandwich layers held together by special high-tensile bolts that run from top to bottom of the engine, and there is always the risk that someone inexperienced in the specialized techniques and materials involved could cause problems through ignorance – although that is hardly a problem unique to this engine.

More important, however, is the fact that part of the brilliance of the engine is down to its extremely low mass, including the use of an unusually low coolant volume, which in itself results in less weight being carried around. The downside of this is a potential vulnerability

MG CLUBS AND SPECIALISTS

The K-Series engine, hidden away in the centre of the MG*F* and MG *TF*, can be easy to neglect. Thankfully the head gasket problems that have been a problem in the past can be fixed. (Rover Group)

of the unit to any loss of engine coolant, a particular concern in a mid-engined car where the power train is both buried away from sight and likely to get especially hot at times.

Head gasket failure, sometimes as a result of simple neglect but also at times due to problems with the interface between the head and the block, has become the bête noire of the K-Series engine and has led to much bad press for the unit, despite the fact that the engine is in other ways almost bullet-proof and has been used by other companies such as Lotus with considerable success. The fact remains that, even if some of the failures might be attributable to poor maintenance, the experiences of MG*F* and Land Rover Freelander owners over the years demonstrate that various things were allowed to go wrong at key stages, leading to issues that were unacceptable to the customer.

Ian Pogson believes that the head gasket was, in his words, merely the 'fuse' that failed in the system. There were other problems: the cooling systems, for example, were hard to de-gas, which in turn could lead to servicing problems when garages tried to refill the engines. Added to this,

> The original black-coloured inlet manifold gasket was not even capable of resisting fuels, oil and temperature! Hence the change to the current green one, with visible tags so it could be recognized from outside.

Furthermore, unwise 'cost savings' were forced through against engineering judgement:

> some idiot – who should be hung by a shredded gasket seal bead – sanctioned, as a pathetic cost saver, the idea of changing the original steel head dowels to plastic. That should have been fought by Engineering over dead bodies.

In due course, the steel dowels were reinstated, but not before the level of in-service failures had damaged both engines and the K-Series's reputation.

Various changes have been made over the life of the MG*F* and MG *TF* to resolve these issues and so for the owners of newer cars, or ones that have been extensively overhauled, these problems should no longer be a real issue. Thankfully for owners of older cars, suitable service packs are available – in particular those from XPart, whose Multi-Layer Steel (MLS) Gasket Kit can allow fitting of upgraded gaskets and other parts to solve the problem. The K-Series engine, which was regarded by BMW as 'legacy technology' (they planned to replace it with their new engine range from the new factory at Hams Hall), has lived on in its new guise as the EEC-IV compliant N-Series, now manufactured in China, and new engines are on the horizon that build upon the lessons learned by this remarkable unit.

appendix

Specifications

MGF

Model	1.8i	1.8i Steptronic	18.i VVC
Type	K Series	K Series	K Series
Position	Mid-mounted transverse	Mid-mounted transverse	Mid-mounted transverse
Head/block material	Alloy/Alloy	Alloy/Alloy	Alloy/Alloy
Main bearings	5	5	5
Cylinders	4	4	4
Configuration	in-line	in-line	in-line
cc	1796	1796	1796
Bore × Stroke (mm)	80.0 × 89.3	80.0 × 89.3	80.0 × 89.3
Compression ratio	10.5:1	10.5:1	10.5:1
Valves per cylinder	4	4	4
Camshaft configuration	DOHC	DOHC	Multi-cam with Variable Valve Control
Camshaft drive	Belt	Belt	Belt
Fuelling type	multi-point injection	multi-point injection	multi-point injection
Fuel specification	EN228 95 RON ULG	EN228 95 RON ULG	EN228 95 RON ULG
Maximum power			
kW	88	88	107
PS	120	120	145
@rpm	5,500	5,500	7,000

SPECIFICATIONS

Model	1.8i	1.8i Steptronic	18.i VVC
Maximum torque			
Nm	165	165	174
lb ft	122	122	128
@rpm	3,000	3,000	4,500
Max engine rpm	6,800	6,000	7,100
Gear ratios	5 speed	6 speed	5 speed
1st	3.166	2.416	3.166
2nd	1.842	1.520	1.842
3rd	1.307	1.123	1.307
4th	1.033	0.845	1.033
5th	0.765	0.681	0.765
6th	–	0.518	–
Reverse	3.000	2.658	3.000
Final drive	3.938	4.050	4.200
Drop gear ratio	–	1.423	–
Km/h/mph per 100rpm in top	35.6/22.2	35.4/22.0 (Steptronic) 41.4/25.7 (CVT mode)	33.4/20.8
Acceleration (seconds)			
0–100km/h/0–60mph	9.0/8.5	10.0/9.5	7.7/7.0
30–50mph in 4th	6.6	–	6.2
50–70mph in 4th	7.0	–	6.5
Top speed km/h/mph	193/120	190/118	209/130
Fuel consumption ltr/100km/mpg			
Urban	10.2/27.8	11.6/24.4	11.2/25.2
Extra-urban	5.7/49.3	6.4/43.9	5.8/48.8
Combined	7.4/38.3	8.3/34.0	7.8/36.3
Kerbweight (kg) minimum	1,060	1,100	1,070
GVW	1,320	1,320	1,320
Distribution	45/55	45/55	45/55
Power to weight (bhp per tonne)	111	107	136
Wheels and tyres (2000 Model Year given – other years vary)	15-inch eight-spoke	15-inch 'Square six-spoke'	16-inch 'Square six-spoke'
Front	185/55 VR15	185/55 VR15	215/40 ZR16
Rear	205/50 VR15	205/50 VR15	215/40 ZR16
Spare	175/656 T14	175/656 T14	175/656 T14

SPECIFICATIONS

MG*F* 1.6

Specification similar, but for engine and transmission details, see MG *TF*115

All Models

External dimensions (mm)	
Wheelbase	2,380
Length	3,910
Width excluding door mirrors	1,630
Width including door mirrors	1,780
Height (hood up)	1,270
Front track	1,400
Rear track	1,410
Internal dimensions (mm)	
Legroom	1,090
Headroom	690
Shoulder room	1,240
Luggage	
Capacity cubic metres	0.21
Fuel tank	
Capacity litres/gallons	50/11
Aerodynamics	
Cd/CdA	0.36/0.62

Suspension	
Front	Double wishbones, interconnected Hydragas units, shock absorbers and anti-roll bar
Rear	Double wishbones, brake reaction rods, interconnected Hydragas units, shock absorbers and anti-roll bar
Steering	
Type	Electronic Power Assisted, rack and pinion
Turns lock-to-lock	3.1
Turning circle (kerb-to-kerb)	10.5m (34.7ft)
Brakes	
Front type	Ventilated discs
diameter	240mm (9.5in)
Rear type	Solid discs
diameter	240mm (9.5in)
Circuit type	Diagonal dual circuit
ABS type	Bosch 5.3

SPECIFICATIONS

MG *TF* 2002–2005

Model	115	120 Stepspeed	135	160
Engine type	K1.6	K1.8	K1.8	K1.8 VVC
Position	Mid, transverse	Mid, transverse	Mid, transverse	Mid, transverse
Head/block material	Alloy/Alloy	Alloy/Alloy	Alloy/Alloy	Alloy/Alloy
Main bearings	5	5	5	5
Cylinders	4	4	4	4
Configuration	in-line	in-line	in-line	in-line
cc (as certified)	1588	1796	1796	1796
Bore × Stroke (mm)	80.0 × 79.0	80.0 × 89.3	80.0 × 89.3	80.0 × 89.3
Compression ratio (as certified)	10.5:1	10.5:1	10.5:1	10.5:1
Valves per cylinder	4	4	4	4
Camshaft configuration	double overhead	double overhead	double overhead	double overhead
Camshaft drive	belt	belt	belt	belt
Fuelling type	multi-point injection	multi-point injection	multi-point injection	multi-point injection
Fuel specification	EN228 95 RON unleaded	EN228 95 RON unleaded	EN228 95 RON unleaded	EN228 95 RON unleaded
Battery output	63 amp/hour	63 amp/hour	63 amp/hour	63 amp/hour
Alternator	85 amp	85 amp	85 amp	85 amp
Maximum power				
kW	85	88	100	118
(PS)	(116)	(120)	(136)	(160)
(bhp/hp)	(114)	(118)	(134)	(158)
@ rpm	6,250	5,500	6,750	6,900
Maximum torque				
Nm	145	165	165	174
(kgm)	(14.8)	(16.8)	(16.8)	(17.7)
(lb ft)	(107)	(122)	(122)	(128)
@ rpm	4,700	3,000	5,000	4,700
Maximum intermittent engine speed (rpm)	6,800	6,000	6,800	7,100

SPECIFICATIONS

Model	115	120 Stepspeed		135	160
Gear ratios					
1st	3.167	2.416		3.167	3.167
2nd	1.842	1.520		1.842	1.842
3rd	1.308	1.123		1.308	1.308
4th	1.033	0.845		1.033	1.033
5th	0.765	0.681		0.765	0.765
6th	–	0.518		–	–
EmCVT [electromechanical constantly variable transmission] max.	–	0.443		–	–
Reverse	3.000	2.658		3.000	3.000
Overall final drive	3.938	5.763		4.200	4.200
Km/h (mph) per 1,000rpm in top		6th	EmCVT		
15-inch wheels	35.6 (22.2)	35.9 (22.3)	42.1 (26.1)	33.4 (20.8)	–
16-inch wheels	35.1 (21.8)	35.3 (22.0)	41.4 (25.7)	32.9 (20.5)	32.9 (20.5)
Acceleration (secs)					
0–60mph	9.2	9.7		8.2	6.9
30–50mph in 4th	8.3	–		6.7	6.4
50–70mph in 4th	9.0	–		6.9	6.6
50–70mph in 5th	14.0	–		10.7	10.2
Top speed (mph)	118	118		127	137
0–100km/h	9.8	10.2		8.8	7.6
80–120km/h in 4th	11.3	–		8.6	8.2
80–120km/h in 5th	17.9	–		13.5	12.8
Top speed (km/h)	190	190		205	220

Model	115		120 Stepspeed		135		160	
Fuel consumption	ltr/100 km	mpg	ltr/100 km	mpg	ltr/100 km	mpg	ltr/100 km	mpg
Urban	9.7	29.2	11.6	24.3	11.2	25.3	10.6	26.7
Extra-urban	5.6	50.4	6.4	43.8	6.0	46.9	5.7	49.6
Combined	7.1	39.8	8.3	33.9	7.9	35.6	7.5	37.6
CO_2 g/km	169		199		189		179	
Unladen weight (kg)								
min	1,095		1,125		1,105		1,115	
max	1,150		1,180		1,150		1,180	

SPECIFICATIONS

All Models

Suspension

Front	Coil spring over gas-filled damper located by double wishbones
	Anti-roll bar diameter 20mm
Rear	Multi-link. Coil spring over gas-filled damper
	Anti-roll bar diameter 18mm
Optional Sports Pack	Trim height reduced by 10mm. Uprated dampers with revised valving and springs

Steering

Type	Speed sensitive electric power-assisted rack and pinion
Turns lock-to-lock	2.8
Overall ratio	17.5 : 1
Turning circle (kerb-to-kerb) (m)	10.56
Steering wheel diameter (mm)	355

Brakes

Front type	Ventilated disc with pin-slider calliper
diameter	240mm disc, 48mm piston
Rear type	Solid disc with pin-slider calliper
diameter	240mm disc, 38mm piston
Circuit type	Front–rear split
ABS type	Bosch 5.3 three-channel
Uprated front brakes (standard on 160)	MG/AP Racing brakes: 304mm ventilated discs with stiffer four-piston opposed red callipers; 32mm diameter pistons

Wheels and Tyres

15-inch (various alloy styles)	6J × 15 wheel with 185/55 R15 front, 205/50 R15 rear
16-inch (various alloy styles)	7J × 16 wheel with 195/45 R16 front, 215/40 R16 rear
Spare (all except 160)	5.5J × 14 steel space-saver with 175/65 R14 tyre
160	Instant Mobility System
160 option	7J × 16 alloy wheel with 195/45 R16 tyre for temporary use
Fuel tank useable capacity	50ltr (11 gallons)

SPECIFICATIONS

External dimensions (mm)		
Wheelbase	2,375	
Length	3,943	
Width excluding door mirrors	1,628	
Width including door mirrors	1,807	
Front track (all except ultra lightweight wheel)	1,404	
(optional ultra lightweight wheel)	1,408	
Rear track (all except ultra lightweight wheel)	1,410	
(optional ultra lightweight wheel)	1,414	
	Standard suspension	**Sports Pack 1**
Height unladen (hood up)	1,261	1,249
(hood down - to header rail)	1,219	1,207
(hardtop)	1,264	1,252
Ground clearance	124	114
Aerodynamics		
Cd	0.36	0.35
CdA	0.62	0.61
Internal dimensions (mm)		
Maximum legroom	1,084	
Maximum headroom (hood up)	956	
Maximum shoulder room	1,240	
Boot		
Capacity (litres VDA)	210	
Loading weights (kg)	115/135	120 Stepspeed/160
Maximum laden weight	1,320	1,390
Front axle load (maximum)	600	610
Rear axle load (maximum)	740	790
Maximum boot lid load (applies when approved luggage rack fitted)	20	

Key Changes for 2009 Model Year

Engine now EEC-IV compliant and known as 'N-Series'. Only the 1.8-litre 135 engine tune is available.

Key Changes for 2010 Model Year

- Enlarged door mirrors to meet new legislation.
- 115 of the 150 cars built fitted with 'Twist of Pepper' wheels
- Minor changes to cockpit trim with silver appliqué

TF 85th: Additional Features

- Monotube Bilstein® gas-filled dampers
- Eibach® uprated anti-roll tow set
- Lower ride height

Index

Abingdon Competitions Department 17
Abingdon-on-Thames MG factory 4, 5, 6, 7, 8, 10, 11, 13, 87, 110, 188
AC Ace (Project Kimber concept) 175
Acura (US Honda brand) 65
ACV30 Concept (Mini 30th anniversary concept from 1997) 104
Adams, Eddie 44
ADC (Automotive Development Centre Ltd) 40, 45, 47, 48, 50, 51, 52, 53, 54, 55, 56, 58, 59, 60, 61, 66, 72, 73, 165
Adder see Project Adder
ADO14 see Austin Maxi
ADO15 see Mini
ADO16 (see also MG 1100) 6, 10
ADO20 see Mini
ADO21 (MG mid-engined prototype) 7, 8, 9, 10, 11, 12, 44, 89
ADO23 (see also MG MGB) 89
ADO28 see Marina
ADO34 8
ADO67 see Allegro
ADO70 ('Calypso') 8, 11
ADO71 see Leyland Princess
ADO73 see Marina
ADO88 13, 15, 19
Adventurer 1 (see also PX2) 60, 62
Adventurer 2 (see also PX2) 60, 62
AER-Lola engines 144
Alcantara (simulated suede fabric) 144
Alchemy Partners 118, 121, 123, 124, 128, 156
Alfa Romeo 6, 70
Algarve (Portugal 2002 MG TF press launch) 145
Alias software 163
Allegro (ADO67 Austin Allegro) 13, 15, 23, 132, 134
Allport, Greg 80, 84, 86, 88, 89, 94, 95, 127, 147
Alpina 96
American Sunroof Company, the 31
Anderson, Derek 36
Andrews, Peter 191
Anniversary Concept Vehicles see ACV30
AP Racing 125
AR6 19, 20, 22, 31
AR8 (see also R8, Project YY and Rover 200) 34
Arbuckle, David 129, 134, 135, 136, 137, 138, 139, 141, 142, 147
ARCONA see Austin Rover Cars of North America
Ardmore Air Park, Oklahoma 185
Ardmore Development Authority, the 185
Artega (German sports car brand) 122
ARUP (see also Chapman Arup) 156, 176, 180, 181
A-Series engine 6, 9, 10, 19 ('A' Plus), 29
Aston Martin Lagonda 15, 66
Audi TT 140, 161, 167, 168
Audi 102, 118
Austin Allegro see Allegro
Austin Ambassador 23
Austin brand, the 33, 123
Austin Maestro see Maestro
Austin Marina see Marina
Austin Maxi 8, 9
Austin Metro see Metro
Austin Mini-Metro see Metro
Austin Mini-Minor see Mini
Austin Montego see Montego
Austin Rover (division of BL Ltd from September 1984) 16, 17, 19, 21, 22, 25, 26, 28, 29, 39, 195
Austin Rover Cars of North America ('ARCONA') 33, 65
Austin Rover Design Studios (see also Canley Design Studios – Rover Group Design Studios) 27, 33, 34, 36, 57
Austin Zanda 8, 10
Austin-Healey Sprite 7
Austin-Healey 6, 7, 41, 43, 103, 104, 162
Austin-Morris (subsidiary of British Leyland) 9, 10, 11, 14
Austin-Morris design studio 9
Autobianchi A112 Runabout 10, 11
Autocar & Motor magazine 65
Autocar magazine 32, 93, 96, 158
Automotive Development Centre Ltd see ADC
Autosport Show, the (1996) 97
Autosport Show, the (1998) 95
Autoweek magazine 39
Axe, Royden (Roy) 18, 19, 20, 22, 23, 24, 25, 26, 31, 32, 33, 36, 39, 40, 45, 64, 67

BAe see British Aerospace
Bangle, Chris 85, 86, 103, 104
Banks, Jeff 152
Baoshan (SAIC) engine plant 186
Bartlam, Richard 53
BASF 44
BBC TV 26, 88, 103, 106, 109
Beech, Ian 27
Beijing Auto Show (2006) 186
Beijing Auto Show (2008) 186
Beijing Auto Show (2010) 187, 192
Bentley Arnage 156
Bertone 11, 76
Bilstein 191
Bishop, David 49, 50
BL Ltd (company name from July 1978) 14, 15, 32, 33, 81
BL Motorsports 17
BL Technology 19, 20
BL Zanda see Austin Zanda
Blair, the Rt Hon Tony, MP 118
Blume, David (of Rover Group Japan) 51, 80
Blundell, Mark 93
BMH see British Motor Heritage Ltd
BMW 3-Series 118
BMW AG 28, 76, 81, 82, 83, 84, 85, 86, 88, 95, 96, 97, 102, 103, 104, 117, 118, 119, 120, 121, 122, 123, 124, 132, 153, 156, 172, 191
BMW MINI Speedster concept 104
BMW MINI 28, 103, 104, 122, 128
BMW Mobile Tradition 85
BMW Z07 Concept 104
BMW Z3 roadster 83, 84, 86, 103, 117, 122
BMW Z4 roadster 103
BMW Z8 103
Bonneville Salt Flats, the 106, 107, 109
Bounty see 'Project Bounty'
Braman, Norman 65
Bravo see Project Bravo
British Aerospace (BAe) 36, 37, 38, 40, 44, 81, 82, 83, 102
British Leyland Inc (US subsidiary of British Leyland Motor Corporation) 09
British Leyland Ltd (from 1975) 12, 13, 14
British Leyland Motor Corporation 6, 7, 8, 9, 11, 12

British Leyland Product Planning Coordination Department, the 11
British Motor Heritage Ltd 37, 38, 49, 50, 148
Broadside see Project Broadside
Brooklands Race Circuit, the 115
Brown & Gammons 195
Bruntingthorpe 191
Brussels Motor Show (2002) 144
B-Series engine 6, 10, 29, 74
Buick (brand) 65, 162
Buick (V8 engine – see also Rover) 09

Cadillac 65
Calypso see ADO70
Campbell, Sir Malcolm 106
Canley (see also Triumph Engineering) 14
Canley Design Studios 19, 20, 24, 27, 37, 39, 79
CAR Magazine 22, 33, 48, 52, 93
Carter, Richard 27, 31, 36
Carver, Mike 11
Castle Combe race circuit, the 97
Castrol Oil 106
Caterham 158
CCV see Project CCV
Chapman-Arup (see also ARUP) 127, 175
Chevrolet Corvette 47
Chicago Auto Show, the (1989) 39
Chick, Denis 87
China Brilliance 153
Chrysler 20
City Rover 171
Classic & Sportscar magazine 85
Cofton Hackett (engine plant) 10
Conservative government of Margaret Thatcher, the 19, 33, 36
Cooper Garages (Cooper Metro) 15
Corus 156
Coultas, Fred 40
Coupé Concept Vehicle see Project CCV
Cowley (factory) 5, 15, 89, 110, 122, 191
Cox, Stephen 105, 110, 148, 159

INDEX

Cropley, Steve 33
CVT gearbox see Steptronic

Daewoo 153
Daimler-Chrysler 175
Davenport, John 17
Davis, Tim 40
Day, Sir Graham 32, 33, 34, 35, 36, 40, 44, 52
De Dion suspension 09
De Lorean 175
De Tomaso, Alejandro (and De Tomaso brand – see also Qvale) 132
Dean, James (film actor) 98
Denton, Baroness Jean 33
Der Spiegel (German magazine) 119
Design Research Associates (Roy Axe's studio in Leamington Spa from 1989) 40, 41, 42
Designworks Studio, California 82, 86, 102, 104
Detroit Motor Show, the (2000) 119, 124
Di-Noc film (used to simulate paint finish in clay models) 50, 57, 58, 62, 133
Djordjević, Marek 82, 83, 84, 86, 102
Donington Park race circuit, the 105
Donovan, Mike 40
Dove Company, the 152, 154
Doyle, John 53
DPRS 131
DR1 40, 41, 43
DR2 (see also PR5) 40, 41, 43, 45, 59, 60, 63, 64, 79
DRA see Design Research Associates (later known as Design Research ARUP)
Du Pont 63

Ealing Film Studios, the 79
Earls Court Motor Show (see also Motor Show) 8
ECV3 19, 20, 29
Edscha Group 165
Edwardes, Sir Michael 13, 14
Eibach 191
Eich, Christian 85
Elliott, Ian 25
Elliott, James 85
Ellis-Bextor, Sophie 147
Enever, Syd 6
EPM Technology 156
E-Series engine 8, 09
EuroNCAP tests (see also NCAP) 140, 141, 171
EX181 108
EX234 (MG prototype) 6
EX253 25
EX253 see MG EXF
EX254 see MG*F* Super Sports
EX255 107, 109
EX257 130

EX-E see MG EX-E
EXF see MG EXF
Eyston, George 106

F-16 see MG F-16
Fairhead, Graham 127, 158
Federal safety standards see United States
Fell, Nick 78, 86, 88
Ferrari 308GTB 24
Ferrari 24, 44, 180
Fiat 10, 11, 44
Fiat 128 11
Fiat X1/9 sports car 11
Financial Times, the 118
Foden Trucks 44
Ford Cosworth engine 131
Ford Fiesta 15, 32
Ford Ghia Focus design concept 72
Ford Granada 33
Ford Motor Company, the 32, 36, 102, 131, 159, 172, 174, 195
Ford Sierra 21
Ford StreetKa 166
Frankfurt Motor Show (1985) 25, 26
Frankfurt Motor Show (1993) 82
Frankfurt Motor Show (1997) 110
Frankfurt Motor Show (1999) 115, 116, 117
Frankfurt Motor Show (2001) 132

Gardner, Cpt Goldie 106
Gaydon Test Centre, the (also Design Centre) 19, 45, 50, 51, 64, 74, 93, 98, 122
GE Plastics 44
General Motors 40, 45
Geneva Motor Show (1986) 32
Geneva Motor Show (1992) 67
Geneva Motor Show (1995) 86, 87, 88
Geneva Motor Show (1998) 94, 100, 101
Geneva Motor Show (1999) 111, 116, 117, 118
Getrag gearboxes 102
Goldeneye (James Bond film) 83
Goodwood race circuit, the 105, 112, 114, 117
Goodyear tyres 110, 111
Gould, Jonathan 50, 170, 176, 178
Green, Andy 107, 109
Green, Gavin 22
Gregory, John 71, 72
Gregory, Peter 101, 105
Great British Sports Car Company, the 177, 181
Griffin, Brian 48, 53, 73, 74, 85, 90, 95
Grosvenor House hotel, the 152
GSM 191

Guangzhou Motor Show (2007) 186
Guangzhou Motor Show (2009) 187, 191, 192
Guyll, Adrian 149

Hale, Duke 184
Hamblin, Richard 24, 26, 27, 30, 31, 34, 36, 37, 38, 39, 40, 43, 44, 45, 46, 47, 49, 51, 53, 54, 55, 56, 58, 66, 71, 78, 79, 80, 126, 156
Hams Hall engine plant, the 102, 122, 196
Hardtop see MG MG*F* hardtop
Harper, Steven (Steve) 20, 56, 57, 58, 59, 60
Harriman, Sir George 6, 106
Hart race engine 106
Hasselkus, Walter 103
Hattersley, Roy (MP) 32
Hayter, Don 9
He Xiao Qing 186
Head, Patrick 17
Heitmann, Dr Henrich 119, 122, 124
Heritage MGB see MGB bodyshell
Heritage Motor Museum, Gaydon 22, 26, 29, 73, 88, 110, 117, 193, 194
Hill, Phil 106, 107, 108
Honda 7, 13, 14, 36, 65, 74, 76, 81, 83, 102, 172, 191
 deal with BL Ltd in 1978 14
 ideas of MG cars based on Hondas 14, 16, 22, 40
Honda Accord 14, 102
Honda Ballade 14
Honda Civic 14
Honda CRX 18, 22, 34
Honda CVCC engine 15
Honda Legend (see also Project XX) 18
Honda Rover XX see Project XX
Honda S2000 104
Honda S800 14
Hooper, Ben 156
Horbury, Peter 54, 56
Horner, Vic 27
Howe, Kevin 132, 149
Howell, Geoff 107
Hu Maoyuan 183
Hucknall, Mick 193
Hudson, Richard 9
Hughes, Paul 8, 9, 12, 25
Hunter, Tony 68, 69, 70, 103, 104, 120, 121, 147
Hydragas suspension 76, 127, 134, 139
Hydrolastic suspension 6, 9

Issigonis, Sir Alec 8
Isuzu engines 43

Jaguar 6, 9, 19, 33, 118
Jaguar E-Type 43

Jaguar S-Type 118
Jaguar XJ40 (XJ6) 33
Jaguar XJR15 56, 57
James, David (Baron James of Blackheath) 174
Joe 90 see Project 88
Jones, Colin 154, 158
Jones, Kevin 147, 148
Judge Dredd film, the 100

Karmann (coachbuilders) 7
Kawamoto, Nobuhiko (Honda Chairman in 1994) 87
Kilbourne, Terry 107, 108
Kiley, David 82, 102
Kimber, Cecil 5, 6
King, Spencer ('Spen') 11
Knockhill race circuit, the 127
Krafthaus 96
K-Series engine (see also KV6 and N-Series) 19, 29, 30, 31, 36, 43, 44, 45, 55, 73, 74, 76, 94, 102, 107, 116, 119, 131, 165, 167, 174, 186, 190, 195, 196
Kume, Tadeshi (Honda President in 1978) 18
KV6 engine 157, 158, 159, 161, 166, 167, 186

L'Automobile magazine 144
Labour government of Tony Blair, the 118
Lambury, Lord (previously Sir Leonard Lord, KBE) 106
Land Rover 28, 43, 67, 81, 82, 83, 85, 88, 100, 102, 103, 104, 107
Land Rover Freelander 85, 98, 102, 196
LC10 (see also Maestro) 14
LC8 (see also Metro) 14, 15, 19
Le Grice, Oliver 67, 68
Le Mans 24-Hours race, the 123, 128
Le Mesurier, John (film actor) 106
Lea Francis 157
Leach, Martin 174
Lee, Chris 116, 124
Leonard Lord see Lord Lambury
Lewis, Graham 27, 31, 42
Leyland Australia 10
Leyland Eight mid-engined sports car concept see Rover P6BS
Leyland Motor Corporation (pre-merger) 7, 9
Leyland Princess (ADO71) 134
Leyland South Africa 10
Leyland Trucks 40
Lincoln (brand) 120
Lindley, David 161, 162, 167, 168, 169, 171, 183
LM11 see Montego
Lockheed-Martin Falcon F-16 24
Lola (see also EX257) 130

205

INDEX

Lola MG EX257 *see* EX257
Longbridge 6, 8, 11, 15, 19, 32, 50, 110, 119, 120, 128, 152, 153, 172, 174, 176, 178, 179, 181, 182, 183, 184, 185, 186, 190, 192
Lotus (*see also* models listed) 13, 36, 44, 123, 169, 196
Lotus Elan 39, 43, 56
Lotus Elise 120, 163, 167
Lotus Exige 191
Lotus M250 Project 162
L-Series engine 174
Lutz, Robert (Bob) 32
Lyons, Sir William 9, 95

M16-engine 31, 43, 49
Maestro (*see also* LC10; MG Maestro) 19, 20, 24, 31, 33, 44, 45
Maestro floorpan – as basis of PR1 (*see also* PR1) 45, 46
Magma Holdings 174
Mann, Harris 9
Manton, Stan 24
Marina (ADO28 & ADO73 Austin Marina, Leyland Marina and Morris Marina) 10, 13, 15, 23
Martin, Tim 78
Maxi *see* Austin Maxi
Mayflower Cup, the 127
Mayflower Group plc 63, 76, 77, 78, 83, 85, 142
Mayflower Vehicle Systems 77, 97, 109, 100, 101, 116, 163, 164
Mazda Miata 39, 40, 44, 53, 66, 104, 153, 158, 160, 167, 190
Mazda MX-5 *see* Mazda Miata
Mazda RX-8 168
McGovern, Gerry 20, 24, 27, 30, 36, 67, 68, 69, 71, 72, 87, 98, 110, 111, 120
McWilliams, Bruce 9
Mercedes-Benz 43
Metro (*see also* MG Metro) 9, 13, 15, 16, 17, 19, 24, 33, 44, 70, 76, 83, 123, 134
Metro 6R4 *see* MG Metro 6R4
Metro Cabriolet 46
Metro fascia in PR3 51
Metro floorpan – as basis of PR3 44, 45, 47, 83
Metro Midget concept *see* MG Midget; PR3; AR6; Project 90
Metro replacement (*see also* AR6) 19
Metro van simulators 9, 73, 88, 90, 91
MG 1100 (ADO16) 6
MG 14/28 148
MG 3SW 186
MG 6 187, 189, 190, 192
MG 7 176, 186
MG Awareness Day, the 68
MG badge 5, 69
MG brand, the 4, 33, 47, 81, (BMW) 102–103, 110, 119, 120, 123, 132, 156, 174, 177, 182
MG Car Club of Switzerland, the 88
MG Car Club, the 87, 182, 194
MG Car Company (for period 1924 to 1980) *see* Abingdon
MG Car Company (idea to reconstitute) 45
MG Cars (in Abingdon guise) *see* Abingdon
MG Cars Australia 111
MG Cars of Europe and North America 184
MG CRX roadster 18
MG D, MG D GT *see* ADO21, TR7, MG CRX, MGF
MG EX-E 22, 23, 24, 25, 26, 27, 28, 29, 36, 43, 44, 55, 67, 68, 89
MG EXF Record car 97, 106, 108
MG F-16 concept 29, 30, 31, 34, 35, 36, 37, 39, 40, 43, 45, 46, 47, 53, 89
MG Garages (Australia) 104
MG Global Design Studios 194
MG grille – Peter Stevens' reinterpretation 130
MG GT Concept 152, 153, 154, 161, 172, 185
MG K3 Magnette 101, 105, 106
MG Lola *see* EX257
MG Maestro 16, 29, 37, 67
MG Maestro Turbo 33, 37, 38, 43, 46, 67
MG Magnette – concept 122, 147
MG marque *see* MG brand
MG Metro (*see also* Metro) 15, 16, 17, 18, 67
MG Metro 1300 *see* MG Metro
MG Metro 6R4 17, 24
MG Metro Turbo 16
MG MGA Twin Cam 89
MG MGA 6, 89, 157
MG MGB GT V8 88, 89, 156
MG MGB GT 9, 11, (Jubilee) 149
MG MGB V8 roadster 50
MG MGB 4, 5, 6, 7, 10, 12, 14, 15, 50, 69, 72, 77, 78, 79, 80, 89, 106, 156, 168
MG MGC 6, 89, 156
MG MGF 1.6 125
MG MGF 75th LE 110, 111
MG MGF Abingdon LE 105, 110, 111
MG MGF and MG TF hardtop 97, 111, 134, 146
MG MGF Cheetah (*see also* SP Performance) 94, 95, 96, 97
MG MGF Extreme (*see also* MG MGF XPower 500) 129, 130, 131
MG MGF Freestyle (LE) 131
MG MGF Limited editions 105, 110, 111, 113
MG MGF Silverstone (LE) 113
MG MGF Steptronic 113
MG MGF Super Sports concept 97, 98, 99, 100, 101, 105, 115, 116, 117, 130
MG MGF Targa Trophy (LE) 111
MG MGF Trophy 160SE 125, 126, 134, 138, 139
MG MGF Wedgewood (LE) 124, 125
MG MGF XPower 500 (*see also* MG TF500 and MG MGF Extreme) 131, 133, 142, 144, 187
MG Midget (*see also* X120 & X121) 4, 5, (T-Series) 6, 7, 8, 9, 11, 14, (concept) 20–21, (TC) 22, (TF) 89, (MINI-based) 103, 106, (TC) 120, (TF) 147, 156, 158, 166, 172, 175
MG Midget PR3 *see* PR3
MG Montego 16, 67
MG Montego Turbo 16, 38
MG Motor UK (from 2008) 159, 187, 188
MG Motors Corporation 185
MG MR2 *see* Toyota MR2 (simulators)
MG Old Number One (1925) 148
MG Owners' Club, the 50, 182, 194, 195
MG R8 (*see also* R8 Coupé) 39
MG Rover Group, the (from 2000 to 2005) 118, 124, 128, 130, 131, 132, 133, 134, 136, 137, 140, 141, 145, 147, 149, 152, 153, 154, 155, 156, 160, 161, 162, 163, 172, 173, 174, 182, 183, 185, 186, 190
MG RV8 (*see also* Project Adder) 46, 49, 57, 67, 78, 79, 80, 82, 98, 156
MG SCV *see* Sports Concept Vehicle and MG EX-E
MG Sport & Racing Ltd. 128, 129, 131
MG TF (2002–2010) 134 *et seq.*
MG TF 115 138
MG TF 120 (Stepspeed) 138, 152
MG TF 135 131, 139, 183, 187, 190
MG TF 160 138, 149, 152
MG TF 200 HPD (hybrid concept) 155, 171
MG TF 500 (*see also* MG MGF XPower 500) 144, 145
MG TF 80th Anniversary LE 150, 151, 152
MG TF 85th LE 183, 186, 187, 190, 191
MG TF Cool Blue (LE) 150
MG TF Coupé (LE) 150
MG TF Elegance (LE) 150
MG TF GT *see* MG GT Concept
MG TF Jubilee 148
MG TF LE 500 131, 178, 182, 183, 186, 187, 190, 191
MG TF Limited Editions *see* pages 150–151 and 190–191
MG TF Oxford (LE) 151
MG TF Spark (LE) 150
MG TF Sprint (LE) 150
MG TF Sunstorm (LE) 150
MG TF Swiss Blue (LE) 151
MG TF Vintage Racing (LE) 150, 151
MG version of TR7 13
MG XPower girls, the 133
MG XPower SV 133, 154, 158, 189
MG XPower 129
MG ZA (and ZB) Magnette 147
MG Zero concept car 187, 192
MG Zero Concept 192
MG ZR 130, 145, 147, 156, 180
MG ZS 130, 145, 147, 156, 171
MG ZT 176, 186
MG ZT Extreme 131
MG ZT-T 109
MGA *see also* Michael Gibbs Associates
MGA (sports car) *see* MG MGA
MGB *see* MG MGB
MGB bodyshell – BMH project to bring back into production 37, 38, 49
MGC *see* MG MGC
MGD *see* ADO21 (1969–70) & PR3 (1990–95)
MGF Centre 195
MGF Cheetah *see* MG MGF Cheetah
MGF Register, the 194
MGF Super Sports concept *see* MG MGF Super Sports
MGF 6 *et seq*
Michael Gibbs Associates (MGA) Developments 54, 55, 56, 57, 58, 59, 66, 67
Michelotti (design studios) 13
Mighty Mini *see* ADO88
Milberg, Professor Joachim 103
Millbrook test circuit, the 177
Milltek 95
MINI *see* BMW MINI
Mini 8, 15, 19, 46, 81, 82, 83, 99, 102, 120, 122
Mini Convertible 46
Mini-Cooper 8, 46, 103
Mintex brake pads 96
MIRA (Motor Industry Research Association) 109, 136, 140, 141, 155
Mitchell, Lee 164, 167
Mitchell, Terry 9
Mitchell, Wynne 107
Modern Gentleman – marketing slogan under NAC 181, 186
Monogram paint colours 173
Monte Carlo rally, the 103
Montego (*see also* LM11; MG

206

INDEX

Montego; MG Montego Turbo) 19, 20, 24, 33, 44
Morgan 13, 49
Morgan Aero 170
Morland's Brewery 'Old Speckled Hen' beer 88
Morley, Kevin 34, 45, 50, 52, 60
Morris (cars and brand) 5, 123
Morris Garages marketing slogan in China under SAIC 181, 187, 192
Morris Garages (business in Oxford) 5
Morris, Graham 48, 49, 65, 68
Morris Marina *see* Marina
Morris Mini-Minor *see* Mini
Morris, William (Lord Nuffield) 5
MOSS Europe 195
Moss, Ken 109
Moss, Stirling 107
Motor Industry Research Association *see* MIRA
Motor Magazine 21, 22
Motor Panels Ltd. 40, 45, 46, 62, 63, 78
Motor Show (UK – 1980) 17
Motor Show (UK – 1990) 52
Motor Show (UK – 1992) 80
Motor Show (UK – 1998) 118
Motor Show (UK – 2000) 162
Motor Show Tokyo *see* Tokyo Motor Show
Motorfair (Motorshow) 26
Moulton, Jon (*see also* Alchemy Partners) 123, 172
Musgrove, Harold 19, 22, 25, 26, 31, 32, 33, 34, 81

NAC Group, the (Nanjing Automotive Corporation) 174, 175, 176, 177, 178, 180, 181, 182, 183, 184, 185, 186
NAC-MG *see* NAC
Nanjing Auto and Nanjing Motor *see* NAC
Nash, Daniel, 109
NCAP (*see also* EuroNCAP) 140–141, 160, 171
New Generation (BMW) NG engines 97, 102
Newman, Jeremy 27, 50
NG (BMW) engines *see* New Generation (BMW) NG engines
Nickless, Robin 47
Nissan 350Z 168
Nissan Be-1, Figaro, Pao, S-Cargo 40
Nissan Micra 40
N-Series engine (*see also* K-Series) 190, 196
Nuffield Organisation, The 6, 106

Nuttle, Marc 185

O'Hara, Mike 66
Ogle Design 19, 40, 62
Oklahoma Global Motors llc 185
Oldaker, Rob 50, 124, 128, 129, 130, 135, 136, 144, 153, 155, 156, 157, 158, 161, 172, 176
OMNI Design 67, 125
Opel Roadster (*see also* Vauxhall VX220) 162
Oriental Morning Post newspaper, the 174
O-Series engine 31, 43
Ovens, Dave 75
Owen, Rob 9, 22
OZ alloy wheels 153, 159

Palexpo *see* Geneva Motor Show
Palmer, Stephen *see* Stephen Palmer Ltd & SP Performance
Paris Salon (Motor Show – 2004) 151
Parker, Roger 50
Paveley, David (*see also* DPRS) 131
Peugeot (PG-1) gearbox 19, 102, 117
Peugeot-Talbot 20
Phillips, Alan 191
Phoenix *see* Project Phoenix and Phoenix Consortium
Phoenix Consortium 43, 118, 121, 123, 124, 128, 153, 172, 175
Phoenix Routes (*see also* PR1, PR2, PR3, PR4, PR5) 43, 44, 45
Phoenix Venture Holdings 128, 172, 174
Piëch, Prof Ferdinand 82, 156
Pininfarina 6, 76
Pischetsrieder, Bernd 81, 82, 83, 85, 102, 103, 118, 119
Pizza Vans *see* Metro Van simulators
Pocket Rocket (*see also* PR3) 47, 49, 51, 53, 54, 55
Pogson, Ian 39, 40, 102, 122, 123, 159, 182, 188, 191, 196
Pond, Tony 17, 97
Pontiac 65
Porsche 'Little Bastard' (owned by James Dean) 98
Porsche 911 head-lamps 70
Porsche 911 tail-lamps 61, 70
Porsche 911 50, 82, 168
Porsche Boxster 96, 158, 161, 167, 168
Potter, Steve 159
Powertrain Ltd. 186
PR1 45, 46, 47, 50, 51, 56, 78
PR2 44, 45, 46, 47, 49, 51, 63
PR3 44, 45, 47, 48, 49, 50, 51, 52, 53, (Project 8300) 55 57, 58,

60, 64, 65, 66, 67, 70, 73, 74, 75, 76, 77, 78, 83, 86, 90, 91, 147, 165, 188, 190
PR4 44
PR5/DR2 *see* PR5
PR5 56, 60, 64, 65
Pressed Steel (also Pressed Steel Fisher) 77, 122
Price Waterhouse Coopers (PwC) 174
Project 8300 *see* PR3
Project 90 20
Project Adder 50, 52, 57, 59, 60, 61, 64, 65, 66, 67, 70, 71, 78, 79
Project AR6 *see* AR6
Project Bounty (*see also* Triumph Acclaim) 14, 15
Project Bravo 18
Project Broadside 15
Project CCV 23, 27, 29, 32
Project Drive 154, 172
Project ECV3 *see* ECV3
Project Hawk (VVC engine) 75
Project Kimber 174, 175
Project Phoenix 40, 46
Project TCV 171
Project Viking 157, 170
Project X80 *see* X80 and MG XPower SV
Project XX 18, 19, 23, 25, 26, 27, 32, 81
Project YY (*see also* AR8; R8; Rover 200) 31, 32, 34, 81
Proton 153
Pukuo factory, the 176, 181, 186
PX1 Rover 800-based sports car using standard 800 wheelbase 60
PX2 Rover 800-based sports car using shortened wheelbase 60

Quandt family, the 103
Queen Elizabeth II, Her Majesty 148
Quincey, Julian 69, 71, 103, 104, 115, 116, 117, 157, 160
Qvale Automotive Group, the (*see also* De Tomaso) 132
Qvale Mangusta 132, 158, 171
Qvale, Kjell 132

R17 *see* Rover 800
R3 Rover 200 of 1995-2000 75
R6 *see* AR6
R8 (*see also* AR8, Project YY and Rover 200) 35, (Coupé 'Tomcat') 38, 39, (convertible 'Tracer') 39, (MG R8) 39, 43, (fascia in PR1) 46, 50, (convertible) 67, 81
Racing Car Show, the 9
Randle, Prof. Jim 157, 170
Range Rover 43
RD110 171
RDX100 171
RDX130 170, 171

RDX140 171
RDX21 170
RDX31 170
RDX60 171
RDX65 171
Regnier, Peter 33
Reitzle, Dr. Ing. Wolfgang 81, 82, 85, 103, 119
Reliant Scimitar SS1 45, 47, 51
Reliant 45, 46, 47, 51, 60, 64
Renault Group, the 120
Ricardo (engineering and design consultants) 183
Riley brand, the 103
Rimstock alloy wheels 191
Road & Track magazine 18, 22
Roewe 550 186
Roewe 750 186
Rolls-Royce brand 82
Rolls-Royce Phantom (of 2003) 84, 86
Rolls-Royce Silver Seraph 57
Rotrex supercharger 96
Routes 1, 2, 3, 4, 5 *see* Phoenix Routes
Rover 200 (R3, from 1995) *see* R3
Rover 200 (R8, from 1989) 35, (Coupé) 38, (convertible) 67
Rover 200 (SD3 replacement for the Triumph Acclaim) 32, 34, 74
Rover 25 (*see also* MG ZR) 145, 156, 174
Rover 45 (*see also* MG ZS) 145, 156, 171
Rover 600 102, 123
Rover 75 Coupé Concept 154, 158
Rover 75 118, 123, 147, 168, 174
Rover 800 (R17) 123
Rover 800 (*see also* Project XX) 18, 27, 31, (launch) 33, 34, 60
Rover 800 Coupé (R17) 34, 65, 67
Rover 800 platform – as basis of PR5 60, 62, 63
Rover 800 Sterling (*see also* Sterling Motor Cars) 33
Rover brand, the 9, 66, 82, 120, 174
Rover CCV *see* Project CCV
Rover Group Design Studios (*see also* Austin Rover Design) 38, 67
Rover Group Directors – assessing the PR1, PR2 and PR3 prototypes 51
Rover Group Europe 68
Rover Group Marketing 52
Rover Group, the (1986 to 2000) 17, 33, 36, 43, 44, 47, 49, 52, 66, 68, 74, 76, 77, 78, 81, 82, 83, 84, 85, 86, 87, 88, 89, 95, 96, 102, 103, 105, 111, 117, 118, 120, 122, 123, 163, 193

207

INDEX

Rover M-16 engine see M-16 engine
Rover Metro see Metro
Rover Metro Cabriolet see Metro Cabriolet
Rover P6BS 9, 25
Rover P9 9, 14
Rover R8 see R8, AR8, Rover 200, Tomcat
Rover SD1 18, 28, 43
Rover Special Products (RSP) 45, 46, 47, 50, 53, 54, 58, 60, 67, 80
Rover Streetwise 186
Rover Tomcat – Rover R8 Coupé see R8
Rover Triumph (division of British Leyland and latterly BL Cars) 14, 15
Rover T-Series engine see T-Series engine
Rover V8 engine (see also Buick) 17, 43, 45, 47, 49, 107
Rover XX see Project XX
Royal College of Art, the 20
RSP see Rover Special Products
Ryder Plan, the 13

Saddington, David (Dave) 20, 27, 102, 103, 115, 120
SAE Show, Detroit (2000) 122, 128
SAIC Group, the 149, 153, 162, 174, 182, 183, 186, 187, 191, 192
SAIC Motor UK Technical Centre, the 187
Scheele, Sir Nick 102
SCV see Sports Concept Vehicle and MG EX-E
Sheet Moulding Compound (SMC) 44, 47
SIM1, 2, 3, 4 see Metro Van simulators
Simpson, George 48, 82
Simpson, Neil 132, 156
Sked, Gordon 24, 27, 40, 67, 68, 71
Smart Roadster 51, 166, 175
SMC see Sheet Moulding Compound
Smith, Andy 51
Smith, Sir Roland (BAe Chairman) 36
Snowdon, Mark 18, 33
Sowden, John 53
SP Performance Ltd. 95, 96
Sparco seats 154, 159
Spartanburg, South Carolina BMW factory 83
Specialised Mouldings of Huntingdon 21, 22, 24
Speedweek event, the 107
Sports Concept Vehicle [SCV] (see also MG EX-E) 23, 24, 29
Sprintex supercharger 74

S-Series engine 31
St. Modwens Properties 186
Stadco 77, 163, 182, 184, 185, 186
Stephen Palmer Ltd. (see also MGF Cheetah & SP Performance) 94, 95, 96
Stephenson, Frank 120, 121
Stephenson, John 47, 66
Stephenson, Nick 40, 45, 59, 85, 118, 124, 134, 153, 154, 161
Stepspeed gearbox see Steptronic
Steptronic gearbox, the (Stepspeed from 2000) 113, 116, 127, 131, 138, 186
Sterling Motor Cars 26, 27, 28, 29, 36, 43, 48, 62, 65, 66, 67, 68
Stevens, Peter 56, 57, 97, 124, 127, 128, 131, 132, 133, 141, 152, 154, 158, 188
Stokes, Lord (Donald) 6, 7, 9, 11, 12
Stone, Roger 74
Straman, Richard 18
Stucky, Wes 185
Styling International 50, 52
Suckling, Jonathan 109

Takada Kogyo 40
Targa Tasmania road race, the 111
Tata Group, the 171
Taylor, Merrick 40
Tesla Roadster 163
Thatcher, Rt Hon. Margaret, MP (Prime Minister – see also Conservative) 32, 33
Thornley, John 89
Thurston, John 38, 106
Tickfords 38
Tokyo Motor Show (1993) 80
Tomcat Rover R8 Coupé see R8
Towers, John 45, 51, 103, 123, 124, 153, 172
Toyota Corolla 40
Toyota engines 159
Toyota MR-2 simulators 73, 74, 88, 90, 91
Toyota MR-2 40, 44, 167
Toyota SV-3 concept car 40
TR7 see Triumph TR7
TR9 see MG CRX
Tracer Rover R8 convertible (see also R8) 39
Triumph Acclaim (see also Project Bounty; Honda) 14, 15
Triumph brand BMW ideas to resurrect 106
Triumph Bullet 11, 12
Triumph Engineering (Canley) 7, 11
Triumph GT6 7
Triumph Herald 8

Triumph Lynx 11
Triumph Spitfire 7, 8, 9, 11
Triumph sports cars in general 28
Triumph TR5 7
Triumph TR6 7
Triumph TR7 rally programme 17
Triumph TR7 The Untold Story book by author 15, 175
Triumph TR7 4, 10, 11, 12, 13, 15
Triumph TR8 15
Truett, Richard 65
T-Series engine 43
Turbo Technics 96
Turin Motor Show, the 10, 32
Turner, Anthea 194
Turner, Phil 159, 190
TVR 13, 47, 64
Twemlow, Patrick 40
TWR Group, the 132, 158

Unipower GT 8
United States of America emissions & safety legislation 10, 12, 76
US emissions see United States of America emissions & safety legislation
US safety see United States of America emissions & safety legislation

V64V engine (MG Metro 6R4) 17
Vacuum Assisted Resin Injection (VARI) 44
Valmet 85
Vanden Plas 28
VARI see Vacuum Assisted Resin Injection
Variable Valve Control see VVC engine and Project Hawk
Vauxhall 45
Vauxhall VX220 162
Vickers Group plc 82
Viking see Project Viking
Vollath, Wolfgang 119, 121
Volvo 55, 56, (480ES Sports Coupé) 57
von Kuenheim, Eberhard 82
VVC engine 74, 75, 76, 94, 95, 125, 139, 159
VW AG 36, 102, 156, 162
VW G-Lader supercharger 74

Wadhams, Michelle 22
Walkinshaw, Tom see TWR Group
Wang Haoliang 183
Wang Hong Biao 177, 182, 186
Ward, Daniel 21, 22, 32
Warming, Anders 104

Webster, Harry 9
Wharton, Les 34
Whitby, Cllr Mike 182
Williams Engineering 17
Williams-Kenny, Tony 183
Wills, Barrie 127, 128, 175
Wiseman, John 66
Wolseley brand, the 123
Wood, John 155
Wood, Jonathan 148
Woodcote Green paint option on MG RV8 80
Woodhouse, David 98, 99, 100, 101, 105, 106, 107, 109, 117
Woollard, William 26
Wyatt, Don 66, 67

X10 170
X100 see RDX100
X11 170
X12 170
X120 56, 156, 159, 160, 161, 164, 165, 168, 169, 171, 172
X121 75, 161, 162, 163, 164, 165, 166, 167, 171, 172, 180
X122 161, 165, 166, 167, 171, 172
X123 161, 165, 167, 169, 171
X13 170
X130 see RDX130
X14 170
X140 see RDX140
X15 109, 170
X20 170
X21 see RDX21
X30 170
X31 see RDX31
X40 170
X50 170
X60 see RDX60
X65 see RDX65
X70 156, 157, 158, 171
X71 156, 158, 171
X72 171
X80 131, 132, 133, 158, 171
X81 171
X90 171
XP20 XPower Le Mans engine 130
XPart 196
XPower brand, the 131
X-Trac gearbox 131
XX see Project XX

Yea, John 66, 67
York, Sarah, Duchess of 95
Yu Jianwei (NAC Chairman) 182, 184, 185
Yuejin (parent company of NAC) 183, 186
YY see Project YY

Zanda see Austin Zanda
ZF gearboxes 102
Ziebart, Wolfgang 119, 122